Theo-
logy
&
Life

# THEOLOGY AND LIFE SERIES

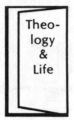

Theo-
logy
&
Life

*Volume 10*

# Biblical and Theological
# Reflections on
# *The Challenge of Peace*

*Edited by*

*John T. Pawlikowski, O.S.M.*
*and Donald Senior, C.P.*

Michael Glazier, Inc.
Wilmington, Delaware

Theo-
logy
&
Life

# CONTENTS

# Editors' Preface

This book is intended as a response to the urgent appeal made by the United States bishops in their Pastoral Letter on war and peace: "We address theologians in a particular way because we know that we have only begun the journey toward a theology of peace; without your specific contributions this desperately needed dimension of our faith will not be realized. Through your help we may provide new vision and wisdom for church and state" (*The Challenge of Peace*, #304).[1]

The essays that follow are not designed as "commentary" on the rich and provocative contents of the bishops' Pastoral; instead they use various aspects of the Pastoral as a starting point for further theological reflection and discussion, thereby hoping to nudge the Catholic community further along the "journey" the bishops have so courageously begun.

The essays included here originated as papers in a faculty seminar at the Catholic Theological Union in Chicago where as members of the theological community and as Christians concerned with the issues of peace and war we struggled with the complex and urgent questions raised by the bishops. All of the papers have been revised in the light of our discussions to make their contents and format more

[1]Unless otherwise noted, all references are to the final text of the bishops' Pastoral, *The Challenge of Peace: God's Promise and Our Response.* Paragraph numbers cited refer to the official edition published by the United States Catholic Conference, 1983 and found at the end of this volume.

accessible to a wider audience of Christians and people of good will concerned with the awesome questions surrounding the realities of war and peace in a nuclear age.

The contributors, each a member of the faculty of Catholic Theological Union, represent a wide range of theological vantage points. Not all are in agreement among themselves or with every aspect of the bishops' Pastoral. Such pluralism is not only to be expected (as the bishops themselves anticipated in their Pastoral) but it is salutary: only from vigorous discussion and interaction can the complex issues of war and peace be responsibly dealt with.

The chapters of this book fall into three major subdivisions: (I) *The Biblical Viewpoint* (chapters 1-4). Four essays consider the biblical foundations for a theology of peace. Dianne Bergant, C.S.A., Associate Professor of Old Testament, examines two sets of traditions related to the peace issue: the image of God as a warrior God and the quest for harmony. These aspects of the biblical tradition are cited in the Pastoral but receive further reflection here. Carroll Stuhlmueller, C.P., Professor of Old Testament, takes up the prophetic traditions and their crucial significance for a theology of peace. His essay not only develops the appeal to the prophetic texts in the Pastoral but illustrates how the bishops themselves exercise the prophetic vocation on the peace issue. Leslie Hoppe, O.F.M., Associate Professor of Old Testament, reminds us of the pluralism on the question of war and peace inherent within the community of Israel and their scriptures. Donald Senior, C.P., Professor of New Testament, concentrates on what he considers the core of New Testament tradition on peace, the teaching on enemy love and non-retaliation. This essay, too, develops a biblical text appealed to by the Pastoral.

(II) *The Ethical Viewpoint* (chapters 5-7). Three essays consider war and peace from the vantage point of Roman Catholic moral theology. A bridge between the biblical materials and ethical reflection is provided by John Pawlikowski, O.S.M., Professor of Social Ethics. From his background in the Jewish-Christian dialogue, he reflects on the issue of "power" and its use within a societal framework. Two essays, one by Paul Wadell, C.P., and the other by Thomas Nairn, O.F.M., both Instructors of Moral Theology, take up the two different tracks of moral reflection on war and peace found within Catholic tradition; pacifism and the just war approach. All three of these essays illustrate the tensions within the Roman Catholic community over the proper Christian response to violence.

(III) *The Pastoral and Ecclesial Viewpoints* (chapters 8-11). The remaining four essays consider some of the remarkable pastoral implications of *The Challenge of Peace.* John Szura, O.S.A., Assistant Professor of Psychology and Theology, faults the Pastoral for not giving more attention to the mass media and its use by governments and other interest groups to create a context for war. Kathleen Hughes, R.S.C.J., Assistant Professor of Liturgy, tends to another dimension of the church's "communication" by showing how liturgical renewal reflects a new consciousness about war and peace and can serve as a powerful source of proclamation. Archimedes Fornasari, M.C.C.J., Associate Professor of Ethics, reflects on the pastoral significance of the historical consciousness implicit in the bishops' approach to the peace issue. Finally, John Linnan, C.S.V., Associate Professor of Doctrinal Theology and President of CTU, concentrates on a spin-off from the Pastoral that may go beyond even the far-reaching consequences of a theology of peace. He contends that the process used by the bishops and their manner of reflecting on war and peace reflect a Vatican II conception of church that is now bearing fruit.

Numerable unjustified accusations have been levelled against the bishops' Pastoral from some within and without the Catholic church. For that reason we feel compelled at the outset of this volume to state the firm support of all the contributors for the moral leadership shown by the American bishops. The points raised by the various authors should be understood as an attempt to deepen and nuance the consciousness-raising process on war and peace questions stimulated by the bishops. We are grateful for their courage and foresight in making peace not only a Catholic question but a focus of national discussion. The greatest disservice that Catholic theologians and ministers could perform relative to the Pastoral would be to harden it into stone. Its continuing vitality will depend on the same kind of ongoing exegesis and reflection we have profitably applied to the basic books of our biblical tradition.

Our desire to continue the process of reflection on Catholic attitudes toward war and peace through this volume flows directly from the spirit that pervaded the composition of the Pastoral. Staff persons at the United States Catholic Conference have indicated to us their deep conviction that nothing will ever be quite the same in terms of Catholic episcopal statements after the process used to formulate the Pastoral. What they are saying is that the widespread consultation principle on major policy statements has now been fully rooted as operative procedure. This reality, however, represents at least implicitly more than a mere procedural change. It touches the question of the very nature of the church and its teaching authority. John Linnan explores this aspect of the question in further detail in his contribution.

This methodological and theological change actually began in earnest with several earlier documents. Among the crucial ones was the statement on energy (*Reflections on The Energy Crisis*, 1981). The extensive consultation with a broad range of the Catholic polity (and significant non-Catholics as well) represents a major re-thinking of how moral authority operates in the contemporary church, even though neither the energy document nor the Pastoral on war and peace directly reflect on the theological implications of their methodology. To employ an analogy from biblical studies, the bishops were far more the redactors of the documents rather than their direct authors.

The one area where the energy document may have gone further was in the interaction process it utilized. The Peace Pastoral process basically involved "hearings" and "individual commentary." What remains rather unique about the energy statement was that the United States Catholic Conference brought together various experts and gave them the opportunity not only to offer input into the writing of the document but to interact with one another as well. The energy document was in a very real way the child of this intense interaction. This procedure was not repeated in quite the same way in the construction of the Peace Pastoral. If it had been, perhaps some of the polarization within the Catholic community might have been overcome.

The important process difference between the energy document and the *Challenge of Peace* leads into another related question of significance. Is the function of the bishops' conference to be primarily prophetic and challenging or is it to help reconcile viewpoints within the Catholic community? We would put the emphasis on reconciling. Reconciliation, we need to insist, does not rule out prophetic challenge and even confrontation at times. Reconciliation is not what the theologian Paul Ricoeur has termed the "ideological screen" of conciliation at any price. But reconciliation is different from a purely prophetic posture. We would encourage the bishops' follow-up committee on the Pastoral to search for further ways of incorporating such efforts at reconciliation into the ongoing study of the document.

The spirit of the Pastoral, both in composition and in content, is due to the leadership of many bishops and USCC staff people. But in a special way it is reflective of the ecclesiology and social concern of the Pastoral's drafting committee chairperson, Cardinal Joseph Bernardin. It is a spirit he has already clearly manifested in the church of Chicago. As a part of the Catholic community of Chicago the CTU faculty wishes to dedicate this volume to Cardinal Bernardin in deep appreciation for his personal service of so many and for the ecclesial ethos he has created for all of us. He has truly made us feel a part of a vibrant church with peace at the core of its faith expression.

John T. Pawlikowski, O.S.M.
Donald Senior, C.P.

# The Contributors

All those who have contributed chapters to this book are faculty members of Catholic Theological Union in Chicago.

*Dianne Bergant, C.S.A.* is Associate Professor of Old Testament Studies and Director of CTU's Master of Theological Studies Program. She is also a member of the Committee on Faith and Order of the National Council of Churches and a Lectionary Subcommittee for the Bishop's Committee on the Liturgy. She has authored a commentary on *Job and Ecclesiastes* in the *Old Testament Message* series for Michael Glazier, Inc.

*Archimedes Fornasari, M.C.C.J.* is Associate Professor of Ethics. He is a member of the Comboni Missionaries and has been involved in education and formation work for his congregation for many years.

*Leslie J. Hoppe, O.F.M.* is Assistant Professor of Old Testament Studies. He recently completed a commentary on *Joshua and Judges* for the *Old Testament Message* series.

*Kathleen Hughes, R.S.C.J.*, is Assistant Professor of Liturgy and serves on various commissions such as the International Commission on English in the Liturgy and the Advisory Board of the Bishops' Committee on the Liturgy. She is a member of the editorial committee for the liturgy volumes of *Concilium* and has published widely on liturgical subjects.

**John E. Linnan, C.S.V.** is Associate Professor of Doctrinal Theology and is currently President of Catholic Theological Union. His specialization is ecclesiology.

**Thomas A. Nairn, O.F.M.** is Instructor in Ethics and is completing his doctoral disseration at the University of Chicago.

**John T. Pawlikowski, O.S.M.** is Professor of Social Ethics. He is the author of several volumes including *Christ in the Light of the Christian-Jewish Dialogue* (Paulist, 1982), and has served as principal theological consultant for the Catholic Bishops' Energy Statement. He was appointed by President Carter to the United States Holocaust Memorial Council.

**Donald Senior, C.P.** is Professor of New Testament Studies and Director of CTU's Israel Study Program. He is the author of several books and numerous articles on biblical subjects. He is co-editor of *The New Testament Message* (Michael Glazier, Inc.) and was one of the biblical scholars invited to give testimony to the Bishops' Committee that drafted *The Challenge to Peace.*

**Carroll Stuhlmueller, C.P.** is Professor of Old Testament Studies and editor of *The Bible Today.* He is past President of the Catholic Biblical Association and of the Chicago Society of Biblical Research. He has authored numerous books and articles and recently completed a two volume commentary on the Psalms for the *Old Testament Message* series, for which he is co-editor.

**John Paul Szura, O.S.A.** is Assistant Professor of Psychology and Theology, and Director of CTU's Master of Divinity program. He has been active in the leadership of Pax Christi and has written and lectured widely on issues of peace and justice.

**Paul Wadell, C.P.** is Instructor in Ethics and is completing his doctoral dissertation at Notre Dame University.

# Part I
# The Biblical Viewpoint

# 1

# Peace in a Universe of Order

*Dianne Bergant, C.S.A.*

"A theology of peace should ground the task of peace-making solidly in the biblical vision of the kingdom of God." (#25) Thus the bishops write in *The Challenge of Peace: God's Promise and Our Response.* Following this direction, the present chapter is an investigation of one part of that biblical vision. Two themes will be treated. One, that of warrior-God, has been explored within the Pastoral itself. (#31, 32) The other, harmony in all of nature, is only mentioned in passing. (#27, 32, 36, 37, 38) These themes have been chosen for two reasons. First, it is the position of this study that, though quite different in perspective, they both grow out of faith in the sovereign and universal reign of God. Second, a closer look at both themes can enhance our appreciation of their importance in a theology of peace.

Several pressing questions will be raised but not answered within this article, which attempts merely to examine the biblical tradition that must influence the way we formulate our answers.

Any serious examination of the issue of peace really requires that the question be properly situated within the broader perspective of universal order or harmony. The past may have been able to endure a compartmentalization of reality; the present certainly cannot. In fact, the modern sciences, both physical and social, have confirmed the ancient pre-scientific view of cosmic interrelationship and interdependence. As far as we know, the same natural laws govern the galaxies as regulate the tides or the momentum with which a child's ball rolls down the hill. We all recognize that family, tribal and national loyalties serve to bind people together for the well-being of the individual and the welfare of the group. However, as societal involvement expands to cosmopolitan proportions, such more parochial interests must give way to global concerns. What may at first appear as relinquishment of national autonomy or prosperity may very well contribute to international progress or enhancement. Thus the world is gradually moving toward a fresh realization of cosmic interrelationship and interdependence.

Limiting our consideration to certain societal or physical concerns, we might do well to ask ourselves some very straightforward questions. Why are we really concerned about peace? Are we afraid that armed conflict will disrupt our social life? Threaten our economic prosperity? Challenge our national reputation? And what of the physical world? Do we admit any responsibility for the preservation and future vitality of our environment? Or are we only interested in exploiting it to serve our fancies? In our discussions of peace do we deal with issues of justice and of societal structures that are enabling? Are we willing to meet legitimate human needs by redistributing the goods of the earth? How often have we pondered our obligations of stewardship of the natural riches of our world? Is peace a value in itself or a means to an end, that end being material comfort?

We are a people who claim a religious tradition. We are informed by this tradition, informed not merely in an intellectual sense but in a fuller sense. This tradition is meant to permeate our minds and hearts and thereby to effect everything about us. It ought to inspire us, animate us, shape us, transform us. It should direct us as we engage in dialogue with our world. The outcome of this dialogue may indeed be shrouded in the mystery of the future, but the values that are brought to bear in this dialogue originated in the past and have been brought into the present by fidelity to the tradition. The result of the interaction between contemporary life experience and traditional religious values may well result in a slightly different or an innovative articulation of these values. This is due especially to the uniqueness of our life experiences. We are faced today with multiple threatening situations that demand careful yet immediate attention. As we face these crises we can neither uncritically restate theological formulations of the past nor hope facilely to apply principles that have little bearing on the complexities of the present. This situation could very well mean that there are no easy answers to religious questions about peace in our day.

A cursory glance at the Scriptures suggests that two prominent themes reflect biblical Israel's struggle with and understanding of social and environmental order. They are: the reign of God in the lives of women and men; and order in the universe based on the sovereignty of the creator. Actually, these two themes are not distinct from each other, but are slightly different manifestations of one and the same belief — God rules all and we must live in harmony with that rule.

## *"Yahweh is a warrior" (Ex 15:3)*

The Pastoral states that the image of warrior-God gave way to "a more profound and complex understanding of God." (#32) This study offers a slightly different interpretation. True, the image changes as Israel's life experience is altered. But is the deeper theology behind the image set aside? The following investigation attempts to discover this deeper theology and then to suggest that it is not.

The ancient Near Eastern world cherished a mythical pattern that provided an explanation of the origin of the

world and some of the laws that governed that world. This
pattern described a primordial battle between two gods.
One of these gods, a valiant warrior, was the embodiment of
order while the other, a monster of the sea, was a comparable embodiment of disorder or chaos. Although some of the
details of the myth may have varied with different civiliza-
tions, basically the story always followed the same line.
There was a fierce and resolute battle that threatened the
very foundations of the universe. Chaos was finally conquered and its forces were restrained. However, they were
never fully vanquished, thus future conflict remained a
possibility. In the meantime, the victorious warrior-god
secured the cosmic order that had been threatened, entered
in triumphant procession into the royal city, and established
himself as divine ruler in his temple-palace. Thus he ensured
peace for all those who showed him reverence and fealty.
With few exceptions, this divine conqueror was portrayed
as a male deity. This was due primarily to the social structures of the people wherein the ruler was king.

Biblical Israel incorporated this myth into its treasury of
religious imagery to be used again and again in various ways
as the creative inclination of the people saw fit. It appears in
liturgical expressions:

> Who is this King of Glory?
> The Lord, strong and mighty,
> the Lord, mighty in battle.   (Ps 24:8)

in historical narrative:

> Let us flee from before Israel: for the Lord fights for them
> against the Egyptians.   (Exod 14:25b)

and in prophetic denunciation:

> Behold, I am against you,
> Pharaoh, King of Egypt,
> the great dragon that lies
> in the midst of his streams,

that says, "The Nile is my own;
I made it."   (Ezek 29:3)

The God of Israel was the victorious warrior who had overthrown the nation's adversaries, both cosmic and national, and had re-established order in the universe and peace among the peoples. This image of a warrior-god has frequently dismayed women and men of faith, especially now when so many are looking to the Scriptures for inspiration and direction in their efforts for peace.

The issue is further complicated by the fact that there are vastly different reasons for engaging in forms of armed conflict. We have all been victims to, if not involved in, struggles for justice, liberation and freedom. We have been encouraged in our striving by biblical theology which proclaims the divine preferential option for the poor and which repeats the prophetic promise of deliverance from oppression. On the other hand, we are also well acquainted with the international vying for world ascendancy and the wars of aggression that often stem from this rivalry. Aggression for the sake of security and prosperity is a prominent theme in the biblical accounts of the occupation of the land. In fact, the people appear to be merely following the will of God as they wrest the land from those already living there. In the face of this, what does the biblical tradition have to say to the contemporary problem of armed conflict? Does the Bible really foster a message of peace, or is its theology arbitrary? Truly bellicose?

There is no denying that the Hebrew Scriptures relate accounts of tribal and national battles. There is no denying that they portray Yahweh in the forefront, leading the people in the conflict. There is no denying that the people credit their God with the final victory. Therefore, there is no denying that biblical Israel did indeed perceive Yahweh as a warrior-god. The narratives recounting liberation from the oppression of Egypt as well as those describing the occupation of the land of Canaan include details of violence either perpetrated or condoned by Yahweh. How are we to understand these traditions, much less draw impetus from them?

A look at the traditions may provide some insight. The central theme of the historical tradition is the Exodus. It testifies to Yahweh's commitment to justice and right order. It paints a picture of the victimization of one people by another and the intervention of a savior-god to counter this exploitation. The ritual reenactment and celebration of this victory is a commemoration of deliverance, not of conquest. Justice, not dominance, was to be served even at the expense of violence and death. Were there another way of achieving this goal, surely the tradition would have lauded it.

A second theme, and perhaps one difficult to appreciate, is the occupation of the land by means of aggressive military campaign. Recent biblical scholarship has claimed that the settlement was accomplished by other than military means which included: support from slaves in revolt against petty kings; incorporation of mercenary troops as well as oppressed serfs; commitment through treaty to other Canaanite peoples or groups already related by distant ancestral ties. These insights notwithstanding, the aggression and violence that are extolled cast serious doubt on the revelatory significance of the traditions. Even if the occupation was viewed as a struggle for independence similar to the deliverance from Egypt, can one conclude that armed conflict is an acceptable, even theologically desirable, means of achieving justice? This question must be answered first from the perspective of biblical Israel before we can respond from the point of view of the contemporary scene.

Three important points must be made at the outset. First, one of the early characterizations of Yahweh was that of a victorious warrior who won sovereignty by overcoming the forces of chaos. Second, this same God was the special patron of the people of Israel, ready and willing to intervene on their behalf. Third, those nations that appeared to threaten Israel were considered enemies of Yahweh as well. Thus, belief in the sovereignty of Yahweh, the personal character of the covenant, and the idea of divine election all influenced the nation's theological interpretation of history.

Given the ancient Near Eastern mythological concept of a

primordial cosmic battle, the theology of Israel cast Yahweh in the role of victor, far surpassing all other gods in power and wisdom and creative ingenuity. If, as was held, this cosmic battle had ramifications on national and societal levels, then Yahweh's conquering force would be unleashed in history and in society as well.

Further, Israel believed that its patron God was present in every detail of its history, from the secret ponderings of the human heart (Ps 139:1-6) to the momentous selection of the divinely graced king (1 Sam 16:1). Yahweh was a God who caressed with tenderness (Hos 11:3-4) and also chastised with severity (Hos 11:5-7); a God who meekly endured rejection (Mic 6:3-5) and furiously punished infidelity (Mic 6:13-16). We should not be shocked to find Yahweh present and active in the midst of battle, or at least perceived as such. Like it or not, human history is a record of personal and societal failure as well as success. If Israel believed in the all-encompassing presence of God, then they had to deal with this presence in the midst of dilemmas where the only options were between various evils and not between evils and goods. They believed that God was there, inspiring them to seek what was best in situations where, from our perspective, nothing looked good.

Finally, reflecting on their history and conscious of the survival and prosperity that they enjoyed, the people saw themselves as especially blessed by their God. Gradually, as their concept of this God took shape and assimilated to itself characteristics of other deities, Israel considered itself a special people because they had been chosen by this preeminent God. Fealty to any other god needed to be eradicated from the face of the earth, and the people may well have felt that such an eradication was their solemn and sacred duty.

Returning to the questions that seem to plague us — Does the Bible really foster a message of peace, or is its theology arbitrary? Bellicose? Are the traditions of a warrior-god revelatory? Can armed conflict be an acceptable, even theologically desirable, means of achieving justice? These questions do not admit to simple answers. However, if we search for the faith that lies behind the Bible's literary expressions, historical accounts, and theological themes of armed conflict we will be better prepared to understand our religious heritage and bring it to bear on our current situation.

In view of the circumstances of the ancient Near Eastern world and biblical Israel's experience in that world, conquest imagery may well have been the most meaningful way of articulating the nation's faith in a God who surpassed all other gods, who was present to the people amidst hardship and trial, and who bestowed blessings on them far beyond their imagining. At another time in history, this same theology may have been expressed in different terms and other imagery. Remembering this we can address the pressing questions.

The bible *does* foster a message of peace. This can be seen in both the Hebrew and the Christian Scriptures (Isa 9:2-7; Eph (2:14-22). It does not, however, give us detailed instructions on how to achieve it. Each generation in turn must commit itself to the struggle and, depending upon circumstances, arrive at its own conclusions. This commitment means that the generation is far from being arbitrary; it is being faithful to the tradition and to the times.

Warrior-god traditions *are* revelatory, but they reveal the splendor of God, not of war. They tell of a God of unprecedented majesty and unsurpassed solicitude. Here is a God that is not only with the people, but for the people as well.

The final question over which we agonize today is: Can armed conflict ever be an acceptable means in our struggle for justice? It is not enough to say: "Yes, the Scriptures sanction it." One can just as easily find admonition condemning any call to arms. Rather, we as individuals and as a community must search behind the biblical articulations to discover the faith that inspired these expressions. We as individuals and as a community must also probe the reality of our own life experience, examine our motivation, and consider the consequences of our actions. We must bring our religious values to bear on our examinations. Only then can we hope to answer the questions of our age with an honest and religious integrity worthy of our dignity and our commitment.

## *"And God saw that it was good!" (Gen 1:25b)*

Although there is no explicit development of the theme of harmony in nature, the Pastoral does refer to it. Societies around the world are beginning to appreciate the importance of this issue. No longer is it viewed as the exclusive concern of "nature-lovers." It is central to every movement that is working toward the establishment of some form of world order. It has ceased to be seen as secondary, much less unimportant. Hence, it behooves us to examine our biblical tradition in this regard.

Most of the theology of early Israel flows from its experience as a people. Traditions about its birth, growth and decline, its cult and its law all contribute to a kind of religious history. It has become almost commonplace to hold that this *Heilsgeschichte* or "salvation history" is the basic framework of ancient Israelite thought. There is, however, another theme the significance of which is becoming more and more evident. This is the theme of creation. Scholars are reevaluating the ancient Near East's preoccupation with world order. They are beginning to see that order and its opposite (chaos) were primary concerns of biblical Israel and were not merely peripheral ideas. The current view sees the doctrine of creation attendant on covenant theology. The new perspective suggests that creation is the dominant theme within which all other views move. The first position could be called anthropocentric with a particular people as a focus. The second might be characterized as cosmocentric with the universe as the point of reference.

This second point of view is prominent in the wisdom tradition and can be seen in such books as Proverbs, Job, or the Wisdom of Solomon. One of the major themes of this tradition is order. It seems that the ancients believed that there was a definite order in the universe and that it concluded the cosmic, the historical/societal, the interpersonal, and the personal realms. All things were to be in proper relationship within its own sphere and with elements of all other spheres. Only then could one be assured of peace. The wisdom writings of the ancient Israelites indicate that they did not seem to differentiate between these spheres as we might today. They believed in a basic "world order" which regulated all of reality, even the world of the gods. Everything was to accommodate itself to this "world order." To understand the structure of the order was to have wisdom.

What was this "world order"? Whence did it come? Who or what was responsible for its stability and endurance? Puzzled by passages like Proverbs 8:22-31, some biblical theologians have defined it as a divine attribute, a personification of God, or even a lesser deity. Whatever the sacred author intended by the passage, this mysterious wisdom had its origin in God and embodied the primordial secrets of creation. Women and men have been in perpetual search of this elusive wisdom but have been forced to reconcile themselves with the acquisition of empirical knowledge. This coveted primal wisdom may have been hidden within creation itself far from reach of human beings, but its manifestations of order and regularity have not been hidden. They can be observed, predicted, understood. The lessons learned from the observation of and reflection upon the order and regularity of the universe and all that is within it comprise the treasures of the knowledge of the ages. We continue to search and are more confirmed in our conviction of cosmic interrelationship and independence.

One might ask how this understanding corresponds with the picture painted in the creation account of Genesis 1. There the blessing bestowed upon humankind is joined to a commission: "Be fruitful and multiply, and fill the earth and subdue it; and have dominion over the fish of the sea and over the birds of the air and over every living thing that moves upon the earth" (Gen 1:28). Is this not an indication that women and men have the earth and its creatures at their disposal? Do not "subdue" and "have dominion" imply conquest? How can a vision of interrelationship and interdependence be reconciled with an attitude of subjugation and mastery? A closer look at the context of the Genesis account will suggest an answer to this question.

First and foremost, we are creatures of the earth. We do not transcend it; we come from it and we return to it. During the short span of life that is given to us, we live on the earth and are sustained by it. We are subject to the laws of growth and development as is every other living creature, and we fall victim to the forces of death and decay. True, we are also endowed with the powers of consciousness, but even they depend upon our corporeal being for their functioning. This kinship with the material world should make us sensitive to the part we play in the drama of survival. We may have learned some of the workings of the world, but we are still subject to its laws and, try as we may, we can manipulate them only so far.

There is no question about the superiority of humankind over the creatures of the earth. It would appear from the biblical text that this superiority is somehow related to the image of God according to which humankind was created. The text says very little about the nature of this image, giving more attention to its function. Even this is not clearly stated and there are many scholarly opinions on the point. As was the case in neighboring cultures, so in Israel, this image/likeness had relational significance. The ancient ruler was often spoken of as the image of the god, thought to be a physical descendant of the deity. The earthly sovereign acted in the place of the god as ruler in the land and over the land. It is in this manner that the human being should be understood in the Genesis 1 account. Not a menial slave such as is found in the creation myths of ancient Near Eastern cultures, this creature is the representative of God in the realm of creation. As image of God, the human being exercises dominion in the place of God. Such an exalted distinction does not allow for total disregard of the animals or of the land. There is still considerable limitation and restriction in the human exercise of authority. The delegated sovereign is to act as a regent of the true sovereign and not as an absolute ruler independent of God.

Responsibility for the earth and the things of the earth along with accountability to the creator are implied in the concept of image of God. What some have erroneously interpreted as unrestricted mastery over the rest of creation is really responsibility for it. Rather than to exploit the riches at its disposal, humankind was meant to exercise responsible stewardship over them. This stewardship demands that the laws governing the interrelationship and interdependence of the created universe be respected and observed. It further suggests that no component of the natural world will be irresponsibly sacrificed for the satisfaction of another.

The moral implications of this point of view are many. We may be both herbivorous and carnivorous, but does this entitle us to disregard the need for replenishment of the natural world? Do we have the undisputed right to rape the earth and the atmosphere, stripping them of resources in order to indulge in vain pleasure or gratuitous experimentation? May we contemplate the possibility of sacrificing the delicate balance of nature to the idol of national supremacy? On the other hand, should environmental preferences stand in the way of legitimate human need? Should conscientious research be halted because it involves risk? Do we not have the right, indeed the duty, to defend ourselves against military aggression?

Once again we are faced with questions that strain us to our limits. As religious people we must take our tradition seriously and open ourselves to its demands regardless of the cost. At the same time, we are people of the twentieth century with its advantages and its dilemmas. Not only religion but science too is reminding us of our responsibility and warning us that disregard of this admonition could result in devastating consequences.

## Conclusions

This brief study of two biblical themes is offered as a beginning of reflection on our religious tradition in the face of a pressing concern of the day. This concern — peace — is considered from both a societal and an environmental perspective. The traditions — Yahweh, a warrior-god, and the harmony in nature — have been examined with an eye to an appreciation of the theology underlying the imagery and articulation as well as the relevance of this theology for today.

The first tradition was a specific way of understanding the sovereignty of Yahweh, the personal character of the covenant, and the special care which was bestowed upon Israel. The second tradition had much in common with the ancient Near Eastern world view of order and balance. Both traditions point to biblical Israel's faith and trust in Yahweh the almighty God and the harmony within which all must live.

Events of our time lead us to conclude that the peoples of the world are in dire need of an expanded worldview. No longer can we be concerned with exclusively regional or national issues. We are citizens of the world, affected by international affairs as well as local events. This does not deny the legitimacy of a country's interests, but it seeks to measure these interests in view of the welfare of the entire human family.

This worldview will embrace the entire created universe. It will call us to reclaim our rightful place within this universe, a place wherein we can value our commonality with the rest of creation as well as our uniqueness within it.

The time is ripe for fostering attitudes of peace: interdependence rather than independence; communion rather than mastery; justice rather than exploitation; stewardship rather than manipulation; cooperation rather than competition; compassion rather than indifference. *How* we do this is the challenge of our time. *That* we do this is the urgency of the moment.

## For Further Reading

Thomas Berry, "The Ecological Age," *Whole Earth Papers #12* (East Orange, NJ: Global Education Associates, 1979) 4-11.

Peter Craigie, *The Problem of War in the Old Testament* (Grand Rapids: Eerdmans, 1978).

Patricia Mische, "Toward a Global Spirituality," *Whole Earth Papers #14* (East Orange, NJ: Global Education Associates, 1982) 4-14.

Rudolf Smend, *Yahweh War and Tribal Confederation* (Nashville: Abingdon Press, 1970).

# 2

# The Prophetic Price for Peace

*Carroll Stuhlmueller, C.P.*

This chapter explores the prophetic insight into peace and the prophets' long journey towards a universal call to peace. This journey led the prophets through winding ways of politics, through political success and achievement as well as through the dark ways of intrigue and disappointment. Finally, the journey seemed to stop on a mountain peak of vision. Yet here as always prophecy was grounded on faith in God and on a wholesome concern for the poor.

## The Human Path towards Peace

Prophecy evolved with the changing scene of Israel's national existence, with the variety of Israel's political leaders and across a complex international panorama. This shifting scene of politics makes prophecy difficult to read and interpret. Yet, the prophets are not to blame. They spoke out clearly, unable to contain at times, as Jeremiah confesses, the "fire burning in my heart, imprisoned in my bones" (Jer 20:9). Or again, as Amos declares:

The lion roars —
who will not be afraid!
The Lord God speaks —
who will not prophesy!

Amos' words are not presented as questions; the *New American Bible* rightly ends each couplet with a defiant exclamation mark! Amos must prophesy clearly and forcefully. Difficulty in catching the meaning of the prophetic message lies both in a literary style, at times apocalyptic and very symbolic, as well as in the complexity of politics. Finally, the prophetic solution is not found in politics nor in rhetoric, but in faith. Israel's religious heritage offered a dream to be achieved humanly, and therefore through politics and economics. Yet it was a dream of faith, divinely inspired and reached only by heroic faith, by firm confidence and ultimately by God's special intervention.

One prophetic preacher compared this dream and its way of fulfillment to the image of rain. In this poem the prophet spoke first of God's thoughts and ways, "as high [above us] as the heavens are above the earth." Yet God's thoughts and words come down "from the heavens [gently like] rain and snow [and] soak the earth, making it fertile and fruitful, giving seed to the sower and bread to the one who eats." The prophet then concludes:

So shall my word be. . .
It shall not return to me void
but shall do my will. (Is 55:9-11)

The American bishops, in their Pastoral on peace, are proceeding on a prophetic course: struggling within the changing and meandering ways of human politics; sustaining social justice and the rights of the defenseless; and themselves sustained by an intuition of faith which reaches beyond human efforts and is to be achieved by God alone. As they wrote in one of the opening paragraphs of the Pastoral:

It was part of [covenantal] fidelity to care for the needy and helpless; a society living with fidelity was one marked by justice and integrity. Furthermore, covenantal fidelity demanded that Israel put its trust in God alone and look only to him for its security. When Israel tended to forget the obligations of the covenant, prophets arose to remind the people and call them to return to God. True peace is an image which they stressed. (#34)

We now delay over four important moments of Old Testament prophecy, to recognize how a supernatural "dream" or divinely inspired intuition of faith led through Israel's political arena to a vision of peace when —

> They shall beat their swords into plowshares
>     and their spears into pruning hooks;
> One nation shall not raise the sword against another,
>     nor shall they train for war again. (Is 2:4)

We explore: *first*, the early history of prophecy and its struggle for social justice and for adequate political structures; *then*, we turn to the first of the "classical prophets" with books to their names, an individual named Amos, whose preaching evolved from social justice for Israel to a strong hint of universal cooperation and peace; *third*, to Isaiah whose memoirs are located in chaps. 1-39 and who recognized that at times peace or in one instance non-action is the only moral solution; and *finally*, to Second Isaiah, author of chaps. 40-55, who during the painful Babylonian exile found peace in a faith for world salvation.

## The Complicated Path of Early Prophecy

The origins and early development of prophecy, like all of its later history, are located in a double phenomenon, one intensely religious, the other unequivocally political! Their call for peace is a divine summons within human and even international patterns of life.

The first prophet clearly to appear in the Bible is the foreigner Balaam, whom the Moabite king, Balak, asked to "come and curse this people [Israel, who] are stronger than we are. We may then be able to defeat them" (Num 22:6). We notice at once the contributing factor of politics and war in the prophetic quest for peace. It will eventually become politics for peace, but that is a long distance from Balaam who beheld in a trance "a star [that] shall advance from Jacob [and] smite the brows of Moab, and the skulls of all the Shuthites" (Num 24:17).

The other factor, strong in the formation of prophecy, comes also from early Mosaic days. This was Moses' intuition of Yahweh as "a merciful and gracious God, slow to anger and rich in kindness and fidelity" (Exod 34:6), especially towards "the affliction of my people [and] their cry of complaint against their slave drivers" (Exod 3:7). There was also Moses' championing of individual rights to receive the spirit and to speak a divine message. Such was the case of elders who decided cases of social justice and settled people's complaints. "The Spirit came to rest on them [and] they prophesied" (Num 11:25), even on two of them not present at the original investiture of elders. When Joshua jealously complained, Moses' reply was direct and simple: "Would that all the people of the Lord were prophets!" (Num 11:29). Prophecy, therefore, was frequently a divine intervention for the needy and helpless. Such was a clear marker on the prophetic path towards peace.

Prophecy, however, was not to show up most forcefully among the institution of elders but among a group called, in Hebrew *benē-nebī'īm*, a prophetic guild which clustered around great shrines like Gibeah, Ramah, Gilgal, Mizpah and Jericho, where great prophetic leaders lived, Samuel, Elijah and Elisha (1 Sam 10:5-8; 10:17; 2 Kgs 2-6). We witness the prophetic action for peace as a way to save Israel from social disintegration and other injustices towards the poor.

When Israel was collapsing and falling apart under the mighty, iron-weaponed Philistines, "all the elders of Israel

came as a body to Samuel at Ramah and said to him,
'...appoint a king over us, as the other nations have, to
judge us'" (1 Sam 8:4-5). Several important factors emerge
clearly: a) royalty which was to become an important religious symbol, even for the messianic age of peace, originated as a foreign, secular importation; b) royalty
amounted to a radical departure from the style of leadership
inherited from earlier days, including those of Moses, and
an acceptance of a Canaanite or Egyptian form against
which Israel had fought bitterly upon entering the land, as
God said to Samuel, "It is not you that they reject, they are
rejecting me as their king" (1 Sam 8:7); c) a prophet like
Samuel was responsible for this innovation; and d) the
change was necessary because Israel was losing its political
and economic independence, and consequently its ability to
secure peace with integrity.

When the prophet Samuel anointed the first kings, Saul
(1 Sam 10:1; 11:12-15) and later David (1 Sam 16:13), he
began a tradition by which prophets made and unmade
kings (1 Sam 13:13-14; 15:26; 1 Kgs 1:11-14; 2 Kgs 9:1-10).
Prophets even sanctioned the *ḥerem* or holy war (1 Sam
15:3; see the chapter of Professor Dianne Bergant). The
prophets' political power gradually led to abuses in their
ranks, so that prophets announced as divine oracles whatever the kings wanted. Eventually, *prophet* was arguing
publicly *against prophet* (the title of a book on this subject
by Simon John DeVries, 1978) and their credibility was
certainly waning, as we see in 1 Kgs 22. It was from such
venal, ambitious prophets that Amos (7:14), Micah (3:5-8),
and Jeremiah (chap. 28) suffered greatly.

Yet, the guild prophet or *benē-nebî'îm* still continued as
God-fearing individuals in the person of Elijah who
defended the right of Naboth to his vineyard, a family
inheritance, even facing down King Ahab and Queen
Jezebel with the extermination of their royal line (1 Kgs 21).
The prophets paid and demanded a price for peace. It was
not to be peace at any price!

The prophetic demand for quality-peace, for peace with

social justice and divine ideals, was inherited by a new type of prophet, the "classical" ones with books to their name. We now study their contribution to peace.

## Amos: Prophet of Justice and Salvation

Amos (around 760 BCE) may seem an awkward candidate for a study of peace. He never uses the Hebrew word for peace, *shālôm*, and derivatives occur only in somewhat different meaning (1:6, 9) or else as a liturgical sacrifice to be rejected: "nor do I consider your stall-fed peace offerings" (6:22). Yet, in his fierce condemnation, Amos enabled prophecy to take a vigorous step forward towards world peace, peace that is worthy of God's dreams for it.

First of all, Amos condemned the ruthless, inhuman ways of warfare and he considered the Israelites just as guilty as the foreigners for their cruelty towards the poor. Gentile nations were to be punished for their barbarous actions: cutting a bloody path "with sledges of iron" through people's homes and families (1:3) or making a profit from captive soldiers by selling them as slaves to another country (1:6, 9) or "ripping open expectant mothers" (1:13). Amos did not condemn war outright, but he denounced practices normal at time of war. This judgment was not based upon any specific piece of biblical revelation but upon the deep-seated humanity of everyone created by God.

Amos, moreover, finds the Israelites equally guilty as their foreign neighbors. Amos calls their action "a crime," in Hebrew *pesha'*, a word not used in the Mosaic lawcodes but reaching back into pre-Mosaic days, to the ancient clan traditions as in Exod 22:8 (where the Hebrew text attests polytheism among Israel's ancestors). The *pesha'*, committed by Israel, consisted in: selling the poor into slavery because of insignificant debts, using the pledge, taken from indigent people, to get drunk and to perform illicit sex in the sanctuary (2:6, 8). Other social crimes are enumerated by Amos:

— trampling upon the weak by exacting levies of grain
    (5:11);
— accepting bribes and repelling the needy at the gate
    (5:12);
— fixing the scales for cheating (8:5).

Because of these crimes, Israel had forfeited the rights of
the covenant and was to be punished severely. Despite the
benefits of God's wisdom in the covenant (3:1-2), Israel
acted no differently than the other nations. Here is where
Amos, by divine inspiration, arrives at an extraordinary
insight for world peace and salvation. Israel's exodus, he
claims, is no different from the migration of other nations:

> Are you not like the Ethiopians to me,
>   O men of Israel, says the Lord?
> Did I not bring the Israelites from the land of Egypt
>   As I brought the Philistines from Caphtor
>   and the Arameans from Kir? (9:7)

This "one-liner" or isolated statement within an appendix to
his preaching (9:7-10) declares that Israel's religious institutions and symbols can be transferred into the culture and
political history of other nations/peoples. All are capable of
salvation; each has experienced a migration which can be
seen as a sacred "exodus" leading to a promised land and to
peace. World religions must dialogue and compare religious
intuitions and so lay a religious groundwork for universal
peace.

## Isaiah: The Immorality of Action

Isaiah (740-690 BCE) has been immortalized across the
world by his vision of peace:

> In days to come,
> The mountain of the Lord's house
>   shall be established as the highest mountain

and raised above the hills.
All nations shall stream toward it,
    many peoples shall come and say:
"Come, let us climb the Lord's mountain,
    to the house of the God of Jacob,
That he may instruct us in his ways,
    and we may walk in his paths."
For from Zion shall go forth instruction,
    and the word of the Lord from Jerusalem.
He shall judge between the nations,
    and impose terms on many peoples.
They shall beat their swords into plowshares
    and their spears into pruning hooks;
One nation shall not raise the sword against another,
    nor shall they train for war again. (Is 2:2-4)

This vision of Isaiah can be understood only within the context of Jerusalem, its temple on Mount Zion and its dynasty in the Davidic family. By struggling for God's ideals of justice and peace within these political and religious institutions — institutions which led Israel to war and which suffered catastrophically from the eventual defeat of Israel's armies — Isaiah like Amos arrived at a vision of true and lasting *shālōm*. The focusing of this vision took a long time.

*First*, it was never to be peace at any price, nor for that matter religion at any price. In chap. 1, a summary in many ways of the entire corpus of Isaiah's preaching in chaps. 2-39, Isaiah threatens the temple and city with such devastation that "daughter Zion is left like a hut in a vineyard, like a shed in a melon patch." The offerings at the temple were considered "worthless" and "your incense loathsome to me," says the Lord. To correct this cultic situation, Isaiah turns to social justice:

Make justice your aim: redress the wronged,
hear the orphan's plea, defend the widow (1:16)

A temple will not be left standing on Mount Zion and therefore no instruction about peace flow from it, unless the orphan and the widow, the proverbial symbol of the poor and the defenseless, are cared for.

*Second*, Isaiah leads us through the most complicated moment of Jerusalem's political history and arrives at a very simple solution: quiet trust in God and thereby peace. Jerusalem is being attacked by the combined forces of Damascus and the northern kingdom of Israel (2 Kgs 16) who intend to replace the Davidic King Ahaz with an usurper called Ben Tabeel. The situation is so serious, that "the heart of the king and the heart of the people trembled, as the trees of the forest tremble in the wind" (7:12). Morally, there was nothing that King Ahaz could do. He was militarily too weak to march against the invaders. Nor could he ethically turn to Assyria for help, for in doing that, he would barter away Jerusalem's independence to save his royal privilege. Yet that was already what he had done! Isaiah gave the only advice, morally acceptable, yet humanly very heroic to accept, the advice which led to interior peace and thereby to national peace and well-being:

> For thus says the Lord God,...
> By waiting and by calm you shall be saved,
> in quiet and in trust your strength lies.
> But this you did not wish.
> "No," you said,
> "upon horses we will flee."
> — Very well, flee!
> "Upon swift steeds we will ride."
> — Not so swift as your pursuers....
> Yet the Lord is waiting to show you favor,
> and he rises to pity you;
> For the Lord is a God of justice:
> blessed are all who wait for him! (30:15-18)

In this long passage, crucial for understanding Isaiah's prophecy, the way to peace was total and absolute, even heroic, in its expectation of faith; it was also the *only* way. At times, no matter the price of peace, it must be paid in terms of trust and even of risk.

Despite such heroic expectations of religious faith, Isaiah remained within the realm of politics. King Ahaz' son, Hezekiah, continued the dynasty. Isaiah wrote a magnificent poem to be sung at his coronation. It is comparable to other anointing formulas like Pss 2 & 110. The English translation only faintly resonates the golden tones of the Hebrew text:

> For a child is born to us, a son is given us;
>     upon his shoulder dominion rests.
> They name him Wonder-Counselor, God-Hero,
>     Father-Forever, Prince of Peace.
> His dominion is vast
>     and forever peaceful. (9:5-6)

Though peace was God's gift, it would come, like the child Immanuel, through a human parent, whether this be the royal dynasty at Jerusalem or the virgin Mary of Nazareth.
    In still another passage, Isaiah projects the vision of peace into the distant future. The passage reads in part:

> But a shoot shall sprout from the stump of Jesse,
>     and from his roots a bud shall blossom.
> The spirit of the Lord shall rest upon him:...
> He shall judge the poor with justice,...
> Then shall the wolf be a guest of the lamb,...
> The baby shall play by the cobra's den,...
> There shall be no harm or ruin on all my holy
>     mountain....    (Is 11:1-9)

The main ingredients of Isaiah's prophecy merge in this vision of peace: Davidic dynasty, the holy mountain of Jerusalem with its temple, justice especially for the poor, the fulfillment of all promises, plus the stories about paradise in Genesis 2-3 that circulated in the Davidic-Solomonic court (we call them the "J" or Yahwist tradition). The price of peace was faith and heroic expectation, justice at all costs, wholesome family life, an ecumenical vision of worshipping together at the holy mountain. Religion was expected to bring to the surface of political and sociological thinking the supreme ideal of God's hope and God's gift of peace.

## Second Isaiah: The Servant of Peace

We make one final step along the way of Israel's prophetic tradition towards peace, this time during the Babylonian exile. Despite the eloquent preaching of pre-exilic prophets, Jerusalem collapsed under the Babylonian war machine, in fact twice, in 597 (2 Kgs 24:8-17) and in 587 BCE (2 Kgs 25). Jeremiah announced it this way:

> Small and great alike, all are greedy for gain;
>     prophet and priest, all practice fraud.
> They would repair, as though it were nought,
>     the injury to my people:
> "Peace, peace!" they say,
>     though there is no peace.
> They are odious; they have done abominable things,...
>     in their time of punishment they shall go
>     down, says the Lord.    (Jer 6:13-15)

We are never allowed to forget the prophetic price for peace. It was paid during the Babylonian exile, in fact, according to the prophet we call Second Isaiah, "double for all her sins" (Isa 40:2).

The prophet, responsible for chaps. 40-55 in the scroll of Isaiah, remained anonymous, called Second or Deutero-Isaiah, or even the Great Unknown. His preaching leads up to the magnificent phrase: "the chastisement that makes us whole," or in Hebrew *mûsar shelômēnû*. The first word, *mûsar*, indicates suffering that is disciplinary, purifying and strengthening; one of its derivatives occurs frequently enough in Jeremiah (2:19; 31:18) and Proverbs (19:18; 29:17). The other word, *shelômēnû*, is literally peace (*shā-lôm*) of us (*-ēnû*), or "our peace." In this phrase Second Isaiah accepted the nation's and his own sorrows and losses, each experienced either as Israel's price for injustice and infidelity or as his own price for exalted ideals of world unity and salvation, and saw in this suffering a disciplinary force for true peace.

In a few short years, between 550 and 537 BCE, Second Isaiah took a long journey. He began his career, enthusiastically announcing to the poor and needy (41:17-20) a new exodus back to the homeland (43:1-7), honestly recognizing Cyrus the Persian as God's anointed leader to achieve this wonder for Israel (45:1-7). He was ridiculed by his own people for giving this role of a new Moses to the foreigner Cyrus (45:9-11), but patiently and silently suffered for his good tidings to the nations (42:1-4) and eventually realized that God wants "salvation [to] reach to the ends of the earth" (49:6). For this ultimate ideal of world salvation and universal peace, he was rejected (52:13—53:12), yet his message remains in the Hebrew Scriptures, forever announcing that such "chastisement [is] for our peace" (53:3).

This summary hardly does justice to the grandiose vision and rhapsodic poetry of Second Isaiah. Limitations of space restrict us in still other ways. In our study of the prophetic way to peace, we stop mid-way, at the end of the Babylonian exile, with more than 500 years ahead before "the fullness of time" (Eph 1:10).

## In Conclusion

We saw how prophecy developed out of the stern desert days of the founder Moses, and out of foreign religious groups like that represented by Balaam. Already with Balaam politics had a stake in prophecy. Early prophetic groups, the *benē-nebî'îm*, fell heavily on the side of the poor. When all Israel was left helpless under the Philistine invasion, prophecy championed the radical change towards royalty. When royalty oppressed the poor, they too were condemned and removed. Amos saw the entire northern kingdom of Israel, like other foreign people, under sentence of extermination for violating social justice and human decency. Yet, this world scene which leveled Israel to the situation of all other people gave Amos a transient vision of universal salvation and therefore of world peace.

Isaiah enabled us to see another, heroic demand in the way of peace, the moment to do nothing as one waits upon the Lord. Yet, Isaiah did very much, with rhetorical elegance and energetic championing of the rights of "orphans and widows," to glimpse world peace that centered in Jerusalem and in the dynasty. Isaiah is the master politician for peace.

Second Isaiah accentuates the role of suffering for one's ideals in the name of a compassionate God who controls world-order for all peoples. Peace results from disciplinary suffering.

These stages of the prophetic quest for peace within the Hebrew Scriptures delineate major moments of United States history. Without denying this parallel to other peoples and countries, we point out the "exodus" days of Moses in the early migrations from Europe and our early religious leaders who like Balaam saw a vision of future glory through the politics of the new land. Immigrants generally clustered together in language groups, protected by their own Elijahs and Elishas against plutocratic industrialists. Like the *benē-nebî'im* of early Israel the immigrants secured justice and basic human dignity.

Then came the American parallel to the classical prophets, when individuals with a fierce rage for righteousness condemned the descendants of the immigrants for opposing social justice towards new groups within our country. This new breed of prophets dared to question the non-negotiable principle of American life: that every American war was for justice and world peace.

Prophecy continues to evolve in USA as in ancient Israel. The period of the classical prophets continues with the American bishops' Pastoral on peace. Here with eloquence and strategy, with consultation with a host of experts, there emerges clearly and supremely the demand of faith. The risks of war are so immoral in their consequences and so imminent in their possibilities that peace must be risked at all price, even at the price of suffering that humiliates and disciplines us as servants of the Lord.

Today an Isaiah is crying out with prophetic strength: "By waiting and by calm you shall be saved." The action of war is immoral and self-destructive. We are not alone in our waiting. We are reassured: "The Lord is waiting to show you favor." Therefore, how "blessed we are who wait for him."

## For Further Reading

Walter Brueggemann, *The Prophetic Imagination* (Philadelphia: Fortress, 1978).

James Limburg, *The Prophets and the Powerless* (Atlanta: John Knox Press, 1977).

Carroll Stuhlmueller, "What Price Prophecy?" *The Way* 20 (1980) 167-175.

_____, "The Prophetic Combat for Peace," *The Way* 22 (1982) 79-87.

_____ with Donald Senior, *Biblical Foundations for Mission* (Maryknoll, NY: Orbis Books, 1983).

J. Carter Swaim, *War, Peace and the Bible* (Maryknoll, NY: Orbis Books, 1982).

# 3

## Religion and Politics:
## Paradigms from Early Judaism
### Leslie J. Hoppe, O.F.M.

### Introduction

One criticism made of the bishops' Pastoral letter is that it
mixes religion and politics. Those who raise this objection
are not so naive as to think that the two can never mingle.
There is just too much evidence to the contrary. How many
sanctuaries in America have the national flag hanging
within them? Political conventions, legislative debates and
judicial sessions usually begin with an invocation of the
deity. The objection regarding the mixing of religion and
politics results from the bishops' attempt to contribute to
the national debate regarding nuclear arms. Those who
criticize this attempt prefer the church to stay out of the
debate until the question is settled on the political level.
Then, of course, religion can be used to support and legitimate the political consensus arrived at without "interfer-
ence" from the church.

The people who produced the Bible had quite a different
view of the relationship between religion and politics. The

Bible is not a collection of timeless truths nor is it the work of objective historians. On the contrary, the individual books which make up the Bible emerged from very specific historical situations. The Bible reflects the religious experiences of people who lived in certain places and at specific times. While the Bible does offer certain emphases and patterns, negations and affirmations which have been accepted by the church as normative, these were not formulated outside the political arena. This is especially true of the Hebrew Scriptures whose interest in history reflects an interest in politics. Kings are anointed, criticized, deposed, assassinated. Prophets judge the political actions of both Israel and the nations.

The New Testament too makes political statements. A portion of the Passion Narrative may have been composed to refute the view which considered Jesus to have been a threat to the state (Luke 23:13-15; John 18:38). Advice is given to Christians as to how they are to relate to the Roman government (Rom 13:1-7; 1 Pet 2:13-17). The Book of Revelation is a scathing attack on Roman persecution of the church. It is not too far off the mark to consider the Bible to be a political manifesto.

What is true generally about the biblical tradition is quite obvious in the texts, both canonical and extracanonical, which were produced by early Judiasm. The literature that was composed in the midst of the Jews' struggle against the Hellenistic Empire of the Seleucids in the 2nd century B.C. is as political as any in the Bible. The conquest of Alexander the Great deprived nations throughout the ancient Near East of their national monarchies. Naturally these nations nurtured the hope that their own dynasties would be restored some day. In the Jewish tradition this hope is called messianism. However Jewish messianic expectations were not unique in the Hellenistic world. Egyptian, Persian and Babylonian texts likewise display a fervent hope for the restoration of their own respective monarchies. Such literature is nothing less than a charter for political resistance in which religion and politics are not only mingled but fused.

This fusion was inevitable since kingship in the ancient Near East was primarily a religious concept. The rule of the king was simply the terrestrial counterpart of the heavenly rule by the national god.

Though wary of the dangers which Hellenism posed for their ancestral religion, the Jews lived peaceably under Greek domination for more than 150 years. The Jews had some measure of self-government and were free to practice their religion. With the accession of Antiochus Epiphanes (175-164 B.C.) the situation changed abruptly. This Seleucid king desecrated the Temple and proscribed the practice of the Jewish religion under pain of death. His actions precipitated a revolution. The despotic actions of Antiochus, however, were merely the immediate causes of the Jewish resistance to his political order. The rejection of the king's policies went much deeper than a reaction to unjust laws. It was a question of the entire political order in which the rule of Antiochus usurped the rightful rule of Judah's God. In the resistance to Antiochus religion and politics were one and the same since the ideology of the resistance was taken from the religious traditions of ancient Israel. Hellenism and its political order had to give way to a resurgence of the ancestral religion of the Jews.

Though there was a general agreement among Jews that the rule of Antiochus must be replaced by an ideal religious and political order, there was a variety of viewpoints regarding how resistance to the Seleucids was to proceed. There were those who insisted upon armed revolution while others preferred non-violent resistance and even martyrdom as the way to restore the rule of God over the Jews. Within the Jewish resistance movement, there was a striking divergence of views regarding the most appropriate way to replace the evil rule of Antiochus with the benevolent rule of God. This article will consider four of the options presented in some of the literature inspired by the crisis with Hellenism: the militancy of 1 Maccabees, the value of martyrdom according to 2 Maccabees, the non-violent resistance of Daniel and the pacifism of the Testament of Moses.

## The Militancy of 1 Maccabees

First Maccabees is a history of Israel which recounts the events in Judah from the accession of Antiochus in 175 B.C. to the accession of John Hyrcanus I, a Jewish high priest and king, in 134 B.C. This book is the principal source of material for reconstructing the history of the Jews in Palestine during the mid-second century B.C. Its purpose is to legitimate the rule of the Hasmoneans, a Jewish priestly family, by showing how they were able to defeat the Seleucids, end the persecution of the Jews, reinstate the observance of the Law and usher in a period of peace and prosperity.

The militant ideology of the book is clear enough from the description of the revolution led by its protagonists against the Seleucid empire. A certain Mattathias began the revolt when he killed a collaborator (1 Macc 2:23-26) and began guerrilla operations against the forces of the enemy. Before his death Mattathias urges his sons to continue the revolt. He predicts the fall of Antiochus (2:61-63) and exhorts his sons to be the instruments of the evil king's punishment (2:50, 66-68). The description of the battles which comprise the revolution led by Mattathias and his sons is modelled after that of wars of conquest found in the Books of Joshua and Judges. In these accounts, it is quite clear that the outcome of any battle is determined by God who fights for Israel; nonetheless, there is a strong emphasis on the human contribution to the victories of God. The army must take the field; its role is crucial.

First Maccabees gives ample evidence of the same type of synergism which marks the holy war ideology of the biblical tradition. The primacy of divine activity is evident in 1 Macc 3:17-19: the size of the army is of little consequence since its strength comes from God. On the other hand, the Jews will be exterminated unless they decide to fight (2:40). Military action is the key to survival and national salvation (3:8). Individual military leaders are given high praise (1 Macc 3:3-9; 14:4-15). It is an understatement to say that 1 Maccabees attaches great importance to the armed resistance to the Seleucids.

The goal of this armed resistance was to bring an end to Antiochus' rule over Judah and to restore political and religious independence to the Jews (2:19-21). Mattathias states that his motivation is strictly religious (2:20). The means to achieve this end is a holy war in which the Jews will fight for and with God. The outcome of the revolution will be an era of peace and prosperity. The Maccabees bring Israel "peace through strength." Their fundamental ideology was a fusion of politics and religion.

## Martyrdom in 2 Maccabees

Second Maccabees is not a continuation of 1 Maccabees but a condensation of a no longer extant multi-volume history of Israel covering the years 180-161 B.C. There is some overlap with 1 Maccabees and comparing their respective descriptions of the same situations makes it clear that 2 Maccabees looks at the revolution against the Seleucids from a somewhat different perspective. The ideology of holy war is present here. The Jews can fight with confidence since they fight along with God (8:18) and angelic armies (10:29-31). But to the usual notions associated with holy war, 2 Maccabees adds the idea of martyrdom as another way the faithful might contribute to the ultimate victory over the Seleucids. In other words, military action is not the only way that humans can participate in the holy war. The book devotes chapters 6 and 7 to the sacrifice of the martyrs of the revolution. When the armies of the Jews take to the field, their leader calls upon God to attend to "the blood that cries out to him" (8:3). Military prowess is not the only way to victory. The blood of martyrs cries out to God for vengeance and thereby seals the ultimate victory for the Jews. Though this book modifies the holy war ideology of 1 Maccabees, it too fuses politics and religion by calling for martyrs to lead the way to victory over the Seleucids.

## The Non-Violent Resistance of Daniel

The Book of Daniel purports to detail events in the life of a certain Jew named Daniel who was exiled in Babylon during the reigns of Nabuchadnezzer and his immediate successors. The book was actually composed during the persecution of Antiochus and reflects the circumstances of those perilous times. The author's use of mythological symbols in the visions recounted in chapters 7-12 attests to the belief that Antiochus' policies were actually rebellion against God. The purpose of these visions was to announce the intention of God to end the rebellion and inaugurate a great era of peace and salvation for the Jews. The Book of Daniel really describes two levels of reality which are clearly separate but nonetheless related. What is happening on earth has repercussions in the heavens and vice versa. When Antiochus persecutes the Jews, he is actually rebelling against God. When God judges Antiochus, his fall is inevitable. Daniel labels the deliverance of the Jews as God's victory — the triumph of divine judgment.

Like the Books of Maccabees, Daniel reflects the traditions of holy war. It is Daniel's belief that the real conflict takes place not on the earthly but the heavenly plane that sets this book off from the other two. As a consequence, Daniel does not have a high regard for the militancy represented by the Maccabees. Certainly resistance to Antiochus is necessary but this resistance is non-violent. It expresses itself in a willingness to undergo suffering and even death. The book can offer non-violent resistance as an option because of its confidence that the faithful will rise again and "shine like the brightness of the heavens" (12:2-3). The actual warfare against the forces of evil is left to God and Michael (12:1). The first vision (chap. 7) sets the tone of the entire book. The conflict between Antiochus and the Jews is resolved in a dramatic judgment scene. Here the evil king's fall is decreed and his kingdom will be given to "the people of the saints of the Most High" (7:26-27). This is hardly a call to arms. The saints do not need to fight since Antiochus' fate has been already sealed. All they need to do is to stand up to the king by not complying with his orders to abandon the God of Israel. They must be ready to endure whatever suffering will result from this non-compliance. Daniel's attempt to locate the real conflict in heaven enables him to find hope even in the deepest crisis. Daniel wishes to show his readers that there is another reality beyond this world. The promise of resurrection assures the faithful that they can experience this higher reality. The promise of resurrection enables the faithful to accept suffering and even death.

Daniel does not positively exclude hopes for national restoration which is the goal of the Maccabean revolution; rather, his own visions really cannot be fulfilled by any revolution. The kingdom Daniel hopes for is a heavenly kingdom. Its victory will be the work of God and the heavenly host led by Michael. The faithful simply prepare themselves for the ultimate triumph of God by accepting suffering and death which will come their way because of their non-compliance with Antiochus' laws. The kingdom of God does not require militancy of its human subjects but only their fidelity unto death.

## The Pacifism of the Testament of Moses

A fourth response to the Seleucid crisis is found in the Testament of Moses, a non-canonical text also known as the Assumption of Moses. The bulk of this work comes from the time of the persecution of the Jews by Antiochus though the book's present form dates from the early part of the 1st century A.D. The Testament was inspired by the final chapters of Deuteronomy (31-34) which are re-interpreted and rewritten to have Moses describe specific events associated with Antiochus' persecution which is presented as God's punishment of Israel's sins (8:1). Those who accept a martyr's death during this persecution rather than "transgress the command of the Lord of Lords, the God of our Fathers" (9:6) lead to God's direct action on behalf of the Jews (9:7; 10:2).

The Testament has no room for the militancy of the Maccabees. The expected deliverance will come by direct divine intervention. The catalyst for the deliverance of the Jews is the death of those who remain faithful to God and the Law. The victory of God, however, does not consist in the re-establishment of a Jewish state and a national monarchy. What the faithful wait for is Israel's separation from the nations and its exaltation in the heavens (10:8-10).

While 2 Maccabees has a high regard for martyrdom, the Testament presents it as the very stimulus which moves God to exalt Israel to the heavens. In 2 Maccabees the Jewish armies are instruments of the kingdom while the Testament attributes Antiochus' downfall to an angel who acts without any human instrument (10:1). The martyrs of the Testament are quietists who attain their goals by submitting to death. This is the only role that humans can play in a holy war. Though Daniel does not treat of martyrdom explicitly, the book stands in basic agreement with the Testament since both attempt to encourage faithful Jews in a crisis which did mean death for many of them. Though pacifist in its orientation, the Testament of Moses is nonetheless a powerful political statement.

## Conclusion

The range of responses to the religious crisis provoked by Antiochus' persecution is striking. On one end of the spectrum there was the nationalistic militancy of 1 Maccabees which fought for the restoration of the Jewish state. On the other end was the pacifism of the Testament of Moses which embraced martyrdom as the only way to move God to save Israel and exalt her to the heavens. In the middle were 2 Maccabees which glorified both martyrdom and armed resistance and Daniel which supported non-violent resistance. While there were diverse responses to Antiochus' persecution from within the Jewish community, it is important to note that each of them was political, i.e. each demanded a specific stand against the political power of the day. At the same time they were religious since they drew their inspiration from the religious traditions of the ances-. tral religion of the Jews. While the specific response advocated by each of these four texts may have been different, they were all political statements since the Seleucid crisis did not permit the Jews the luxury of withdrawing into the secure realm of a purely private form of religious expression.

The resistance against Antiochus was dominated by the militancy of the Maccabees but the evidence of non-violence and pacifism cannot be denied. Daniel and the Testament of Moses reinterpret the holy war tradition so as to insure that the defeat of Israel's enemies is left entirely to God without the aid of any human instrument. The Jews are to play their part by remaining faithful to the Lord though their fidelity will mean death. When Jesus came proclaiming his message, he used that blatantly political word *Kingdom*. Perhaps that is why the Romans had no hesitancy in executing him as a threat to their hegemony over the Jews of Palestine. Jesus, however, did not reflect the militancy of the Maccabees with its concern to restore the Jewish monarchy. But like those who resisted Antiochus, Jesus had a basic concern for the political order. At the same time, however, Jesus' teaching of the kingdom was one that pointed to dimensions beyond time and space. The followers of Jesus need to have his concern for the political order, but the expression of that concern ought to reflect their faith in the certainty of God's victory and the transcendence of the Kingdom.

The bishops Pastoral is remarkable in its sensitivity to the paradoxical nature of Jesus' approach to the political order. The bishops have considered the question of nuclear policy so important that they found it necessary to participate in the national debate over this issue. Their Pastoral letter is a call for all American Catholics to make their own contribution to resolving this grave matter that calls for a decision on the part of this nation. Yet the bishops' contribution to the national debate is unique because it flows from the assurance of faith that God will be victorious over the power of evil. This assurance does not prevent the bishops from taking their courageous stand regarding the nuclear question; rather, it has impelled them to offer the American people a special perspective on the question — the perspective of believers who look hopefully and confidently to the victory of God's Kingdom — a kingdom of justice, peace and love.

## For Further Reading

R. H. Charles, "The Assumption of Moses" in his *Apocrypha and Pseudepigrapha of the Old Testament* (Oxford: Clarendon, 1913) 407-424.

John J. Collins, *The Apocalyptic Vision of the Book of Daniel* (Missoula: Scholars Press, 1977).

George W. Nickelsburg, *Jewish Literature between the Bible and the Mishnah* (Philadelphia: Fortress, 1981).

_____, *Studies on the Testament of Moses* (Cambridge: Society of Biblical Literature, 1973).

# 4

# Jesus' Most Scandalous Teaching

### *Donald Senior, C.P.*

The root of the word "scandal" is the Greek term "*scandalon*" or "obstacle." "Scandal," in this root sense, means something that gets in the way and blocks us. In the Gospels, Jesus' hometown people of Nazareth had a hard time believing the great things he did because they found him to be a "scandal" (Mark 6:3). No doubt many of Jesus' contemporaries had a similar experience; Jesus did not fit the mold and, therefore, he was difficult to accept.

The issue of peace will, I suspect, bring out the scandal in Jesus in a way few other contemporary issues can. Of all the provocative things Jesus had to say, perhaps none is more difficult than his teaching on *love of enemies*. This aspect of Jesus' teaching on peace is mentioned in the bishops' Pastoral letter:

> Jesus also described God's reign as one in which love is an active, life-giving, inclusive force. He called for a love which went beyond family ties and bonds of friendship to reach even those who were enemies (Matt 5:43-48; Luke 6:27-28). (47)

By all counts, the proposal to actively love an enemy is a difficult, "scandalous" teaching. One can sense this if the abstraction "enemy" were to be translated into the raw circumstances of today's world: Americans are to actively love Russians; Derry Catholics must love the Ulster Defense Force; the Cambodians should love the Khymer Rouge; and so on. Things get no better if individual and personal cases of "enmity" are thought of: parents should love the drunken driver who ran over their only child; a raped woman should love her assailant; the owner of a home should love the intruder who ransacked and robbed it.

Considering circumstances like these, many devout Christians would either dismiss the injunction to "love your enemies" as pious drivel or, worse, as dangerous insensitivity to the rights of the victim and the obligations of justice. In connection with the issue of nuclear arms, one outspoken critic of the bishops' Pastoral declared that no bishop would make her love the Russians; she deserves credit for sensing what ultimately may be at stake when we search the New Testament as part of our efforts to build a theology of peace.

Since the "enemy love" tradition is so "scandalous" and because it is, in fact, an important and characteristic teaching of the New Testament, I would like to consider this single facet of the biblical foundations for peace.[1]

## *"Enemy Love" in the New Testament*

First of all, we should make it clear that the command to "love your enemies" is, in fact, a capital part of the New Testament. The explicit saying "love your enemies" is found in the Gospels of Matthew and Luke. Similar exhortations about blessing and doing good to enemies rather than reviling or doing evil toward them are found in three of Paul's letters (1 Thessalonians, 1 Corinthians and Romans) and in the First Letter of Peter. The evidence suggests that there

---

[1] I have discussed these materials in a related but different format in "Enemy Love: The Challenge of Peace," *The Bible Today* 21 (1983) 163-169.

was a steady stream of tradition on this point in the early church, a tradition rooted in the teaching of Jesus himself.

## The Saying in Matthew and Luke

Most scholars believe that Matthew and Luke have preserved the original saying of Jesus that stands behind this remarkable New Testament tradition on dealing with enemies. Each evangelist has adapted Jesus' teaching to their own particular circumstances but the substance of the original is intact.

The saying in Matthew is found in 5:44. I will quote the material in its full context (5:43-48):

> You have heard that it was said, "You shall love your neighbor and hate your enemy." But I say to you, Love your enemies and pray for those who persecute you, so that you may be sons [and daughters] of your Father who is in heaven; for he makes his sun rise on the evil and on the good, and sends rain on the just and on the unjust. For if you love those you love you, what reward have you? Do not even the tax collectors do the same? And if you salute only your brethren, what more are you doing than others? Do not even the Gentiles do the same? You, therefore, must be perfect as your heavenly Father is perfect.

It should be noted at the start that this remarkable teaching comes at a climactic point in the Gospel. It is found in the Sermon on the Mount as the final "antithesis" (e.g. "You have heard it said, but I say to you . . .") in a series of six, each of them illustrating how Jesus has come to bring the law of Israel to its fullest expression (cf. Matt 5:17). Matthew presents Jesus as the Messiah, the one who discloses in word and deed the will of God for his people. Jesus' teaching on enemy love serves as the final and most provocative expression of what the law intends.

In Matthew's presentation, Jesus' teaching is put in contrast with previous interpretation of the Law ("you have heard it said"). The injunction "You shall love your neighbor" is taken from Leviticus 19:18; but the phrase "hate your enemy" is not found in the Hebrew Bible. It probably reflects the sectarian mentality of some groups in Israel at the time of Jesus. The strict Jews who formed a monastic life at Qumran on the Dead Sea in reaction to the compromises of the ruling class spoke of lawless Jews and Gentiles in bitter condemnatory language (especially against the Romans who occupied Israel at this time). Jesus' own teaching, by contrast, does not speak of vengeance towards the enemy but of "love." This phrase may be part of Matthew's adaptation of the original saying of Jesus. Matthew's own church had experienced persecution from the Pharisees. Following the Jewish revolt against the Romans in A.D. 66-70, culminating in the siege of Jerusalem and the burning of the Temple by the victorious Roman troops, the Pharisees had become the leaders of Judaism, enabling it to rebuild and survive. But relationships between the Pharisees and the Jewish Christians became soured and the two religious groups moved further and further apart. Missionary activity of Jewish Christians among Jews was opposed. Thus the "enemy" for Matthew's Christians was no longer the "enemy" (presumably the Romans) that Jesus had encountered. Now that enemy was defined as "those who persecute you."

The crucial part of the saying in Matthew comes with the motivation offered. The disciple is to love the enemy because that makes them truly children of "your Father in heaven." God himself is indiscriminately gracious: letting his sun shine and rain fall on both good and bad, just and unjust. Mere reciprocity is not enough: even "tax collectors" and "Gentiles" (symbolic of the unconverted person in Matthew's Jewish-Christian context) are capable of loving those who love them. The Christian must be as gracious as God is, loving those who do not love you. In this way the disciple becomes "perfect" as God is "perfect" (5:48). The Greek word used here is *teleios* which has the connotation of

"complete" or "whole." What Matthew's text implies, therefore, is that God's nature is best expressed in his indiscriminate and gracious love; and the disciple who seeks God will
find full life in experiencing and sharing this same kind of
love.

Therefore, for Matthew's Gospel love of enemy is not an
isolated saying but one that expresses God's very nature
and, at the same time, the ultimate criterion of genuine
discipleship.

Luke's version of the saying is similar but, as in the case of
Matthew, bears the imprint of the evangelist's own circumstances and style.

> But I say to you that hear. Love your enemies, do good to
> those who hate you, bless those who curse you, pray for
> those who abuse you... If you love those who love you,
> what credit is that to you? For even sinners love those
> who love them. And if you do good to those who do good
> to you, what credit is that to you? For even sinners do the
> same. And if you lend to those from whom you hope to
> receive, what credit is that to you? Even sinners lend to
> sinners, to receive as much gain. But love your enemies,
> and do good, and lend, expecting nothing in return; and
> your reward will be great, and you will be sons of the
> Most High; for he is kind to the ungrateful and the selfish.
> Be merciful, even as your Father is merciful. (Luke 6:27-
> 28, 32-36)

In Luke, too, this teaching of Jesus has pride of place: it
comes at the very beginning of Jesus'"Sermon on the Plain"
and serves as the first and most demanding of Jesus' instructions to his disciples.

The basic saying "love your enemies" is repeated twice
(6:27, 35). Luke multiplies the phrases which define the
"enemy": "those who hate you," "those who curse you,"
"those who abuse you," and apparently those who borrow
your goods without returning them (6:34-35)! At the same
time Luke amplifies just what "love" is to mean: "do good
to," "pray for," "lend to." Connecting enmity with borrow-

ing and lending is a unique feature of Luke's text and ties
into an emphasis of his Gospel as a whole. His Gospel is
lined with parables and sayings that warn of the corrupting
influence of riches (see, for example, 12:13-21, 41-48; 16:19-
31; 18:18-30, etc.). By linking the question of sharing one's
goods ("lending") with "enmity" Luke further adapts the
original saying of Jesus and applies it to "enemies" created
through economic tensions.

Luke retains the crucial connection between the teaching
on enemy love and one's experience of God. To love an
enemy makes the disciple a son or daughter of God "for he is
kind to the ungrateful and the selfish" (v. 35). Through the
terms "ungrateful" and "selfish" (different from Matthew's
"bad" and "unjust") Luke retains his focus on the issue of
sharing possessions. God is lavish in his gifts; so must his
children be. To love the enemy makes one "merciful, even as
your Father is merciful" (6:36); Luke's term "merciful" is
more immediately expressive than Matthew's "perfect."

We might note that both Matthew and Luke seem well
aware of the "cost" of enemy love. To refuse to return
violence for violence and to actively love the enemy can only
be done on the basis of radical commitment to the values of
God's rule. This is clearly demonstrated in the passion
narratives of both Matthew and Luke where Jesus himself is
presented as refusing to take up arms in his own defense. In
Matthew's story of the arrest (26:47-56), Jesus tells his
disciples to put their swords back into their scabbards, "for
all who take the sword will perish by the sword," a refusal of
violence and retaliation that coincides with Jesus' own
teaching in the Sermon on the Mount (cf. Matt 5:38-39,
43-48). In Luke's account, when the disciples ask, "Lord,
shall we strike with the sword?" (22:49) and one of them cuts
off the ear of the high priest's slave, Jesus commands, "No
more of this!" and heals the slave's ear (22:51): words and
action that clearly demonstrate Jesus' own teaching in the
Sermon on the Plain (Luke 6:27-29).

In both instances Jesus' refusal to take up the sword in his
own defense leads ultimately to the cross.

This quick survey of the materials in Matthew and Luke

might be summarized in the following observations about the love of enemies texts:

1. Both evangelists place those sayings at crucial places in the structure and conceptual framework of their Gospels. Love of enemies is not presented as a peripheral teaching of Jesus but at the heart of his message.

2. The teaching is rooted in an experience of God as gracious, merciful and indiscriminately loving. This element, common to Matthew and Luke, was surely part of Jesus' own teaching: his boundary-breaking ministry to outcasts and sinners, his many parables about the mercy of God, and his interpretation of law with love and compassion as first principles all reflect Jesus' own experience of God as lavishly merciful.

3. "Love" of enemies is defined in active terms: praying for, blessing, doing good to, lending to, etc. It is not an abstraction or a merely passive attitude.

4. The teaching of Jesus is not left by the evangelists as an abstract, timeless principle; it is adapted to the concrete circumstances of their communities. Both the meaning of "enemy" and the meaning of "love" take on new connotations in different social and political contexts.

## The Tradition on Enemy Love in Paul and 1 Peter

The exhortation to love the enemy rather than returning evil is also found in several New Testament letters. Here the provocative expression "love your enemies" is not found but the substance of Jesus' teaching is clearly present.

Two brief expressions of the tradition are found in 1 Thessalonians 5:15 and 1 Corinthians 4:12-13. The text in 1 Corinthians is not a direct exhortation to the community but is part of Paul's reflections on his experience as an Apostle: "When reviled, we bless; when persecuted, we endure; when slandered, we try to conciliate...." The words Paul uses ("revile," "bless," "persecute") are, as we shall see, stock terms of this New Testament tradition.

The text in 1 Thessalonians comes near the conclusion of

the letter as Paul instructs the community on how they are
to live in the world: "See that none of you repays evil for evil,
but always seek to do good to one another and to all." The
phrase "and to all" shows that Paul intends this instruction
to apply not simply to relations within the community but
also to outsiders, to those who might harass or slander the
Christian community. Of critical importance for understanding this text is the *basis* of Paul's exhortation. Earlier
in the same chapter as he begins a series of instructions to his
young Christian community, Paul reminds them that they
are "all children of light and children of the day; we are not
of the night or of darkness" (5:5). Paul refers to a fundamental part of the Christian vision: the Christian lives not in a
world of despair and alienation but in expectation of God's
coming triumph. The Christian believes that God's power
has radically destroyed the grip of evil over creation. The
believer lives in full hope of redemption; therefore the values
that animate the Christian are not those of violence and
enmity but of love and peace (cf. Paul's listing of these
virtues in 5:12-22).

Although the language is quite different, the motivation
for enemy love that Paul offers here is, in fact, quite similar
to that presented in Matthew and Luke. It is the experience
of God's gracious and transforming love that impels the
Christian to live by a set of values that directly challenge the
world's logic.

Paul's most complete discussion of non-retaliation is
found in Romans 12:14-21:

> Bless those who persecute you; bless and do not curse
> them. Rejoice with those who rejoice, weep with those
> who weep. Live in harmony with one another; do not be
> haughty, but associate with the lowly; never be conceited.
> Repay no one evil for evil, but take thought for what is
> noble in the sight of all. If possible, so far as it depends on
> you, live peaceably with all. Beloved, never avenge your-
> selves, but leave it to the wrath of God; for it is written,
> "Vengeance is mine, I will repay, says the Lord." No, "if
> your enemy is hungry feed him; if he is thirsty, give him

drink; for by so doing you will heap burning coals upon his head." Do not be overcome by evil, but overcome evil with good.

There are a number of observations that can be made about this passage. First of all, similar to the text in 1 Thessalonians, it comes at a key point in the letter where Paul begins a series of instructions to the Roman Christians on their life in the world. Paul's exhortation applies not only to relationships within the community but to "all," including the outsider and the "enemy" (note that Paul explicitly mentions the enemy in 12:20). And the entire instruction follows Paul's reflection on the overwhelming mercy of God (cf. 11:29-36; 12:1). The Christian who has experienced God's mercy is to live accordingly.

The language Paul uses in the passage is strikingly similar to the Gospel tradition, especially that of Luke: "bless those who persecute," "repay no evil for evil," "do good," etc. Here we see strong continuity with the tradition rooted in Jesus' own teaching.

There are some special features in this text. One of the motivations Paul seems to suggest for not retaliating is that God will do so on the final day. Paul quotes Deuteronomy 32:35, "Vengeance is mine, I will repay, says the Lord." This is similar to the reasons offered for not retaliating against enemies in a number of Jewish writings contemporary with the New Testament period. But in the subsequent verse Paul seems to step away from the note of God's vengeance. Quoting Proverbs 25:21-22, the Christian is told "if your enemy is hungry feed him; if he is thirsty, give him drink; for by so doing you will heap burning coals upon his head." Although its precise meaning is obscure, many scholars believe that "heaping coals upon the head" stems from an Egyptian ritual signifying the attempt to change one's viewpoint. Paul's meaning, therefore, would be that the Christian by doing good to the enemy ("feeding," "giving drink to") will transform them from enemy to friend. That is what Paul says in the conclusion to the passage: "Do not be overcome by evil, but overcome evil with good." This text vividly illustrates that the New Testament tradition on enemy love was never viewed as a passive stance but as an active and transforming expression of good towards the enemy.

A final example of the enemy love tradition is found in 1 Peter 3:9-12.

> Do not return evil for evil or reviling for reviling; but on the contrary bless, for to this you have been called, that you may obtain a blessing. For "He that would love life and see good days, let him keep his tongue from evil and his lips from speaking guile; let him turn away from evil and do right; let him seek peace and pursue it. For the eyes of the Lord are upon the righteous, and his ears are open to their prayer. But the face of the Lord is against those that do evil."

This beautiful passage, which has striking similarity to Paul's instructions and to the Gospel traditions of Matthew and Luke, fits into the mood of the entire letter. The author of 1 Peter writes to Christian communities in northern Asia Minor who are small outposts of faith surrounded by an often hostile majority culture; he calls them "exiles" and "aliens" in their own world (cf. 1:1, 2:11). Instead of adapting a defensive posture, the letter urges the Christians to be involved in society, to be good citizens and to live in such a way that their good conduct will win over their critics (cf., for example, 2:12).

The passage we have cited above comes near the conclusion of the letter where the author is instructing various groups within the community. In this passage he addresses the community as a whole. In language typical of the enemy love tradition, he exhorts them "not to return evil for evil" but "to bless." This stance, the author insists, is the meaning of the Christian vocation: "to this you have been called." A quotation from Psalm 34:12-16 ("He that would love life. . .") reaffirms that the Christian call is not mere abstinence from evil but the active pursuit of peace (3:11).

## Conclusions for a Theology of Peace

Our quick survey of these New Testament texts may help us consider some of the implications of this biblical material for a theology of peace in a nuclear age.

1. First of all, as Christians we have to wrestle with the fact that "love of enemies" and prohibitions against retaliation are important New Testament teachings, rooted in the very words of Jesus himself and taken up in a steady stream of teaching within the early church. At the very least, it cannot be ignored or dismissed if one wants to have a biblical foundation for our contemporary Christian life.

2. The taproot of this tradition is the Christian experience of God. Here is the radical intuition that gives force to the teaching: God's own relationship to humanity, as revealed by Jesus, is one of indiscriminate, gratuitous mercy and compassion. This experience is basic to Jesus' own mission of proclaiming the coming rule of God. The God who was coming is, in fact, a God not of vengeance but of mercy. All reality, all structures and human relationships, must ultimately be transformed in the light of this reality. This fundamental dimension of the enemy love tradition seems to suggest that a Christian theology of peace cannot be constructed only on the basis of common sense or natural law. It is the core religious experience of Christianity, which discloses both the nature of God and the value of the human person that fires the scandalous proposal to love an enemy.

3. "Non-retaliation" and "enemy love" are not understood in the New Testament as passivity or non-action. The whole thrust of the tradition in its various expressions is that the "enemy" is to be addressed in a vigorous and transforming manner. Enemy love does not mean abandonment of the pursuit of justice or devaluing the defense of authentic values. At issue are the means appropriate for the Christian pursuit of justice. This New Testament tradition rules out "reviling," returning evil for evil, cursing the enemy. The Christian is not to adopt destructive violence as a way of transforming the world. Instead, the Christian is to confront

the "enemy" with goodness. They are to be "blessed," "prayed for," "fed," "given drink," "lent to," "healed." The New Testament is not naive about the aggressive power of evil; after all, it connected the enemy love tradition with the cross. To love an enemy is, in a very real sense, an eminently aggressive act; it seeks to totally transform the nature of the relationship; it does not allow the enemy to remain enemy.

4. The tradition on enemy love must not be made an abstract ethical principle detached from the social and political milieu of those who attempt to live the Gospel. Exhortations about non-retaliation against enemies are not unique to the New Testament or Christian tradition. Stoic philosophy (especially as represented in the writings of Seneca) also spoke of doing good to the enemy, as did a number of Jewish writers. A key element in such exhortations is societal relationships between the one who proclaims enemy love and the ones to whom it is addressed. The powerful could be advised not to retaliate against their enemies in order to demonstrate superior virtue; they do not need to bother with insignificant enemies. The poor and defenseless, such as the slaves or minorities or captive peoples, could be warned not to retaliate against their enemies because they might incur more harm. Or those repressed could be told by the powerful to love their enemies as a means of defusing a just pursuit of their rights.

In none of these instances does "love your enemies" represent the Gospel, no matter how pious the language used to trumpet the message. The Gospel tradition on enemy love does not spring from a desire to express superior virtue, nor is it a means of defense against further abuse, or a subtle way of suppressing dissent. The Gospel tradition is based on a religious experience of God as overwhelmingly gracious and merciful. That experience gives a new vision of how we stand before God and each other; it is the ultimate reality against which all other human values and strategies are to be judged. In many ways, it is the oppressed themselves, those who experience real enmity, who are best equipped to insure that the call to "love your enemy" is in the spirit of the Gospel. For example, North Americans, many of whom do not hesitate to build an armory of incalculable violence to protect their rights, are not in a good position to preach love of enemies to the Christians of Latin America. When those who experience enmity from another are able to respond without retaliation or enmity — not simply to save their skin or out of fear — then the Gospel is being preached.

5. The New Testament tradition of enemy love is based on a vision of the world's ultimate destiny. Almost all New Testament ethical teachings are "eschatological," that is, based on a conviction about the ultimate destiny of humanity and creation. Violence, injustice, enmity, and death itself belong to the "old world," to "the darkness." But through Christ humanity is called to a life of peace, justice and love. This Christian vision is rooted firmly in the hopes of Israel, and deeper still, in the very longings of the human heart. The paradoxical stance of the Gospel is that the disciple of Jesus is called to live *now* by the values of a world that is yet to come. For the modern, existentially inclined human being this eschatological framework is undoubtedly difficult to comprehend. But little of the New Testament teachings can be understood without this perspective. The Christian is not commanded to love the enemy as if imposing a new and impossibly rigorous law. Nor is this merely pious rhetoric based on religious fantasy rather than raw facts. For the believer the human destiny of ultimate peace is just as real —even if only partially glimpsed and fleetingly experienced —as the palpable experience of evil that dogs our world. That destiny is based not so much on convictions about the evolutionary progress of humanity or verifiable trends toward enlightenment, but on faith in the God revealed through the death and resurrection of Jesus Christ.

Therefore, the call to "love your enemy" is a vivid expression of the Christian vocation as a whole. The Christian is to actively pursue peace because peace is our God-given destiny; it is "our call."

What can this scandalous teaching of Jesus mean in a nuclear age? The New Testament, of course, knew nothing of modern national security states, nor of nuclear arms, nor did it have any experience or conception of warfare on the scale of modern conflicts. There is no "biblical" answer to the issue of nuclear warfare or instructions on how to extricate ourselves from this world-destructive threat. Christ's injunction to "love your enemies" is, as we have stated, not an abstract ethical principle applicable in homogeneous fashion in all times and places. The biblical call to peace, of which enemy love is the most vivid expression, is at once a vision of the world's destiny and a compelling invitation to discipleship. Only we who are citizens of the nuclear age and followers of Jesus can construct the answer through the power of God's Spirit among us. Some Christians will serve that process by a prophetic way of life that immediately eschews all compromise with violence. Others, immersed within the ambiguities of our contemporary social and political structures — structures entwined with violence — will painstakingly attempt to move away from nuclear weapons and to find other means of achieving peace and justice. No Christian who claims to live by the Gospel can stand still, content with our present situation or simply paralysed by fear.

The Pastoral letter of the American bishops endorses both the prophetic vocation of pacifism and the pursuit of peace through negotiation and gradual disarmament as authentic expressions of Christian peacemaking. Ultimately, it could be said that both courses of action, even though at times in apparent tension with each other, are rooted in Jesus' scandalous teaching, "love your enemies."

## For Further Reading

C. John Cadoux, *The Early Christian Attitude to War* (New York: Seabury, 1982).

Victor Paul Furnish, *The Love Command in the New Testament* (Nashville: Abingdon, 1972).

Martin Hengel, *Victory Over Violence: Jesus and The Revolutionists* (Philadelphia: Fortress, 1973).

Pheme Perkins, *Love Commands in the New Testament* (New York: Paulist, 1982).

John Piper, *"Love Your Enemies" Jesus' Love Command in the Synoptic Gospels and the Early Christian Paraenesis* (New York: Cambridge University Press, 1979).

Luise Schottroff, "Non-Violence and the Love of One's Enemies," in Reginald Fuller (ed.), *Essays on the Love Commandment* (Philadelphia: Fortress, 1978).

Donald Senior, C.P., "Enemy Love: The Challenge of Peace," *The Bible Today* 21 (1983) 163-169.

# Part II
## The Ethical Viewpoint

# 5

# Power and the Pursuit of Peace: Some Reflections

*John T. Pawlikowski, O.S.M.*

## The Hebrew Scriptures and Peace

I come to an analysis of the Pastoral both as a social ethicist and one who has been deeply involved in the Christian-Jewish dialogue for well over a decade. From the latter perspective in particular the Pastoral's emphasis on the peace vision of the Hebrew Scriptures is indeed welcome. Stress is properly placed on the continuing evolution of peace as a central religious category within biblical Israel. And, very importantly, this peace perspective from the Hebrew Scriptures is presented not simply as background reflection but as a continuing mandate in faith for Christian believers. From the standpoint of the Christian-Jewish dialogue this represents a significant step in the process of restoring the Hebrew Scriptures to the center of Christian spirituality as they were for Jesus himself. This emphasis might have been further strengthened if the final draft had adopted the recommendation that the term "Old Testament" be replaced by "Hebrew Scriptures." This would have

further underscored the theological point that any comprehensive Christian theology of peace must view the Torah
tradition as central, not merely as preliminary and
peripheral.[1]

There are some crucial areas where further discussion is
necessary with respect to the Pastoral's use of the Hebrew
Scriptures in the construction of a theology of peace. For
one, too great a distinction continues to be made between
the peace perspective of Jesus and the Hebrew Scriptures,
and even within the Hebrew Scriptures themselves between
the pre-exilic and exilic periods. There is little doubt that
there exists some significant evolution within the Hebrew
Scriptures regarding the divine image and the divine-human
person relationship. This also holds true for the Second
Temple period in Judaism, the constructive era between the
two testaments which saw the coming of Jesus and the
development of the church. As time went on, the intimate
relationship between the Creator God and each human
person was increasingly recognized and made a central
focus of the divine-human encounter. God as Father, a
pivotal image for both Pharisaic Judaism and Jesus, gave a
decidedly different cast to faith identity and faith expression
than God as mighty defender of the nation.[2] In this theology
the individual person assumed a far greater significance,
though not to the total exclusion of the survival of the
community. And as the dignity of the individual person
assumed higher priority warfare, even in legitimate defense
of the country, became much more problematical.

This intense stress on the dignity of the human person was
unquestionably present in Jesus' call for reconciliation, for
love of enemies, which even the Jewish scholar of the New
Testament David Flusser had admired for its uniqueness:

---

[1] For more on the significance of "Hebrew Scriptures" rather than "Old Testament" cf. my "Why the Old Testament Needs a New Name," *National Catholic
Reporter* 14 (April 21, 1978) 11.

[2] For more on the development of Pharisaic Judaism and the teachings of Jesus,
cf. my *Christ in the Light of the Christian-Jewish Dialogue* (New York: Paulist,
1982) 76-135.

It is clear that Jesus' moral approach to God and man...
is unique and incomparable. According to the teachings
of Jesus you have to love the sinners, while according to
Judaism you have not to hate the wicked. It is important
to note that the positive love even toward the enemies is
Jesus' personal message. We do not find this doctrine in
the New Testament outside of the words of Jesus Himself
.... In Judaism hatred is practically forbidden. But love
to the enemy is not prescribed.[3]

The Pastoral's highlighting of this developing dimension
of peace and reconciliation is indeed welcome. But it is not
the whole story. Upon further examination it is clear that
the development line is not simplistically straight-forward.
And inattention by the Pastoral to the significance of the
social conditions at least partially responsible for this development leads all too easily to an exclusive focus on "peace in
Christ" which may result in an overly individualistic, hence
greatly limited, concept of peace. Such a focus tends to
concentrate too much on the peace witness of the individual
person which, while crucial, is inadequate by itself.

A fully-honed theology of peace needs to wrestle with
how a community with leaders actually engaged in governing might incorporate a peace perspective as its fundamental orientation. Exilic Israel and the Jewish community of
the Second Temple period of which Jesus was a part were
not in a position to govern. These were people under occupation. This was also true during the first centuries of
Christianity, a time when many of the Church Fathers
expressed strong peace sentiments. But unless we are willing
to renounce all societal leadership roles as Christians the
church needs a theology of peace that can adequately direct
the use of the power that all states acquire in varying
degrees.

Societal leadership also involves the judicious use of such
power in confronting threats to national existence. Many

---

[3]"A New Sensitivity in Judaism and the Christian Message," *Harvard Theological Review* 61 (1968) 126.

peace activists judge St. Augustine too harshly for moderating the pacifist orientation found in an overwhelming number of earlier Church Fathers. What they fail to acknowledge adequately is that Augustine faced a new problem as an ethical thinker. He had to produce moral guidelines for a community now in charge of preserving a people and a culture, not for a group under alien political domination as was the Christian church in earlier times. The struggle of Israel as a faith community to maintain its national destiny and religious mission in pre-exilic times thus must be seen not merely as outdated political theology, totally irrelevant for a peace perspective today, but as an important, continuing complement to the peace perspective of exilic and Second Temple Judaism as well as of Jesus. This continuing significance of the Hebrew Scriptures for a theology of peace was clearly acknowledged by Augustine. The Hebrew Scriptures expose us to a religious community which dealt with war/peace issues in a variety of political situations; the New Testament discussion of peace (as that of the Church Fathers) was confined to a single political experience — occupation. That is why the Hebrew Scriptures are vital for filling out any biblical theology of peace.

The initial tendency of the Pastoral's drafting committee, as of many peace groups, was to ignore these war texts. Ensuing revisions have now brought them into the discussion, but barely. The Pastoral now stresses some of the positive dimensions of these "war" or "liberation" themes —God's continuing faithfulness to His people even in times of social struggle; the people's expression of trust in God; God as source of security. Yet, despite these advances, the Pastoral tends to push these texts too far into the background in terms of a contemporary theology of peace. While they stand in need of redefinition, they were not merely supplanted by later understandings of the God-human person relationship as the Pastoral claims. The positive contribution of these texts to an authentic spirituality of justice has been recognized during the past several years by any number of the theologies of liberation. One of the significant drawbacks of the Pastoral is its failure to meaningfully engage liberation theology in the construction of its peace theology.

In not grappling in a comprehensive way with the "God as Liberator" texts, the Pastoral tends to bypass a thorough discussion as to whether any use of power and force is conducive to peace. Or are peace and power to be construed as antonyms? It needs to be stressed at this point that the first part of the Pastoral appears to be laying out an over-arching theology of peace, not one merely applicable to the more limited question of *nuclear* warfare. Hence it must deal both with the responsibility Christians may assume for conserving a society as well as provide guidelines for the Christian caught in the mesh of dictatorial governments. While some criticisms of the Pastoral have been overdrawn on this point, its initial construction of a theology of peace seems unduly influenced by a perspective common in sectarian Protestantism which argues that the function of the church and its individual members is to stand permanently over against secular culture and the state in faithful witness as saved remnant. Any involvement in the affairs of the state will seriously corrupt that witness.

But this is not the mainstream Catholic tradition which has defined Christian witness as much more directly involved with the actual governance of society. It should be emphasized that this latter perspective tends to predominate in the subsequent sections of the Pastoral where the bishops address specific issues related to nuclear warfare. But this reality does not eliminate my concern about the opening part of the Pastoral. For any religious group that does not eschew involvement in the continued governance of society as contrary to biblical faithfulness the power question becomes of vital concern. The sectarian Protestant peace witness, though valuable as prophetic challenge, has been conditioned far too much by an experience of church on the fringes of secular society and by an ethos which generally rejects governance in society. So its more individualistic theology of peace is incapable of providing sufficient direction for the Catholic tradition and experience on the peace question. Its response to the power question is marked by an unbending renunciation that will not fully meet the demands of societal leadership.

Some further thoughts on the power question are in order at this point. What is not fully clear in the Pastoral is the bishops' basic ecclesiological vision and its relationship to the use of power. Delineation of ecclesiological vision is crucial to a peace theology. And traditional Catholic ecclesiology and the ecclesiology of sectarian Protestantism do not blend easily. How one looks at the ecclesiological question will be a fundamental determinant of a stance on power. And there are clearly a variety of ecclesiologies operative within the religious peace movement, some of which are not easily reconcilable. Somewhere along the line one must clarify his/her ecclesiological perspective. Too many peace activists have failed to do so. Either the church and its members become directly involved in the governance of society or essentially maintain a prophetic posture over against the state. If the latter, then the power question is naturally mute. But if the former, then the power question needs to be met head-on. Certain configurations and concentrations of power, including any use of nuclear weaponry, may indeed by rejected on moral grounds within the latter perspective. But the use of power as such cannot be totally abrogated.

Karl Rahner has argued that physical force, though of sinful origins and a potential source of future sin, "is not itself sin but a gift of God, an expression of His Power, an element of the reflection of God in the world."[4] While Rahner is wrong in implying that absolute rejection of power automatically constitutes an abandonment of a Catholic's responsibility for creation, he is correct in maintaining that the use of power, including physical force, is integral to the overall process of human salvation. The bishops in the Pastoral rightly assert that peace will not come about simply by proclaiming peaceful ideals or praying for it. The building of the structures of peace is a *sine qua non* requirement as Pope Paul VI insisted in several of his

---

[4] *Theological Investigations*, Vol. 4 (Baltimore: Helicon, 1966) 197.

important writings on the subject. But if this is the case, then we must recognize that such structures of peace can sometimes only be built realistically after the destruction through power of the entrenched structures of injustice.

A Catholic theology of power, while it may leave open the pacifist option for some, must concentrate far more on the humanizing of power rather than merely rejecting its use. The words of Romano Guardini, written some years ago, remain a useful guide:

> In the coming epoch, the essential problem will no longer be that of increasing power — though power will continue to increase at an even swifter tempo — but of curbing it. The core of the new epoch's intellectual task will be to integrate power into life in such a way that man can employ power without forfeiting his humanity, or to surrender his humanity to power and perish.[5]

Any use of nuclear weapons may indeed constitute the kind of surrender to power of which Guardini speaks. But the rejection of this form of power should not be automatically linked to the rejection of all forms of power, whether military, economic or otherwise. The real challenge is to find ways of expressing power in the service of justice that will not destroy all sense of human dignity and worth, whether our own or that of our opponent.

Returning to the "war" texts of the Hebrew Scriptures it is necessary to underline that in general they do not stand in opposition to the drive for peace in the world unless one has *a priori* ruled out all use of power in that quest. Most of the biblical war texts refrain from any glorification of war as such. Those that seemingly do so should be discarded as inauthentic revelation for today. Nor do these texts in the main elevate warfare to an ultimate value for the believer. Rather the ultimate value of the kingdom for the authors of the Hebrew Scriptures, as the bishops rightly insist, is peace with justice.

[5] *Power and Responsibility* (Chicago: Henry Regnery, 1961) xiii.

What Christians need to understand and profit from in reflecting on the question of power in the Hebrew Scriptures is their particular spirituality which is deeply and unalterably rooted in the realism of history. One of the dangers involved in peace activity is that it can easily be caught up in peace slogans that have little connection with historical reality. The hardheadedness of the Hebrew Scriptures can prevent such potential flight into fancy. One of the realities the Hebrew Scriptures clearly recognize is that people are born into a world in which power is unevenly distributed, frequently resulting in widespread injustice. The question before the believing community is then how shall such injustice be overcome. This was the question, for example, before the Christians of Cuba and Nicaragua before their revolutions. This is a burning question confronting the churches of South Africa.

The "liberation" texts in the Hebrew Scriptures are telling us that power maldistribution in society will sometimes only be corrected through warfare and that God is with the people when they undertake such a redeeming struggle for their liberation. Neither God nor the believing community rejoice in such a struggle. Certainly there is always need for vigilance against the development of what Roland Bainton has termed the "crusade" mentality regarding war. But warfare is clearly recognized by the Hebrew Scriptures as a reluctant requirement in certain situations.

## The New Testament and Peace

The bishops are certainly to be commended for their clear assertion of the primacy of peace in Jesus' message and for highlighting the centrality of reconciliation in the Gospels. But absent in this section is any thorough engagement with the confrontational side of Jesus' ministry and with the social/political realities of Second Temple Judaism of which this ministry was very much a part. Slight improvement in this regard is evident in the final draft over earlier versions. But the description remains underdeveloped.

There exist sound grounds for rejecting any association between Jesus and the Zealots as the Pastoral does. But the Jesus of the Pastoral still appears as too solitary a figure preaching his notion of peace apart from the social dynamics of the Jewish community that was the context of his work. There is danger the Pastoral may endorse a model of Jesus' ministry developed by writers such as Oscar Cullmann in his *Jesus and the Revolutionaries*[6] where the stress resides almost entirely on internal transformation as a peace ethic without adequately relating such transformation to the destruction of impeding social structures.

To repeat, the Pastoral has moved a little in its acknowledgement of the confrontational side of Jesus. The invasion of the Temple account now receives mention. But unfortunately no attempt is made to spell out the implications of this episode and relate it to the prevailing social circumstances.

Jesus' action in invading the Temple, which some biblical scholars such as Etienne Trocmé[7] argue occurred quite early in the public ministry and set the tone for its remaining years, represents more than a protest against the abuse of worship. It signalled rather a far reaching disagreement on Jesus' part with the inherently exploitative Temple system, some of whose leaders were collaborating with the Roman occupying forces for their self-aggrandizement. The neglect of this activist and confrontational side of Jesus' ministry may well result in an overevaluation of passive resistance as the only valid model for a theology of peace. Such models are certainly commonplace in the peace movement today. While I respect the witness of the peace churches' passive resistance approach, I find it theologically and strategically insufficient. I am also convinced that it is based on an overly selective reading of the New Testament situation.

The comments of ethicist Stanley Hauerwas at an international conference on the Nazi Holocaust at the University

---

[6]*Jesus and the Revolutionaries* (New York: Harper & Row, 1970).

[7]"L'Expulsion de Marchands du Tempe," *New Testament Studies* 15 (1968/69) 1-22.

of Indiana are illustrative of this inadequate approach. Hauerwas, strongly influenced in recent years by the writings of Mennonite theologian John Howard Yoder who has also shaped the theology of many Catholic peace activists, said that if a Christian saw the Gestapo taking away a Jew to the death camps the only moral options available to that person from the standpoint of Christian faith would be to volunteer to replace the Jew or agree to go alongside him or her. For Hauerwas no sort of active attempt to prevent the Nazi soldiers from seizing the Jew would be permissible from a Gospel perspective. I must reject this limitation of moral options as overly narrow for a full Christian peace theology. If there seemed some possibility of rescue it would be perfectly permissible from my perspective to physically attack the Nazi soldiers in the hope of liberating the seized Jew.

What is missing from the peace theology of the Pastoral is any attempt to relate the ministry of Jesus to the power struggles within the Judaism of the period. It is my contention that a definite relationship existed. Jesus was far more interested in the social/political consequences of the "reign of God" than many would care to admit. Though he did challenge people "to recognize in Him the presence of the reign of God," as the Pastoral claims, he did not stop there as the Pastoral seems to imply. Any thorough investigation of this question involves more than a simple dismissal of any association between Jesus and the Zealots which is the extent of the Pastoral's current treatment of the subject. There is need to understand far more comprehensively than the Pastoral does the highly complex distribution of political power in Roman-controlled Palestine.

The Romans always preferred to govern their colonies through local people. Inevitably, therefore, two layers of power existed: (1) ultimate Roman political authority; and (2) everyday governing authority in the hands of indigenous collaborators with the Roman regime. Such a division of power prevailed in the Palestine of Jesus' day. The local group consisted of the ruling clique of the Jerusalem priesthood headed by the high priests Annas and Caiaphas. These leaders not only controlled the religious activities of the Jewish community but also shaped its political and social cast. A picture of them as generally corrupt and interested primarily in their self-preservation rather than the general welfare of the Jewish populace emerges from historians of the period both ancient and modern. During the period of Jesus' active ministry the power of this group was being severely challenged by the widespread reform movement in Judaism begun by the Pharisees. The label "reform movement" will no doubt sound strange to those who have been accustomed to depict the Pharisees as the epitome of legalistic rigidity and moral bankruptcy. It is not possible here to offer a comprehensive account of what the Jewish historian Ellis Rivkin has called the "Pharisaic revolution." Let me point out merely that true Pharisaism little resembled the stereotypical portrayal so widespread in Christianity. Further delineation of this Pharisaic revolution and how Jesus was related to it can be found in several of my writings, including my volume *Christ in Light of the Christian-Jewish Dialogue.*[8]

Basically, the Pharisaic movement represented a revolt of the Jewish laity against the Sadducean priests who kept a stranglehold on the people religiously and polically. By the time Jesus appeared on the scene, the Pharisees had become a formidable group putting considerable pressure on the Temple leadership. The growing strength of the Pharisees, combined with the Zealot threat, was additionally eroding Roman confidence in the ability of the priestly leadership to maintain control over their people.

Such was the political picture in Palestine at the time of Jesus. The point to be stressed is that there were two levels of political authority — the ultimate Roman and the subordinate priestly. Both were under attack. The Zealots went directly after the Roman. Their approach was violent, they were heavily outnumbered, and as is well known they were eventually liquidated in a bloodbath. Apparently, it was

---

[8]Also cf. "On Renewing the Revolution of the Pharisees: A New Approach to Theology and Politics," *Cross Currents* 20 (1970) 415-434 & "Jesus and the Revolutionaries," *The Christian Century* 89 (December 6, 1974) 1237-1241.

their belief that the Messiah would join them and insure their victory despite the staggering odds against them in human terms. The Pharisees, on the other hand, attacked the subordinate authority — the Temple priesthood. Their approach, less eschatological and less violent, was rooted both in a new theological understanding of the God-human relationship as well as a deep desire for greater social justice in Jewish communal life.

Whether out of pragmatism or idealism (probably both), the Pharisees rejected the Zealot approach to political power redistribution. They thought it impossible to eliminate Roman suzerainty over Palestine at that moment in history. Therefore, somewhat reluctantly, they tried to accommodate themselves to it. Unlike the Zealots their eschatological hopes were not of the "imminent" variety; hence they had little reason to risk direct confrontation with vastly superior Roman firepower. Moreover, they recognized that a change in the local political authority would probably bring about an alleviation of the hardships imposed upon the Jewish community by the self-serving priestly elite. Added to this was a pacifist strain in Pharisaism — one evident in the movement's downgrading of the festival of Hanukkah which commemorated the military victory of the Maccabees and indeed in the Beatitudes of the New Testament which are deeply reflective of the Pharisaic spirit. Given this orientation, the Pharisees would hardly have considered people of the Zealot type who were slitting throats in the alleys of Jerusalem as the precursors of a new, humane society.

It is my contention that Jesus conducted his peace and justice ministry not as an isolated figure, but within the general context of the Pharisaic movement's attempt to alter the distribution of power in Jewish society at this time. Along with the Pharisees he showed a deep commitment to peace because of their joint insistence on the fundamental dignity of each human person. His particular spirit of reconciliation further enhanced his proclivity for peace. Following in the footsteps of Jesus and the Jewish tradition that was so much a part of his personal spirituality, the church, as the bishops insist, must have a decided preference for peaceful, non-violent forms of conflict resolution and the achievement of justice. But it is not all that certain that either Jesus or the Pharisees rejected the use of all forms of violence out of hand. It was their considered judgment that violence made no political sense under the conditions prevailing in Roman-controlled Palestine as it may not make sense, for example, anywhere in Eastern Europe today. But it is not so clear that the value attached to power redistribution by both Jesus and the Pharisees would not have led them to contemplate seriously the use of limited military power in certain circumstances. It is wrong to turn the lack of "military imagery" in the New Testament (save for the Book of Revelation) into an absolute theological principle as the Pastoral does. It might be noted that not all biblical scholars would agree with the Pastoral's contention that the "war imagery" of the Book of Revelation refers exclusively to the end-time. It could just as well be a form of veiled prophecy (formal prophecy had ceased by this time) about the anticipated downfall of the Roman regime.

It is also not clear from the New Testament what position Jesus and the Pharisees would have taken if they had achieved political control of their society, if they were in a leadership role or were called upon to give counsel to leaders in whom they trusted. If an enemy attacked, if a Hitlerian-figure arose to challenge the well-being of the people, would peace and reconciliation have been their only word? Based on events such as the invasion of the Temple, I think not. But this was not a question Jesus and the Pharisees had to face realistically. So it is misleading to say with certainty what their responses would have been. Silence on the matter cannot be transformed into theological justification for pacifism as some Christian writers have done. It is a question that the church must decide today based on certain directions in the New Testament — the commitment to use power to change unjust power distribution in society; the basic dignity of each human person; the importance of communal survival; the centrality of reconciliation. It may very well be that these directions will never come together in a way that would allow the use of nuclear military power. But they do not seem to me to come together in a way that rules out all use of non-nuclear military power.

The challenge before us today is the achievement of peace with humanized power, not merely peace without power. The Pastoral has provided us many vital principles for an overarching theology of peace. But further clarification and amplification is necessary on the question of what role can be legitimately assigned to power in the quest for peace.

## A Word on Deterrence

The Pastoral's section on the morality of deterrence has been without doubt one of the most publicized and debated parts of the document. And this is as it should be. For over and above the specifics of this section the fundamental underlying message it contains represents one of the bishops' most important contributions to consciousness-raising in America and the world. Things cannot remain as they are. Even if we were to grant the argument that nuclear stockpiling has prevented a major superpower military confrontation since 1945, a change in basic ethos is desperately needed now. What the bishops have fundamentally called for in this section of the Pastoral, and their emphasis must be preserved despite any reservations one might have with their evaluation of one or another particular issue discussed here, is a clear national reorientation from "preparation for war" to "preparation for peace." The two approaches are not totally incompatible. But a nation has to establish priorities. War preparation continues to claim foremost attention within the United States government. The bishops are urging that there be a thorough reversal in attitude with arms control and disarmament assuming the greater priority. And this for two basic reasons: (1) the inherent danger to humankind of the weapons buildup itself; (2) the staggering costs of the weaponry which has the real danger of destroying the social fabric of this nation and indeed of the world without the explosion of a single nuclear bomb.

This is what stands behind the much discussed connection the bishops have established between deterrence and com-. mitment to serious and far-reaching arms control agreements. The highly publicized vote over the "curb/halt" terminology in the end came down to a strong desire on the part of the overwhelming majority of bishops to state their profound conviction that we cannot go on as we have in the arms race. Most bishops clearly recognized that they were in no position to halt the production of further nuclear weaponry by themselves. But their strong endorsement of the "halt" language was their way of demonstrating their formal break with the prevailing mentality of peace through ever-increasing force.

But having accepted deterrence, however conditionally, as a morally permissible situation the Catholic community will need to give greater attention to the presentation of the "vocation" of those who labor in deterrence. It would be somewhat hypocritical for the church to accept deterrence in principle and then leave the impression that those Christians who are intimately involved with the implementation of this strategy are less than fully moral. We do not need a repetition of the medieval church's handling of usury. There is danger that some peace groups may interpret the Pastoral as completely anti-military. It is not, anymore than it is unilateralist.[9] The real question is whether in the maintenance of an appropriate deterrent capacity a new attitude can be developed. This would involve massive re-training within the military toward a philosophy of peace. It will mean trying to break through the decision-making apparatus which, in the judgment of military leaders such as the former chairman of the British Chiefs of Staff, Field Marshall Lord Carver, led both the USSR and the USA to blunder into an escalation of nuclear weapons in Europe

[9]On the unilateral question it is worth noting that at an international conference on peace in Sweden just prior to the bishops vote on the final draft, the USCC representative was forced to cast a negative vote against the conference's declaration on disarmament because it was deemed too unilateral in its appeal to the West and too exclusively passivist in tone.

which has little to do with the actual enhancement of either's security.[10]

Greater attention will also need to be given to links between weapons decisions and the economic needs of munitions manufacturers. This is something that Admiral Hyman Rickover addressed quite bluntly and directly in his final congressional testimony in which he suggested that it might be better if military hardware production were taken over by the government in order to free us from cost over-runs and the manufacture of weapons purely for the economic well-being of military contractors.[11] These are but a few examples of what the transition to a basically "preparation for peace" perspective would entail within the context of a deterrence stance.

The bishops' Pastoral has put us on the right track, a life-sustaining track, in leading us towards the realistic development of a theology of peace. As the bishops themselves have clearly indicated, the Pastoral marks the beginning of a process, not its termination. In launching the process, the bishops have pointedly reminded us of what an ancient scribe of Athens knew as well — war is an unnatural condition of humankind: "No man is such a fool as to desire war instead of peace; for in peace, sons bury their fathers, but in war fathers bury their sons."

## For Further Reading

Ronald Freund, *What One Christian Can Do To Help Prevent Nuclear War* (Chicago: Fides/Claretian, 1982; volume now published by Twenty-Third Publications, Mystic, CT).

David Hollenbach, S.J., *Nuclear Ethics: A Christian Moral Argument* (New York: Paulist, 1983).

[10]David Fouquet, "European Missile Deployment: A Tragedy of Errors?" *The Christian Science Monitor* (June 21, 1983) 3.

[11]*No Holds Barred. The Final Congressional Testimony of Admiral Hyman Rickover* (Washington, DC: Center for the Study of Responsive Law, 1982).

Willy Brandt, ed., *North-South: A Program For Survival* (Cambridge, MA: MIT Press, 1980).

Alan Geyer, *The Idea of Disarmament* (Elgin, IL: The Brethren Press, 1982).

Barrie Paskins and Michael Dockrill, *The Ethics of War* (Minneapolis: University of Minnesota Press, 1979).

Robert Woito, *To End War: A New Approach to International Conflict* (New York: Pilgrim Press, 1982).

# 6

# Pacifism: A Christian Option?
## Paul Wadell, C.P.

A Christianity that no longer seems strange to us is a Christianity that has lost its nerve. The problem for Christians today is not that the world has changed too fast for us, but that we have lost that delightful sense of strangeness incumbent upon a people whose life is a gift of the forgiveness of God.

There are many things peculiar about Christianity. But perhaps none is so strange as the disturbing fact with which Christianity begins: the love of a God whose forgiveness makes of his enemies something they could never have made of themselves, his friends. The Christian life is nothing more than the ongoing elaboration of what it means to be forgiven, but it is precisely this that should make Christians seem so odd because the last thing any of us want to remember is that we live by the mercy of someone else. To be indebted to anyone is to give her or him a say in our lives, to even let them control us. Christians are people who let the memory of a God who refused to let the gift in us be lost: control, challenge, change and rule our life. As St. Thomas

Aquinas mused deeply in his *Summa,* "Different ideas of how life should be lived come from the various objects that we consider good." The life of Christians should look different, baffling, and even downright odd to others because we insist on considering good, even imitating, a God whose love goes to extremes. Christians are like their God, going to extremes, courting danger, risking abuse and misunderstanding because we refuse to let the good that can save us be chased from a world too deceived to know what is best for it. Christians have to worry not when people find us strange, but when they stop being offended. For it is then we have lost the nerve to live in memory of the love that is ours.

What is troubling about the American bishops' recent Pastoral is that it is not odd enough. On the one hand, the bishops offer a very thoughtful, commanding account of Christian pacifism as the moral position befitting those "trying to live up to the call of Jesus to be peacemakers in our own time and situation," but they hedge on adopting pacifism as normative for the church. Near the beginning of the Pastoral, and again at the end, they straightforwardly assert that "peacemaking is not an optional commitment. It is a requirement of our faith. We are called to be peacemakers, not by some movement of the moment, but by our Lord Jesus." (# 333) But several pages later after analyzing the contemporary relevance of the traditional Catholic doctrine on just war, the bishops speak of pacifism as only an "option" that must be reaffirmed. (#119)

What makes *The Challenge of Peace* frustrating is that is is a beautiful, often inspiring letter that finally leaves the reader confused because there is a contradiction threaded throughout the letter that never gets resolved. Despite its sensitive, well-measured tone, there is something inconsistent about this Pastoral. The problem is the bishops do not follow through on their own logic. If, as they so clearly argue, "we are called to be a church at the service of peace," (#23) and this is simply commeasurate with a life of discipleship, then how can pacifism, at least for the Christian, be optional? What is most troublesome is that the bishops so convincingly demonstrate why pacifism is most in keeping with the convictions that make us Christians, but then relegate pacifism to a choice that is to be respected and admired, but not the kind of requirement that might make Christians offensive.

In this respect, the bishops mirror what is generally true in Catholic moral theology today. As James Finn observes, "On issues of war and peace there are today two principal positions that are legitimized within the Roman Catholic Church as acceptable applications of the gospel message —pacifism and justifiable war."[1] But, as Gordon Zahn responds, that begs the question of coherence. "As a pacifist," he writes, "I am not sure that the Church can rest easily with two essentially contrary interpretations of Christian belief and mission. Objectively, or so it would seem, only one interpretation can be right; either it is always wrong to wage war or under certain conditions it can be permitted, or even obligatory to do so."[2]

Zahn's uneasiness is telling, and what I want to suggest in this essay is that the very incoherence that troubles Zahn will remain as long as Christians, like the bishops, attempt to reconcile the pacifism of the gospel with the just war doctrine of our tradition. What this essay will suggest is that pacifism is the only response to war that does not fundamentally betray our discipleship identity as Christians. This will be developed through three sections: first, an analysis of the bishops' own treatment of pacifism in the Pastoral letter; secondly, a critique of the theological presuppositions, most notably displayed in Reinhold Niebuhr, that commonly support Christian rejections of pacifism; and third, a response to these objections that considers the relationship between the achievement of peace and the virtue of courage.

---

[1] James Finn, "Pacifism and Justifiable War," in *War or Peace? The Search For New Answers*, ed. Thomas A. Shannon (Maryknoll, New York: Orbis Books, 1982) 3.

[2] Gordon C. Zahn, "Afterword," in *War or Peace? The Search For New Answers*, 239.

## Called to be Peacemakers in Our World

In its opening paragraphs, *The Challenge of Peace* promises to distinguish itself from most recent Catholic moral theology by not attempting to fashion its argument on the basis of what is reasonable and acceptable to all members of a pluralistic society. Instead of presuming the best way for the church to be responsible to society is by limiting its position to values that are agreeable to everyone, the bishops hint the approach of their letter will be different. "We write this letter," they tell us, "from the perspective of Catholic faith. Faith does not insulate us from the daily challenges of life, but intensifies our desire to address them precisely in light of the Gospel which has come to us in the person of the risen Christ." A few pages later the bishops add, "From the resources of our faith we wish to provide hope and strength to all who seek a world free of the nuclear threat." (#2) In other words, the bishops want to ascertain a Christian's responsibility in a nuclear age not through a natural law methodology that emphasizes values and norms agreeable to anyone, but through an approach that recognizes how the moral notions that guide our lives are simply expressions of the convictions that make us who we are. The bishops commence their essay on peace "from the perspective of Catholic faith" not because it seems proper to acknowledge God first, but because morality must be guided by the concrete, highly explicit question of how a people must live if they are to be faithful to the traditions and stories that are theirs. What the bishops have to say has universal value not because they speak in a way anyone can instantly understand, for that is probably not the case, but because what they say either is or ought to be consonant with that story to which Christians have committed their lives just because they have found it to be true. Dorothy Day, Peter Maurin, and Daniel Berrigan come to mind as Catholic pacifists of our time who have so beautifully displayed through the witness of their lives exactly what the bishops suggest. They were pacifists not from a desire to be different, but because being a people of peace is integral to the particular story Christians should be trying to live.

But if this is so, even though Christians may agree with other pacifists that war may never supercede a commitment to non-violence, why Christians are pledged to peace and even what they take that peace to be is something unique, something different than the humanist's understanding of peace. How Christians understand peace is a direct result of the religious convictions that form them into a community who learn through Jesus what peace, fellowship, love, and forgiveness mean. And so it is not quite right to say with J. Bryan Hehir that for Christians "implicit in the pacifist position is the conviction that human life has an absolute value; it has such intrinsic worth that no conflict of values justifies taking human life. . . ."[3] That may be why others are pacifist, and certainly it is a rationale of a secular-humanist tradition, but it does not adequately explain why Christians are obliged to be people of peace. As the bishops suggest, Christian pacifism rests not on the absolute value of human life, which is a questionable theological claim, but on the Christian's duty to imitate and embody the ways of God. Christian pacifism is not a measure of the value of human life, but of fidelity to the Christian's vocation to be faithful to the ways of God displayed in Jesus. Christians are peacemakers because that is who we have been called to be by God, because that is who God is, a peacemaker reconciling all men and women in Christ.

In the section of the Pastoral that describes the Old Testament roots of Christian pacifism, the bishops note that peace, "a special characteristic of the covenant," witnesses not so much the sanctity of every human life, but Israel's willingness to "put its trust in God alone and look only to him for its security." (#34) Just as a violation of this peace was fundamentally a sin of idolatry, a refusal to accept Yahweh alone as Lord, so was the presence of peace not directly a human achievement, but the flower of Israel's fidelity to God. Israel was called to peace not so much

---

[3]J. Bryan Hehir, "The Just-War Ethic and Catholic Theology: Dynamics of Change and Continuity," in *War or Peace?*, 30.

because human life is sacred, though that can hardly be denied, but because peace best describes a people who desire nothing so much as God. In this sense, the peace proper to Christians cannot be attained apart from an unflinching fidelity to God. It is a requirement of our covenant as well as fidelity's gift.

Similarly, in the New Testament the Christian vocation to be peacemakers reflects an appropriate awareness of what it means to be part of a covenant wrought from the forgiving love of God. The Cross is the grammar of Christianity, and that means everything in the Christian life ought to express a remembrance of precisely how God loved in order that we may have life. Being a people of peace is the singlemost distinguishing mark of Christians because nothing else so genuinely captures the understanding, the perception, the whole character of a people who realize everything they are is the work of a God who refused to let their enmity prevail. Peace is reverence for the extraordinary, unnerving mercy of God that gives us hope exactly because God's ways are not our ways. Peace is humility because our willingness to love our enemies when it means forgiving them, suffering for them, even being put to death by them, is nothing but a reminder of how God loved us when we were the enemies of God. Peace is a gift of the kindness of God, and as the bishops remind us, "so intense was that gift and so abiding was its power that the remembrance of that gift, and the daily living of it became the hallmark of the community of faith." (#52)

Pacifism is a Christian obligation quite simply because Christians are called to carry on the ways of God. Their life, as John Howard Yoder so nicely puts it, "is not guided by the goals it seeks to reach, but by the God it seeks to reflect." (*The Original Revolution*, p. 39) This means their way of being in the world is different. Christians should always disturb us, baffle us, even anger us because they insist on being ruled by a God whose ways seem perpetually strange. In their Pastoral the bishops say that "Jesus challenged everyone to recognize in him the presence of the reign of God and to give themselves over to that reign." (#42) That is what Christians do. They hand themselves over so fully to the ways of God that the life they live, how they see, think, act, and understand, is a wholly new life, a life so completely taken up in Christ that it is ruled not by the values of the world, but by the standards of the Kingdom.

Christians are strange and unnerving because they do what other people avoid. They live in a way faithful to Christ that not only challenges but very often collapses our customary ways of thinking. As the bishops note, while others may love only those they choose, following Christ, Christians love all who come into their presence, even their enemies, because "such a love does not seek revenge but rather is merciful in the face of threat and opposition." (#47) While others might find it sensible to avenge those who hurt them, Christians follow Christ who "showed the way of living in God's reign; he manifested the forgiveness which he called for. . . . In doing these things, he made the tender mercy of God present in a world which knew violence, oppression, and injustice." (#48) And like Jesus who "refused to defend himself with force or with violence," (#49) Christians endure the violence and threats of others without striking back not because they are cowardly, but because they have learned from Jesus that only non-violence can ever break the hold of violence upon the world by bringing forth into our midst "a peace the world cannot give," a peace "that is a sign to the world that God indeed does reign, does give life in death and that the love of God is stronger even than death." (#50, #51)

Pacifism is the response to violence that gives God the freedom to bring his peace into our world. Christians grant God that freedom to bring his peace, the peace of the Kingdom, to others because they remember it is the very same peace that made their lives whole. As the bishops so beautifully explain, "Because we have been gifted with God's peace in the risen Christ, we are called to our own peace, and to the making of peace in our world. As disciples and as children of God it is our task to seek for ways in which to make the forgiveness, justice and mercy, and love of God visible in a world where violence and enmity are too often the norm." (#55)

And so if we consider only the opening pages of the Pastoral, the bishops offer a beautiful, articulate, and convincing analysis of both why and how Christians are called to be peacemakers in the world. Pacifism is a requirement of discipleship, a necessary means of embodying and carrying on God's ways in the world. And discipleship is not an option, but a vocation — the comprehensive life task of all men and women who claim through baptism to have "put on Christ." Being peacemakers is a difficult virtue to develop because God's peace will never be acceptable to people convinced their most cherished right is to injure those who have hurt them. That is why the bishops, near the end of their letter, remind us that Christians will always seem odd to anyone who has not yet surrendered to this story of God. "We readily recognize," they tell us, "that we live in a world that is becoming increasingly estranged from Christian values. In order to remain a Christian, one must take a resolute stand against many commonly accepted axioms of the world." (#27)

Discipleship begets misunderstanding, hostility, and probably also violence because nothing so threatens the world as the story of how God wants to change it. That the world considers pacifism cowardly and irresponsible only reflects how much we fear letting God have power over us and how greatly we resist being saved from a violence that must eventually destroy us. "In our own country," the bishops conclude, "we are coming to a fuller awareness that a response to the call of Jesus is both personal and demanding. As believers we can identify rather easily with the early church as a company of witnesses engaged in a difficult mission. To be disciples of Jesus requires that we continually go beyond where we are now. To obey the call of Jesus means separating ourselves from all attachments and affiliation that could prevent us from learning and following our authentic vocation. To set out on a road to discipleship is to dispose oneself for a share in the cross." (#276) Still, Christians must be people willing to share in the Cross because, as Jesus showed us, that is the only way for God's peace to enter our world.

With this statement the tone and direction of the Pastoral would seem to be set. Christians are required to be pacifists because that is what discipleship demands. Resorting to violence is not only a sin against the other, but for the Christian, perhaps more glaringly, a refusal to be grateful to the God whose own peacemaking in the Cross made us a people of hope. What is strange about the letter is not its explication of pacifism, which boldly and impressively reflects the logic of faith, but that midway through the letter its pacifist stance is forsaken. What is so strikingly odd about the argument of *The Challenge of Peace* is not its initial conclusion that pacifism is incumbent upon Christians precisely because of what we see in Jesus, suggesting that for the Christian there can be no option, no rational choice between violence and non-violence, but that having established this the bishops could abandon it when they begin their discussion of the "principle of legitimate self-defense." Here the "about-face" in the letter is not the moral conversion to which the bishops exhort us, (#333) but a sudden reversal in their whole methodology, a shift in the principles and notions that fuel their logic. This abandoning of the pacifist perspective in favor of the traditional Catholic teaching on a just war is the bishops' way of addressing the perplexing question of how Christians are to respond to unjust aggression in a way that does not make them seem irresponsible to others. Remembering the words of Pope Pius XII, the bishops write: "A people threatened with an unjust aggression or already its victim, may not remain passively indifferent, if it would think and act as befits a Christian. All the more does the solidarity of the family of nations forbid others to behave as mere spectators, in any attitude of apathetic neutrality." (#76)

Are the bishops hedging on their commitment to pacifism? Are they beginning to fear that as a way of exercising responsibility for peace in the world, pacifism is suspect? In their evaluation of the just war doctrine the bishops assert that "the Christian has no choice but to defend peace, properly understood, against aggression." (#73) But that begs the question of *how* Christians, in keeping with what they believe, are called to safeguard and nurture peace in our world. Earlier in the letter the bishops suggested Christians rightly defend peace by being faithful to the convictions that allow them to be the people through whom God's peace can work in our world. However, faced with the threat of unjust aggression, confronted with the violence of the enemy, the bishops draw back: "We believe work to develop non-violent means of fending off aggression and resolving conflict best reflects the call of Jesus both to love and to justice. . . . But, on the other hand, the fact of aggression, oppression and injustice in our world also serves to legitimate the resort to weapons and armed force in defense of justice." The bishops continue: "We must recognize the reality of the paradox we face as Christians living in the context of the world as it presently exists: we must continue to articulate our belief that love is possible and the only real hope for all human relations, and yet accept that force, even deadly force, is sometimes justified and that nations must provide for their defense." (#78)

Is "force, even deadly force," ever justified for the Christian? Everything the bishops wrote about pacifism would counter that it is not, and yet here the bishops move to another perspective from which the question of war and peace is addressed. Even though they rightly note that in the just war tradition the presupposition always is in favor of peace, and even though they insist that with nuclear warfare the guiding criteria of proportionality and discrimination is lost, and even though they often affirm that any system of nuclear deterrence is "but a step on the way toward a progressive disarmament" (#188), it is hard not to feel that with this shift of perspective something of the vision and imagination of the Pastoral is lost. What bedevils the bishops is knowing how to talk about war and peace to people outside the community, to people who "don't share the same vision of faith." (#17) The bishops' solution is to speak to them not from a "specific perspective of faith," but to seek reasons and arguments that are agreeable to all. In other words, in order to talk about peace in a pluralistic society in which peoples' convictions and values differ, pacifism, the appropriate Christian word about war, must be silenced.

Underlying the bishops' shift in logic is the prevalent but troubling idea that in order to be responsible to others, Christians cannot speak about what they ought to know best, the peace that only God can give, the peace that comes through faithful discipleship, because that is a peace all neither believe nor share. In this way Christians end up reneging on what they have to offer the world because of a peculiar idea of what it means to be responsible to the world. Yet, if the peace of God, the peace that flowed from the Cross, is the only peace that saves the world, why should it be forsaken at the point it is needed most? The answer usually given is that in a pluralistic society Christians must be quiet about what they believe because not everyone believes it; therefore, they can rightly insist only on modes of argument that embody values acceptable to all. Here the bishops' strategy parallels David Hollenbach's. In his *Nuclear Ethics: A Christian Moral Argument*, Hollenbach writes:

> The just war norms do not embody the only Christian approach to warfare. They do, however, hold a privileged place in the Christian community's effort to make a contribution to the formation of public policy. The privileged place of just war norms in policy debate is an implication of theologically legitimate pluralism. Christians could insist that policies be formed on a pacifist foundation only if theological and historical-political argument could establish that the pacifist stance were mandatory for all persons and societies. . . . But public policy in a pluralist society cannot be held to norms for the use of force which are more stringent than those of the just war theory. To do so would be to deny the legitimate plurality of approaches we have argued for. (p. 38)

And so Hollenbach concludes: "The pacifist theological argument from the death of Jesus Christ on the cross to an absolute obligation of non-violence cannot be made the basis for a political ethic for a pluralist society." (p.43) Lurking behind this argument is the suspicion that any Christian social teaching must be dismissed as irrelevant and even immoral because it is incapable of application in the real world of international politics. In our time a source of these suspicions, as well as their most articulate and impassioned spokesperson, has been Reinhold Niebuhr. No one more than Niebuhr has so effectively countered arguments for making pacifism the normative response to war by the church. Any attempt to legitimize pacifism must answer Niebuhr's telling critique. It is to this we now turn.

## A Critique of Pacifism as a "Utopian Illusion"

Reinhold Niebuhr was not always writing stinging criticisms of pacifism. In some of his books, particularly his earlier writings, much that Niebuhr said offers eloquent support to the bishops' reflections of a pacifist church faithfully witnessing Jesus in the world. In the opening paragraphs of an *Interpretation of Christian Ethics*, Niebuhr laments that "Protestant Christianity in America is, unfortunately, unduly dependent upon the very culture of modernity, the disintegration of which would offer a more independent religion a unique opportunity....Therefore the lights in its towers are extinguished at the very moment when light is needed to survey the havoc wrought in the city and the plan of rebuilding....The Christian churches are unfortunately not able to offer the needed guidance and insight." (pp.1-2)

Why has this happened? Because, Niebuhr explains, "in adjusting itself to the characteristic credos and prejudices of modernity, the liberal church has been in constant danger of obscuring what is distinctive in the Christian message and creative in Christian morality." (p.2) Later, in his essay, "The

Christian Witness in the Social and National Order," Niebuhr argues that the task of the church "is to present the Gospel of redemption in Christ to nations as well as to individuals." (p.111) In this way, he says, the church learns "only a small leaven is needed, only a little center of health can become the means of convalescence for a whole community. The fact measures the awful responsibility of the people of God in the world's cities of destruction." (p.116)

However promising, Niebuhr's overtures toward pacifism were silenced by the bombs of World War II. It was during this time that Niebuhr, perhaps more than any other American theologian, argued vigorously that pacifism rested on a flawed interpretation of the gospel that resulted in a "Christian perfectionism" that failed to understand how extensively the doctrine of original sin conditions any theological claims that can be made. Not realizing how much the deeply rooted fact of sin qualifies possibilities of goodness, Niebuhr charged that pacifism, based not on the gospel but the "renaissance faith" in the goodness and perfectability of humankind, was an "utopian illusion" that genuine Christianity disavows. Admitting that pacifists had an important witness to offer society, Niebuhr still persistently concluded that pacifism was an irresponsible, perhaps even cowardly, attempt to sidestep the conflicts and tensions of history.

And yet, what makes Niebuhr's critique problematic is that he is so zealous to emphasize the historic fact of sin which makes peace difficult, that he effectively denies the historic coming of a God who makes peace possible. For Niebuhr, sin so tyrannically rules the world that Christ seems never to have entered it; thus, the law of love unveiled on the Cross remains an "impossible possibility" to which Christians should always aspire, but which they can never achieve. Niebuhr is ready to admit that the law of Christ is, as the perfection of humankind, a final norm for Christians that is absolute and uncompromising, but not a "real possibility in history." For Niebuhr the act of God that revealed this love, the crucifixion and death of Jesus, was not an event in history, but a symbol that represents the final reconciliation, the ultimate healing of all life's tragedy, in the divine mercy which stands wholly apart from and beyond this world.

In this respect, Niebuhr differs with the pacifists not so much in his understanding of sin, but in his Christology. Pacifists are committed to non-violence not because they are optimistic about the possibilities of human goodness, for about this they may well be as somber as Niebuhr. Rather pacifists believe what Niebuhr denies: that the ways of God came into our world in Christ, that the Cross stood not beyond history or on the edge of history, but squarely within history. Thus the law of Christ, the suffering, sacrificial love of the Cross, is not pushed outside the world by the power of sin, but stands exactly at the center of that world as the singular way sin is to be overcome and the world redeemed. In *The Nature and Destiny of Man*, Niebuhr wrote, "The cross is the final norm of human nature that has no final norm in history," (V.2, p.75) and that is just what pacifists deny. The Cross is the final norm of history because in Christ the Cross was an event of history that revealed the key to what is necessary to prepare this history for what is not yet, the Kingdom. In *Love and Justice*, Niebuhr again claims that "the Cross stands at the edge of history and not squarely in history. It reveals what history ought to be, but not what history is or can be." (p.276) And this pacifists must deny too because genuine Christian pacifism sees in the death and resurrection of Jesus exactly that pattern of life, faithfully undertaken and witnessed, which alone can break the vicious, endless cycle of war upon war, violence upon violence, endemic in a world unwilling to believe that while the Cross may not escape tragedy, it is certainly the only way to a peace where tragedy is no more.

Where Niebuhr failed to understand pacifism was in his charge that pacifists try to avoid the suffering and tragedy that is part of a world in sin. Looking to the Cross of Jesus, pacifists do not deny suffering and tragedy; rather, unlike Niebuhr, they want to show what kind of people we must be if these sufferings and tragedies are to be borne in a way they can finally be overcome. To do this requires an extraordinary courage, and if that courage is to be a virtue, it must be a courage for peace. This is an unusual way of thinking about courage, and it must be explained.

## Peace and the Courage It Requires

*Sophie's Choice*, based on a novel by William Styron, was a movie widely acclaimed as a masterpiece. As told through its main character, Sophie, it was also a story about courage and how important courage is if we are not to be deterred from the good that is ours. Often, it is true, we associate courage with the battlefield and think of courage as a virtue particularly requisite for withstanding the horrors of war. However, none of the virtues has a single meaning, for the virtues are intelligible not in themselves, but from the stories we are trying to live. Christians are people who are trying to live the story of God. Courage is just that virtue that enables us to be faithful to that story not only when we are particularly tempted to betray it, but also at those times when so many about us claim the story cannot be told. St. Thomas says courage is the virtue that disposes us to remain steadfast in our good against "whatever wages war upon it." For Christians it is courage that enables us to remain committed to peace, to stand steadfast in the Gospel, when we are almost persuaded the way of discipleship does not apply and peace actually might be gained through war.

The genius of Thomas' moral theology is that it expresses his conviction that whatever we do, we do for the sake of something we love. For Thomas, the virtues, though guided by reason, are not so much expressions of reason as expressions of what we most love. Each of the virtues articulates and embodies the love that rules our life, and courage is the virtue that enables us to pursue what we love, to continue to seek our good, in face of the dangers and threats that would tempt us to believe our good cannot be had. In this sense, courage is a measure of the depth of our love. As Augustine reminds us, courage "is love readily enduring all for the sake of what is loved." Thus Thomas concludes that "the chief activity of courage is not so much attacking as enduring, or standing one's ground amidst dangers."(ST,2a2ae.q123) So it is for the Christian that peace comes through courage. Peace is the harvest of fidelity, the gift of those who endure in their love for the Lord.

What is disappointing in the Pastoral is not so much that the bishops turned to the doctrine of the just war, but perhaps that they did not see clearly enough just what the challenge of peace really is. Peace is the achievement of love. But, as Thomas reminds us, "there only will you have true peace where true good is desired." What Christians try to tell the world is that genuine peace, a peace the world cannot give, comes from desiring only God. Peace is the goal of our life, the perfect enjoyment of what we have always wanted. But genuine peace, a peace that really quiets our desires, is found only in God. And that peace is the achievement of love. "Perfect peace," Thomas writes, "consists in the perfect enjoyment of the sovereign good, which causes all our desires to be united and rest in one," and this peace is "directly the work of charity" because when we have charity we desire exactly what God desires in the way that God desires. (ST,2a2ae.q29) In this sense, peace best describes the kind of people we become when all our desires are focused on God.

But such love is not easily sustained in a world that loves so much more than it loves God. There is war and violence in the world today not because we have no peace, but because the peace we are seeking is different. Ultimately pacifism is threatening to the world not because it abjures violence, but because it calls us to love God above all else. Ultimately pacifism is threatening not because it forgives the enemy, but because it calls us to a peace we have not yet learned to desire. It is no accident that Thomas follows his analysis of courage with a discussion of martyrdom, for he realizes it is just that kind of courage and just that expression of love that might be demanded if the peace of God is not to be lost. As Thomas says, the courage resplendent in martyrdom is the perfection of charity because it so concretely expresses how we love God above all things. But martyrdom also "embraces the highest possible form of obedience, namely, being obedient unto death." And in this sense, Thomas adds, martyrdom is the Christian's way of bearing witness "not to any truth, but to the truth involved in our duty to God, which was made known to us through Christ." (ST,2a2ae.q124) To be a people of peace one can hardly be cowardly; indeed, being committed to peace demands just as much courage as being willing to wage war. But they are not the same virtue, not the same kind of courage. The courage required to be a people of peace is qualitatively different because the good that courage seeks and the love that courage serves is God and God's kingdom.

In *The Challenge of Peace* the bishops have presented the church with a letter of great sensitivity, beauty and depth. Moreover, in their attempt to explain why Christians are pacifists, the bishops have done the church a great service. It can only be hoped that Christians will study this letter in the same perspective of faith from which so much of it has been written. Still, the thrust of this essay has been to suggest that pacifism for the Christian cannot be, as the bishops finally conclude, an option. Pacifism is a Christian's obligation because discipleship is a Christian's vocation. To refuse to be pacifist is a sign that in a world torn apart by the violence of war we no longer believe God's story can be told. The greatest responsibility Christians can exercise toward the world is to be the people through whom God's story of love can be told. Perhaps what the bishops failed to see clearly enough is that for Christians our politics are our virtues, and our virtues are formed at the root of that Cross where God died lest the gift in us be lost.

## For Further Reading

Stanley Hauerwas, "The Church and Liberal Democracy: The Moral Limits of a Secular Polity," in *A Community of Character: Toward A Constructive Christian Social Ethic* (Notre Dame: University of Notre Dame Press, 1981).

David Hollenbach, *Nuclear Ethics: A Christian Moral Argument* (New York: Paulist Press, 1983).
Thomas A. Shannon, ed. *War or Peace? The Search for New Answers* (Mary Knoll, New York: Orbis Books, 1982).
John Howard Yoder, *Nevertheless: Varieties of Christian Pacifism* (Scottsdale, Pennsylvania: Herald Press, 1971).
_____, *The Original Revolution* (Scottsdale, Pennsylvania: Herald Press, 1971).

# 7

# The Peace Pastoral:
# A Product of the Just War Tradition

*Thomas A. Nairn, O.F.M.*

In November of 1980, the National Conference of Catholic Bishops undertook a study which was to result in a Pastoral letter about war and peace in the nuclear age. The three years which followed witnessed three drafts of the document and a final letter which was over one hundred pages in length. During the same period, the bishops found themselves being called either "nuclear heretics" or "mere politicians" depending upon which draft of the Pastoral was being analyzed by whom. The drafts were described either as flights from the prophetic nature of the church or as "flights from good sense." Yet, it should be clear to anyone who reads the letter, *The Challenge of Peace: God's Promise and Our Response*, that the Pastoral is neither an uncritical attempt to justify war nor one which will push Catholicism to "peace church" status. On the contrary, the bishops' Pastoral is almost a classic example of what has come to be known as the just war tradition.

## The Just War Tradition

The Christian just war tradition is generally recognized to have begun with Augustine of Hippo. Prior to his time, the church's attitude toward military service and warfare was best described in the words of Tertullian (c.155 - c.240): "Christ, in disarming Peter, disarmed every soldier." Although there were some exceptions, the general experience of the church in the first three centuries of its existence was pacifist. Several reasons have been given for this attitude. Among the most frequently cited is the fact that there was a greater possibility of idolatry in the military than in civilian life. Yet, there was also a deeper reason for this prohibition. War was seen as contrary to Christian love. Tertullian posed the question in the following manner: "If we are enjoined to love our enemies, who have we to hate? If injured we are forbidden to retaliate. Who then can suffer injury at our hands?" The early church found it impossible to reconcile the Christian command of love of enemies and warfare.

By the time of Augustine (354-430), the state of the question had changed. The church was no longer a persecuted sect but had attained official status within the Empire. Therefore the question posed was no longer that of whether a member of the minority Christian church was allowed to join the military but rather whether a Christian nation had a right to defend itself. Augustine shaped his answer within a context which acknowledged the reality of a sinful world. Because of sin war was inevitable, but war could also be seen as a remedy for sin. War could restrain sinners from evil. By such reasoning, Augustine was able to offer a justification for war from within a context of Christian love. One's *intention* in waging war became the paramount consideration. War had to be fought to prevent the enemy from doing wrong and to defend the innocent. Hatred and revenge were antithetical to a just intention. Nevertheless, love for enemies did not necessarily preclude acts of belligerence. Augustine thus offered a Christian alternative to pacifism, an alternative which both allowed the Christian's participation in war and at the same time attempted to limit such participation. This soon became the dominant theory.

Between the time of Augustine and that of Thomas Aquinas (1225-1274), wars came to be justified with increasing ease. During the early Middle Ages, a war was considered just if it was waged on behalf of God or the Catholic faith. During the age of the Crusades, all means of waging such holy wars were considered licit. The element of sin disappeared from the description of these wars. Bernard of Clairvaux (1090-1153), for example, when preaching on behalf of the Second Crusade, proclaimed:

> [God] puts himself in your debt so that, in return for your taking up arms in his cause, he can reward you with pardon for your sins and everlasting glory. I call blessed the generation that can seize an opportunity of such indulgence as this, blessed to be alive in this year of jubilee, this year of God's choice.

It is clear that another change in attitude toward war had occurred. As Augustine's teaching displayed a change from absolute prohibition to reluctant acceptance due to the reality of a sinful world, the age of the crusades demonstrated a further change from reluctance to positive acceptance, seeing in certain forms of war God's own vindication.

It is in response to this attitude that the medieval development of the just war tradition took place. Although the tradition continued to acknowledge that participation in war could be justified, it also stressed limitations to such participation. Thomas Aquinas, for example, did not condemn the crusades but rather discussed the doctrine of just war in a way which served as a corrective to the crusade mentality. Although he rejected any new dominion of unbelievers over Christians as a scandal and a danger to the faith, his position also recognized that the mere fact that an enemy is an unbeliever was not a sufficient reason for an offensive war. God did not demand that members of the church engage in wars against unbelievers. The medieval just war doctrine justified only genuinely defensive wars.

Furthermore, Christians were bound in charity to act according to principles of discrimination and proportionality. Although these principles were not developed in great detail in Thomas' writings, especially as regards conduct in war, neither were they absent. He urged restraint in dealing with the wicked when they were hidden among the good and was of the opinion that it was better to let God deal with the wicked on the Day of Judgment rather than run the risk of killing the innocent.

From these two examples of Augustine and Aquinas, one sees that in its origins and development the just war tradition tried to keep a middle course between what it considered the dangers of a pacifism which refused to acknowledge a nation's right to defense and a crusade mentality which placed no moral limits upon a Christian's activity in war. As the tradition developed into the modern period, this middle way was systematized into eight criteria:

1) that there be a just cause;

2) that war be declared by a competent authority;

3) that there be a sense of comparative justice which acknowledges the limits to a nation's right to go to war;

4) that a right intention to pursue peace exist;

5) that war always be only a last resort;

6) that there be a probability of success;

7) that the good sought through war be proportional to the evils endured;

8) that just means of proportionality and discrimination be used.

As the tradition continued to develop, the question of just means became more prominent. Hugo Grotius (1583-1645) emphasized the importance of moderation for Christians:

> And even in the sharpest war, there ought to be some grains of mildness and clemency, if it be regulated according to the Christian discipline. The very Philosopher has already pronounced them cruel who, though they have cause, yet know no measure in punishing.

It was only by means of the principle of the double effect that any death of non-combatants could be justified. Since this principle could be misused, theologians claimed that developments in war technology demand that "just means" be given closer rather than less scrutiny. After the first uses of the atomic bomb, Pope Pius XII made a series of strong statements in which he questioned whether the just means criterion could justify the development and use of nuclear weapons. Yet he never condemned the atomic bomb as immoral.

## The Use of Nuclear Weapons

Today, because of the situation created by the continued presence of nuclear weapons, many are re-thinking the validity of the just war tradition. There are those who claim that it is obsolete or even counter-productive. In a speech to the ninth *Pax Christi* National Assembly, Bishop Carroll Dozier said: "The day, if ever there was a day, of the just war theory is over. It must be declared no longer valid as an excuse for war making. Let it perish in the midst of the pages of history. It has been the occasion of sin in country after country." There are others who maintain that the fact that there is an enemy who may not follow the same sense of morality in war that a Christian would follow must affect our preparation for war. They conclude that, because of the motives of the Soviet Union, America must not be too scrupulous regarding the question of the means used in waging war.

Following the middle course exemplified throughout the just war tradition, the bishops' Pastoral tries to steer between both claims. Confronted with the real possibility of nuclear war, the bishops maintain that the just war criteria take on added importance. They place special emphasis on the criteria of probability of success and of just means. The first deals with a consideration made on behalf of one's own nation, the second on behalf of the enemy.

In the Pastoral the bishops reach three conclusions regarding the waging of nuclear war: 1) "under no circumstances may nuclear weapons or other instruments of mass slaughter be used for the purpose of destroying population centers or other predominantly civilian targets" (# 147); 2) "we do not perceive any situation in which the deliberate initiation of nuclear warfare, on however restricted a scale, can be morally justified" (# 150); and 3) regarding the concept of limited nuclear war, "the burden of proof remains with those who assert that meaningful limitation is possible." (# 159)

Each of the above conclusions is placed firmly within the just war tradition by particular recourse to one or more of the criteria mentioned above. In fact, one may say that according to those criteria the bishops' conclusions are rather cautious. Their most unequivocal condemnation regards the bombing of population centers or primarily civilian targets. In reaching this conclusion, the bishops have the backing of an unambiguous tradition. Some trace the principle of discrimination between combatants and non-combatants back to Augustine himself. Aquinas' use of the notion was mentioned above. There is also evidence of the principle in medieval tracts of canon law. Contemporary theologians have used the principle to condemn the saturation bombing of London and Dresden. Pope Pius XII used it to condemn the notion of "total war." The Second Vatican Council in its *Pastoral Constitution on the Church in the Modern World* insisted: "Any act of war aimed indiscriminately at the destruction of entire cities or of extensive areas along with their population is a crime against God and humanity." Clearly, the notion of non-combatant immunity is so much part of the church's traditional teaching on war that, if nuclear warfare cannot make such a discrimination, it must be seen as in principle immoral.

The bishops then condemn a first-use nuclear policy, but this condemnation is less emphatic than that of the use of nuclear weapons against population centers. Since they condemn a first-strike use of nuclear weapons, the bishops seem to be saying that the only possible moral use of such weapons is in retaliation for a previous nuclear attack. The reasoning toward such a conclusion is based upon the principle of proportionality. The argument entails a judgment that the consequences of using nuclear weapons are so dangerous that under no circumstances can it be seen as warranted as retaliation for a conventional attack. This argument itself is based upon an understanding that the distinction between a first use of nuclear weapons and a retaliatory strike is analogous to the distinction between aggression and just defense.

An analysis from the perspective of the just war tradition, however, is more complex than the above distinction indicates. For example, a first strike against an enemy's nuclear arsenal, especially upon indication that the weapons are poised for imminent use, may indeed be defensive and therefore as morally acceptable as a retaliatory strike. On the other hand, the mere fact that a nuclear strike is in retaliation does not make such a strike moral. Such ambiguity forces the bishops to be cautious in their appraisal. This same ambiguity has led many proponents of the just war tradition to consider themselves to be nuclear pacifists.

The third and most cautious conclusion concerns the idea of limited nuclear war. On the one hand, the bishops indicate their extreme skepticism regarding the viability of such a concept; on the other hand, they acknowledge the controversial nature of the issue. They nevertheless conclude that the concept is a dangerous one. Quoting the Pontifical Academy of Sciences (# 145), they argue that there is no way to keep a limited nuclear war in fact limited. This judgment is then used as the basis for a critique of the idea that a nation can both fight and win a nuclear war. If this strategy is impossible, it is prohibited by the criterion which insists that to enter a war there must be a reasonable chance of success. Even if a limited nuclear war were possible, its morality would not be self-evident. Because of high levels of radiation which may affect non-combatants, neutral nations, and even future generations, one may raise other moral questions based upon the criteria of proportionality and discrimination.

These three conclusions serve to limit the justifiability of nuclear war. Both the attempt to limit the justification of the use of nuclear weapons and the tentativeness of the conclusions identify this argument as a form of the just war theory. The tradition has continually rejected absolute claims. The rejection of absolutism, however, is accompanied by a strong reluctance to justify nuclear warfare.

Because of this reluctance, and consistent with the just war tradition, the bishops admit that a nation's development of its conventional forces is a morally acceptable alternative to nuclear arsenals. Yet, the rationale behind the just war tradition attempts to limit participation in all wars, conventional as well as nuclear. Accordingly, the bishops add:

> We believe that any program directed at reducing reliance on nuclear weapons is not likely to succeed unless it includes measures to reduce tensions and to work for the balanced reduction of conventional forces. . . . It is not only nuclear war that must be prevented, but war itself. (# 218, 219)

## Deterrence

The decades since the development and first use of the atomic bomb have witnessed the introduction of a new strategy which complicates any discussion of the morality of nuclear weapons, that of deterrence. Even if one acknowledges that in principle the use of nuclear weapons is immoral, one is nevertheless forced to also examine the morality of nuclear deterrence. The bishops introduce the topic with these words: "Deterrence is at the heart of the U.S.-Soviet relationship, currently the most dangerous dimension of the nuclear arms race." (# 162) The moral concerns surrounding the notion of deterrence are definitely more ambiguous than those dealing with the use of nuclear weapons.

Again, the bishops, following the just war criteria, try to steer a middle course between two opposite claims. Some reason that although the use of nuclear weapons may be immoral, their accumulation paradoxically is the only way to ensure that an enemy will not resort to their use. Others claim that since the use of such weapons is immoral, the threat of such use and consequently the possession and development of such weapons are likewise immoral. The bishops' middle way leads to three conclusions (# 188):

1) If deterrence exists only to prevent the *use* of nuclear weapons, any proposals which go beyond this are to be rejected;

2) the rejection of the concept of nuclear superiority and its replacement with that of "sufficiency"; and

3) the understanding that deterrence must be used only as a step toward a more general disarmament.

These conclusions are consistent with the just war tradition insofar as they endeavor to acknowledge both legitimate defense and the real danger of the possession of nuclear weapons.

The first conclusion addresses a central difficulty with deterrence itself. Deterrence can be successful only if the threat to use nuclear weapons is perceived as real by the enemy. Therefore concrete strategies aimed at deterrence must be judged by the same criteria of discrimination, proportionality, and chance of success which apply to weapon use. This would seem to indicate that the prevalent strategy of deterrence based on "mutually-assured-destruction," the so-called MAD deterrence, is immoral, since it cannot pass such an examination. Not only are certain forms of nuclear deterrence deemed immoral, but the goal and purpose of concrete strategies must constantly be held up for moral scrutiny. If the only acceptable purpose of deterrence is to decrease the likelihood of nuclear war, strategies which in actuality tend to increase the chances of war are shown to be of questionable morality.

The bishops' second conclusion deals with one such strategy, that of nuclear superiority. It is the judgment of the bishops that such a notion of deterrence does not help to keep peace but rather serves only to increase an armament build up, since an enemy then feels threatened and increases its armaments to a "superior" capacity, which in turn threatens the security of the first nation. Nuclear parity may be considered as an analogous situation, since there is no way to ensure real parity. Parity strategies thus degenerate into those involving nuclear superiority. The bishops return to a notion used in the 1960's by then Secretary of Defense Robert McNamara, that of nuclear sufficiency. The logic behind this shift is that the real issues of deterrence are the maintenance of peace and adequate defense. Both issues are addressed by a deterrence strategy based on sufficiency without the risks of war which the notions of both nuclear superiority and nuclear parity bring.

A further criticism of the notions of deterrence mentioned above can be traced back to Pope Pius XII. In his Christmas message of 1954, he spoke of a world situation in which each superpower viewed the other's latest weapon with apprehension while at the same time seeking to turn the other side's fear of its weapons to its advantage by means of propaganda. He concluded: "The current practice, while dreading war as the greatest of catastrophes, at the same time puts all its trust in war."

The bishops' third conclusion responds to this issue of where a nation is to place its trust. If deterrence is ever to promote peace, it must be used as part of a broader strategy of negotiations toward mutual disarmament. Nations must put their trust in the logic of negotiation rather than in weapons of war. By emphasizing the priority of negotiations to relieve world tensions, the bishops are actually following two other just war criteria, those of comparative justice and last resort. No nation is able to have the confidence that its motives are pure while its enemy is lacking all justice. There are never such absolute black and white situations. Therefore all nations must acknowledge that honest negotiations with the enemy are always morally superior to war, especially nuclear war, and to a deterrence based solely on the threat of war.

Thus, it is by means of criteria taken from the just war tradition that the bishops' Pastoral attempts to address the extremely important, and extremely complicated, issues of war and peace in an age which has discovered the destructive power of nuclear weapons.

## The Just War Ethos

There is an often overlooked element of the just war tradition which transcends the mere adherence to certain criteria. This essay has mentioned several times that the just war tradition is properly seen as a middle position. Being a middle position, it eschews simplistic answers. It refuses to speak in absolute terms of "always" or "never." Therefore, even though it find itself compelled to severely limit the circumstances in which the use and even possession of nuclear weapons may be considered moral, the tradition does not evaluate either nuclear weapons or nuclear war as intrinsically evil. The tradition's own inner logic refuses to reject the *theoretical* possibility that under certain circumstances such possession or use may be ethical.

Nevertheless, this theoretical "yes" to nuclear weapons is in tension with a practical "no." Throughout its history, the just war tradition has understood war as a great evil which must be avoided unless its avoidance would endanger or threaten values central to humanity itself. Properly understood, the tradition has not been an excuse to justify any war. The bishops are clear that in spite of a theoretical justifiability of nuclear war the Christian's moral task is its prevention. (# 131)

This theoretical "yes" but practical "no" reveals an attitude which may be called the just war ethos. It demands that the proponent of the just war tradition live in a state of tension. Rejecting the pacifist position, one is in danger of adopting the crusader's solid acceptance of war; and rejecting the crusade mentality, one is in danger of removing the Christian, in the name of pacifism, from genuine dialogue concerning the possible morality of particular wars. The proponent of the just war tradition rather lives with the tensions arising from the complexities of knowing both that war is an evil and that in this less than perfect world there exist values central to humanity which must be defended.

The temptations to remove the tension by going to either extreme are great. Therefore, the proponent of the just war tradition needs the vision of a critical community positively dedicated to peace. In the final sections of the Pastoral the bishops speak of the church as a community with such a vision. It is only a community which reverences life and which endeavors to defend it, which is self-critical but not afraid to enter into public debate, which has nothing to gain by war and everything to gain by peace that can support and foster such a vision. It is only such a community that can ensure that the just war tradition does not deteriorate into an ideology of war.

## The Task Ahead

The just war tradition has helped to nurture the church's attitude toward war and peace for over fifteen centuries. Throughout that time the tradition itself has changed and developed. As one looks back at recent centuries, one sees the systematization of an ethos into a set of criteria by means of which one was able to evaluate the justifiability of concrete wars. If any further development is needed in this tradition, it seems to be the rediscovery that the criteria are indeed based upon a specific ethos.

That the just war criteria can be misunderstood and even misused is apparent. Wars have in face been termed "just" by an application of the criteria which is much less stringent than that espoused by the tradition. That the just war tradition itself has been misunderstood is evident from the initial reaction of many Catholics to the Pastoral.

At the very least, what is needed is the general acceptance by those in the church of the ethos described above. If this acceptance is really to occur, however, another task must first be performed. The bishops call upon theologians to further develop a theology of peace. (# 304) Yet, if the above description of a just war ethos is correct, what is also necessary is the further development of a theology of power so that the Christian community may deal honestly with both elements of political existence. It is by means of both a theology of peace and a theology of power that the church can develop concrete strategies for implementing a balanced application of the principles of the just war tradition.

Finally, what has until now been the task of bishops and theologians must become the task of every member of the church. All are to continue the work of making the church more obviously that critical community dedicated to peace. At this most basic level, the proponent of the just war tradition sees the pacifist as an ally. However, the former also maintains that the church must critically challenge, and be challenged by, other people of good will who do not share its presuppositions. It must engage in public debate and in a continual reading of the signs of the times. If the criteria of just war are seen in light of this ethos within a church which is truly a critical community dedicated to peace, then indeed can this tradition speak to all people not only of war but also of peace.

## For Further Reading

J. Bryan Hehir, "The Just-War Ethic and Catholic Theology: Dynamics of Change and Continuity." In *War or Peace? The Search for New Answers*, Thomas A. Shannon, ed. (Maryknoll, New York: Orbis Books, 1980) 15-39.

James Turner Johnson, *Just War Tradition and the Restraint of War: A Moral and Historical Inquiry.* (Princeton, New Jersey: Princeton University Press, 1981).

William V. O'Brien, "Just-War Doctrine in a Nuclear Context." *Theological Studies* 44 (1983) 191-220.

Paul Ramsey, *The Just War: Force and Political Responsibility* (New York: Charles Scribner's Sons, 1968).

Gerard A. Vanderhaar, "The Morality of Nuclear Deterrence," *Cross Currents* 29 (1979-80) 409-416.

# Part III
# The Pastoral and Ecclesial Viewpoints

# 8

# Vatican II Foundations of the U.S. Peace Pastoral: Source of Strength, Source of Weakness

*John Paul Szura, O.S.A.*

Pope John XXIII convoked the Second Vatican Council to renew the church. He wanted a church able to bring the Gospel to the modern world, but to a great extent the church today is the church of that Council. Almost all facets of the church were touched by the Council, some more powerfully than others, through its sixteen published documents.

Of these documents of Vatican II, perhaps none is so filled with the spirit of renewal as is the *Pastoral Constitution on the Church in the Modern World (Gaudium et Spes)*. Asserting the dignity of the human person and recognizing the profoundly changed conditions of the modern world, the Pastoral Constitution gives solid contemporary guidance on many important matters. One of these is peace. The Pastoral Constitution mandates us to pursue peace and to undertake an evaluation of war with an entirely new attitude. The Second Vatican Council, the Pastoral Constitution, and its mandate have deeply affected today's

Catholic peace movement. They have deeply affected the bishops of the United States as well.

*The Challenge of Peace: God's Promise and Our Response* is thoroughly imbued with the spirit of the Council and of the Pastoral Constitution. We may be thankful for this. Yet there are both the good and the bad in everything human, including the Pastoral Constitution and therefore the U.S. bishops' Pastoral as well. This essay attempts to reflect upon a problem in both documents: that of modern communication. We write in a spirit of support for the U.S. bishops' Pastoral letter but also with a conviction that Vatican II was a point of departure rather than the end of church renewal.

## The Pastoral Constitution and Modern Communication

The Second Vatican Council attempted to deal with modern communication. Its teaching is contained in the *Decree on the Instruments of Social Communication (Inter Mirifica)*. This document concerns an area very important for church renewal because a proper theology and pastoral practice regarding "the word" in the modern world must take into account the human word given unprecedented power through modern techniques. Modern communication, mass media, the arts, forces shaping public opinion, etc., are hardly peripheral to church renewal. A survey of Council concerns and documents would indeed illustrate how central an issue "the word" is to the mission of the church in our modern world so taken up with human words.

However *Inter Mirifica* was not a success. There were several reasons for this failure. It was one of the first documents of the Council, promulgated on December 4, 1963. Thus it was not a mature, well developed product of the Council as were later and more successful documents. Compared to areas like theology, Scripture, liturgy, or social theory, the area of modern communication lacked a pool of competent experts available to the Council. The bishops were occupied with other more pressing issues at the beginning of the Council. Among these were liturgical reform, ecumenism and church unity, and the sources of revelation. Thus the bishops did not devote much energy to this new question of modern communication.

The failure of *Inter Mirifica*, widely recognized by theologians and commentators on Vatican II, has had profound impact upon the church. Theology, spirituality, catechetics, homilies, and pastoral thought and practice in general are not much help to the church confronting the human word in the modern world. The impetus from the Council simply is not there. The documentation is inadequate.

The failure of *Inter Mirifica* also had an impact on the Second Vatican Council itself. Subsequent Council discussions and documents had little effective teaching on modern communication upon which to build further insights for renewal. Moreover, because *Inter Mirifica* did make an attempt to deal with modern communication, no subsequent document made an effort to return to the issue in any systematic manner. This is true also of the Pastoral Constitution. What *Inter Mirifica* dealt with poorly, the Pastoral Constitution did not deal with at all.

Most theologians and commentators would rate the Pastoral Constitution very high. It was promulgated at the end of the Council, December 7, 1965. Thus it was enriched by three years of discussions, meetings, theological and scriptural lectures — in short, by all the experiences that made the Council an education for the bishops. The issues addressed by the Pastoral Constitution were studied for years. Many experts were available for consultation as well. It is little wonder that this document is almost universally considered a success. Yet neither the Pastoral Constitution nor the Council in general give the church effective guidance on modern communication.

This lack of guidance is important for questions of war and peace. In fact it renders incomplete the church's teaching on modern war. The Pastoral Constitution did address modern war. It does condemn the destruction of cities and civilian populations. It gives new respect to older values of pacifism, nonviolence, and conscientious objection. It demands conversion and new attitudes on war. It condemns the arms race and total war. It even asks that peace be built in the new conditions of the modern world. Yet the Pastoral Constitution lacks awareness of the importance of modern communication to modern war.

Modern war is more than war with modern weapons. It is also war that is advertised, marketed, and sold to a public. It is war supported by shaped public opinion, public relations, propaganda, and disinformation. It is war against an enemy made to appear less than human by the power of modern communication — an enemy dehumanized and therefore worthy of being targeted and annihilated. Though we may not be able to judge the motivation behind the modern communication, e.g., fear, malice, enthusiasm, exaggerated nationalism, etc., the effects are the same. As preaching the word incited the Crusades in years past, so in the modern world the human word amplified by modern communication can make our wars into secular crusades.

Vatican II and the Pastoral Constitution contributed greatly to peace especially through the sharpened awareness of the horror of modern weapons. Yet no matter how horrible are the weapons, modern communication can still dehumanize an enemy enough to justify targeting and destruction. This power of the modern pen, greater even than that of the modern sword, was not a focus of the war-peace teaching of the Council. As a result, war-peace teaching is in danger of being drowned out by the power of modern communication. Let us illustrate with a simple example:

Imagine a peace demonstration against nuclear weapons. The crowd loudly condemns these weapons. Historians mourning Hiroshima and Nagasaki document with photographs the death, mutilation, and ruin. Physicians describe in detail the medical consequences of nuclear bombs. Sociologists and psychologists explain the chaos and distress of those unlucky enough to survive. Physicists explain the radiation, heat, and blast effects. Ecologists tell the fate of the earth. Biologists foretell the end of life. Everyone condemns the bomb and its horror — even a representative of the Pentagon in the crowd. This person might say: "Yes, these weapons are terrible and should never be used. I hate them even more than any of you. It really was a shame we had to use them against Japan. I hope we never are forced into using them again, but you know those Russians. We have to be ready because we all know how bad Communists are."

What happened in this imaginary peace demonstration is exactly what happens in reality. Every sane person agrees with the fundamental insight from the Pastoral Constitution. All agree that nuclear weapons are horrible and should never be used. Yet there is a kind of readiness to use even the most horrible weapon when the enemy is dehumanized enough. Though the weapons were critiqued, there was no critique of the process of enemy dehumanization. This is seldom done in society in general. Even in the peace move-ment more skill and energy are put into explaining the Hiroshima bomb and its effects than into understanding the development and consequences of those war movies that made the Japanese look like monsters. Likewise the Catholic peace movement lacks systematic teaching, tradi-tion, or guidance from the church concerning the powerful role of modern communication in modern war.

## The Pastoral Letter and Modern Communication

The Pastoral letter of the U.S. bishops is based upon, and inspired by, the *Pastoral Constitution on the Church in the Modern World* promulgated by the Second Vatican Coun-cil. Speaking about the long and complex Catholic tradition on war and peace, the bishops state in the first part of their letter: "As we locate ourselves in this tradition, seeking to draw from it and to develop it, the document which provides profound inspiration and guidance for us is the *Pastoral Constitution on the Church in the Modern World* of Vati-can II, for it is based on doctrinal principles and addresses the relationship of the Church to the world with respect to the most urgent issues of our day." (# 7)

A reading of the Pastoral letter and a survey of its footnotes reveal how dependent the bishops were on the Pastoral Constitution. The Pastoral comes close to being an application of the Pastoral Constitution to the situation of the United States today. This is one reason why the Pastoral letter is of such high quality and filled with the spirit of church renewal. The Pastoral letter takes seriously the call to evaluate war with an entirely new attitude. We are placed solidly within the tradition and life of the church, challenged with a nuanced analysis of nuclear war morality. Nonviolence and the building of peace in a complex world are brought to our attention compellingly.

However the Pastoral letter is certainly much more aware of the horror of modern weapons than it is of the power of modern communication. Offspring of the Pastoral Constitution, the letter of the U.S. bishops is heir to the failure of Vatican II to lead the church in a critique of war marketing, propaganda, enemy dehumanization, or any process that prepares for war by providing modern weapons with dehumanized — and therefore worthy — targets. Problems arising from this failure are diffused throughout the Pastoral letter in general. The following specific examples may be useful to ponder.

1. *Appreciation of modern communication might prompt a more complete analysis of the church's war-peace history.* The analysis in the Pastoral letter is limited to just war theory and pacifism. When speaking about "Moral Choices for the Kingdom," the Pastoral letter attempts to balance the love that avoids harming even an enemy with the love that protects the innocent. Conditions for just war are set forth as is a brief sketch of pacifism. The letter notes that both Christian options are worthy of respect and in fact "support and complement one another, each preserving the other from distortion." (# 121)

Modern communication, however, has the power to turn a war into a crusade. A crusade is the most vicious war of all. It is a war of righteousness fought against an enemy deserving annihilation. Crusade is a fact of church history every bit as much as just war theory and pacifism. Yet there is little in the Pastoral letter about crusade.

The neglect of any analysis of crusade theory is of great consequence for U.S. Catholics. Their bishops are presenting them a letter on war and peace written in terms of just war theory and pacifism at the very moment that their government (in the judgment of many) is embarking on an anti-Communist crusade. U.S. Catholics need to appreciate the sources, nature, and consequences of violent and uncontrolled crusade just as they need to appreciate the consequences of that violent and uncontrolled nuclear reaction called an atomic bomb. This means an analysis of modern communication.

Some might question the need to analyze crusade theory so thoroughly. It would be possible, in the view of these persons, to resist crusade through a correct application of just war theory itself. Thus extensive communication and crusade analyses would not be needed. However this objection does not seem persuasive. When crusades sweep a nation, application of nuanced, rational requirements of just war theory have little chance of success. It is very interesting to note that the U.S. bishops in an analogous question see little chance that a nuclear war once begun could be kept limited. There is scarcely any possibility that emotionally charged events, whether a crusade or a nuclear war, could be limited by the cool, rational application of rules that theoretically should bring order.

2. *Appreciation of modern communication would perhaps suggest a more complete analysis of the Vietnam War.* This war is mentioned in the section of the Pastoral letter listing conditions to be met for a war to be just. The bishops name proportionality as one of these conditions, explaining that a war cannot be just if there is no proportion between the damage inflicted and the good that might be reasonably expected. Their illustration is Vietnam: "During the Vietnam War our bishops' conference ultimately concluded that the conflict had reached such a level of devastation to the adversary and damage to our own society that continuing it could not be justified." (# 100)

This 1971 declaration against the Vietnam War, reprinted in the Pastoral letter, seems prophetic. Seldom does a bishops' conference state that its nation is conducting an unjust war. However, if the Pastoral letter were written in a tradition sharply aware of modern communication issues, criticisms of the Vietnam War would be broadened far beyond violations of proportionality.

The Vietnam War was advertised, marketed, and sold to the people of the United States. That much would be clear from a study of the *Pentagon Papers*, an investigation of questions surrounding the Gulf of Tonkin Resolution, and exposure during the Watergate scandal of manipulation of public opinion to provide war support. To appreciate the marketing of the Vietnam War, one must grasp how the United States took over the war effort from the French in a series of foreign policy decisions not open to public scrutiny. One would need to analyze the communication events that would move a nation to tolerate a war reminiscent of colonialism. The Pastoral letter, unable to confront the power of modern communication, must be content with recalling a condemnation of the Vietnam War based upon proportionality.

We might also note that a grasp of the role of modern communication in modern war might even anticipate future communication uses of the Vietnam War itself. This war might at some time be made to be perceived as bad not because it was immoral but because it was lost. Vietnam may become a reason to fight the next war with more determination and vigor. New generations of warriors might be motivated to fight all the harder to break the "Vietnam syndrome" of weakness, defeat, and fear of intervention. Just as modern communication may sell a "new improved" soap or detergent, so may it sell a nation a "new improved" war.

3. *Appreciation of modern communication might have prompted challenges to the assumed sharp contrast between the United States and the Soviet Union.* The maintenance of sharp contrast between the two superpowers is a pressing question of modern communication. It is closely related to

the process of enemy dehumanization so necessary for crusade. The Pastoral letter fails to analyze the perceived sharp contrast between the U.S. and Russia that is supported by so much modern communication today. The letter should have been more aware of this problem.

We must further observe that the Pastoral letter even contributes to the sharp contrast between the superpowers. The bishops do indeed criticize certain aspects of the United States and its war plans. They are indeed concerned about the direction our nation is headed and say so. They also admit that our country has faults, both foreign and domestic. Yet an interesting imbalance remains. One can read the entire Pastoral letter without being struck by any indication of current U.S. involvement in conflict in Central America. In contrast the Pastoral letter explicitly mentions Poland and Afghanistan, current Soviet involvements. (# 249)

Yet there is more. In the third part of the Pastoral letter, "The Promotion of Peace: Proposals and Policies," the bishops speak of nonviolent means of conflict resolution. They state, "the heroic Danes who would not turn Jews over to the Nazis...serve as inspiring examples in the history of nonviolence." (# 222) This example of the Danes is truly a shining moment of courage and justice. Yet in the bishops' own United States at the time of their Pastoral letter a growing number of heroic church and synagogue leaders were giving sanctuary to Central American refugees. These religious leaders were risking fines and prison for sheltering from United States authorities people destined for return to their homeland and torture and death. This sanctuary movement, its leaders risking their freedom, and the refugees finding safety in U.S. churches and synagogues were all — unlike the heroic Danes — passed over in silence by the Pastoral letter.

The United States sanctuary movement has the power to critique the perceived sharp contrast between the United States and the Soviet Union so fostered by modern communication. This movement raises disturbing questions far beyond the limitations of the Pastoral letter. Why does the United States treat so differently refugees fleeing Communism and refugees fleeing U.S. allies? If all refugees were treated equally, would this imply criticism of our Central American involvement? Are there parallels between the U.S. and Soviet Union, each in its own sphere of influence? Are there parallels between the U.S. sanctuary movement and the "heroic Danes"? Are there parallels between the Nazis hunting Jews and the United States returning Central American refugees? On these questions the Pastoral letter is powerless and silent.

4. *Appreciation of modern communication would perhaps bring an expanded agenda to the bishops' messages to various categories of people.* At the end of their letter the bishops close with words of support, encouragement, and even challenge to particular groups. While these messages are quite good, an awareness of modern communication would perhaps enrich and broaden them.

For example, a tentative but challenging paragraph of moral guidance is offered to people working in defense industries. In the preparation of the Pastoral letter there was much debate about whether or not such workers were justified in keeping these jobs. This is indeed a complex issue. Yet there was hardly any debate on the fundamental communication issue of naming such industries "defense." In the section of the Pastoral letter on abortion, we have no parallel euphemism such as "termination of pregnancy." It is interesting how the entire tone of the debate on making nuclear weapons would shift if one would use an adjective other than "defense," e.g., "military," "war," "extermination," "genocidal."

The bishops briefly address military chaplains. The Pastoral letter is aware of the value and dignity of the ministry of the chaplain. Yet sensitivity to communication might prompt questions. Does the chaplain communicate, in addition to the Word of God, a certain legitimacy of war? Is the military really interested in the spiritual good of the troops, or do they have their own reasons for wanting a chaplaincy? There are certain subtle communications that enhance morale, a quality necessary for an efficient fighter. Even in E. G. Boring's 1945 classic *Psychology for the Armed Servi-*

*ces* there is stated, "During combat, morale is aided greatly by men's concern for the welfare of others, by prayer, and by hatred of the enemy." (p. 482)

When addressing public officials the Pastoral letter stays well within the boundaries set by the Pastoral Constitution. There is an urging of respect for conscientious objection. There is deep awareness of the importance of the role of public officials in society. Yet there is little awareness of the modern communication issues facing society and its authorities today. These must be probed. For example do public officials frustrate debate by overextending secrecy with the excuse of national security? Do they attempt to manipulate public opinion through systematic news leaks and disinformation? What is the real extent of covert agreements and activities?

The message to men and women of the media is perhaps the most instructive of all — because it is so brief. This message is one short paragraph of encouragement and inspiration. It is sign and symbol of the impact today of the failure of *Inter Mirifica* at Vatican II.

•

The above observations do illustrate the general state of the Pastoral letter with respect to modern communication. However this general state is quite obscure. We so lack a teaching and sensitivity regarding the power of modern communication, that we sometimes fail to see, to ask the right questions.

How often do we reflect on the power of parades and war memorials to inspire a fighting spirit? When do we consider military stunt pilots or bands in their war marketing aspect? Where are the systematic studies, waiting to be popularized, to tell us how and under what conditions do sacrifices like rationing, registration and the draft, and even battle casualties incite to war — as gambling losses incite to more gambling? How many Americans have investigated the *Pentagon Papers* or other records of selling war? How many Christians feel that the age of the crusade is no longer with us? We need to get to know the power of the word.

## For Further Reading

*Documents of Vatican II*, especially *The Pastoral Constitution on the Church in the Modern World* and *The Decree on the Instruments of Social Communication.*

George F. Kennan, *The Nuclear Delusion: Soviet-American Relations in the Atomic Age* (New York: Pantheon Books, 1982).

*The Pentagon Papers.* As published by the New York Times (New York: Bantam Books, Inc., 1971).

Robert Scheer, *With Enough Shovels: Reagan, Bush & Nuclear War* (New York: Random House, 1982).

# 9

# The Voice of the Church at Prayer: A Liturgical Appraisal of *The Challenge of Peace: God's Promise and Our Response*

### Kathleen Hughes, R.S.C.J.

The following reflections from a liturgical perspective are offered in the hope that they might augment the content of *The Challenge of Peace* from two points of view. In a first section the focus will be on the renewed liturgical life of the church as a *neglected source* in the Pastoral's elaboration of a developed theology of peace, a source which strongly confirms and supports the scriptural and theological foundations for peace advanced in the beginning of the document. In this first section we will be examining what the Pastoral letter does not cite, but could add, as the contribution of another sector of the church's life: the voice of the church at prayer. In a second section the focus will shift to Part IV of the Pastoral: "The Pastoral Challenge and Response." In this instance it may be argued that the liturgy is an *underestimated means*. This second section will include specific suggestions for the cultivation of a gospel

135

vision of peace as a way of life for believers and as a leaven in society through the recognition of the transformative power of the liturgical life of the church.

## Liturgy as Neglected Source

In the ancient church, especially in the East, the liturgy was known as *theologia prima*, as distinguished from the more theoretical and speculative formulation of the community's faith, its *theologia secunda*. To speak of "first" and "second" theology, then or now, is not to suggest a pecking order but to underline a fundamental relationship between the church's symbolic language and its theoretical enunciations. To speak of liturgy as "first theology" is to speak of evocative and performative language which gives expression, albeit inchoately, to the community's self-understanding: its relationship with God, the demands of that relationship, the community's desires and hopes and fears on its journey as collaborators with Christ in the establishment of the Kingdom.

Yet another way to view the relationship of liturgy and more formal theological elaboration is to recall that the first meaning of orthodoxy is right praise. Thus liturgy is the doxological dimension of theology, mediating God's claim upon the human community and bringing the community to full and mature encounter with the divine, an encounter which both expresses and continues to enlarge the community's faith. Theological speculation, pastoral letters included, will be enriched by constant dialogue with the community's experience and expression of its faith in the liturgy. Likewise the liturgical experience of faith will be supported, purified and deepened through dialogue with developed and developing theological elaboration. For fullest interpretation the church's *theologia prima* and *theologia secunda* need to be placed in dialogue with each other.

Turning now specifically to the liturgy, it is clear that there has been a dramatic shift in the voice of the praying church following the general restoration of the liturgy in line with the mandate of the Second Vatican Council. According to Antoine Dumas, one of the many collaborators in the post-conciliar liturgical reform, the criteria which governed the revision of the liturgical texts were truth, simplicity and *sens pastorale*, a phrase difficult to translate but which might best be rendered *pastoral appropriateness*. These criteria dictated that the language of the rites reflect not only sound theology and contemporary spirituality but, in addition, the joys and hopes, the grief and anguish of our times, concerns captured by the Council Fathers themselves in the *Pastoral Constitution in the Modern World*.

Peace, and the quest for justice which will make a stable and authentic peace possible, are among contemporary aspirations which have been expressed in the renewed liturgy. Consider and compare the following prayers, those on the left from the English-Latin Roman Missal, 1965 interim translation of the *Missal of Pius V*, those on the right from the post-conciliar *Missal of Paul VI*:

*"In Time of War"*
O God, you destroy wars and by your power you overthrow the aggressors of those who hope in you. Help your servants who appeal to you, so that we may overcome our belligerent enemies and never cease to praise and thank you. Through Jesus Christ.

*"In Time of War or Civil Disturbance"*
God of power and mercy, you destroy war and put down earthly pride. Banish violence from our midst and wipe away our tears that we may all deserve to be called your sons and daughters. We ask this...

*Alternative*
God our Father, maker and lover of peace, to know you is to live, and to serve you is to reign. All our faith is in your saving help; protect us from men (people) of violence and keep us safe from weapons of hate. We ask this...

### "For Defense Against Enemies"

We pray you, O Lord, humble the pride of our enemies and let the might of your right hand crush their arrogance. Through Jesus Christ.

### "For Enemies"

O God, you are the lover and guardian of peace and charity. Grant true peace and love to our enemies, forgive them their sins, and let your might guard us against their deceits. Through Jesus Christ.

### "For the Defense of the Church"

Almighty and eternal God, your hand controls the power and government of every nation. Help your Christians and by the might of your right hand destroy the non-believing peoples who rely on their own cruel strength. Through Jesus Christ.

### "For Peace"

O God, source of all holy desires, right counsels, and just works, grant your servants that peace which the world cannot give so that we may be obedient to your commands and under your protection enjoy peace in our days and freedom from fear of our enemies. Through Jesus Christ.

### "For our Oppressors"

Father, according to your law of love we wish to love sincerely all who oppress us. Help us to follow the commandment of your new covenant, that by returning good for the evil done to us we may learn to bear the ill-will of others out of love for you. Grant this...

### "For Persecuted Christians"

Father, in your mysterious providence, your Church must share in the sufferings of Christ your Son. Give the spirit of patience and love to those who are persecuted for their faith in you that we may always be true and faithful witnesses to your promise of eternal life. We ask this...

### "For Peace and Justice"

God our Father, you reveal that those who work for peace will be called your sons (and daughters). Help us to work without ceasing for that justice which brings true and lasting peace. We ask this...

*Alternative*
God of perfect peace, violence
and cruelty can have no part
with you. May those who are at
peace with one another hold
fast to the good will that unites
them; may those who are enemies forget their hatred and be
healed. We ask this...

The "new" voice of the church at prayer is that of a church
desiring and working for peace, a church no longer self-
righteous and vindictive, a church which recognizes that
violence and cruelty are not of God, a church which fears
weapons of hate. The community no longer asks God to
lead it in battle and to vanquish its enemies; rather, the
community desires to be healed of the violence in its midst,
to return good for evil, and to work for justice which alone
will bring about a true and lasting peace.

The sample of prayers cited above is from the *Sacramentary*'s collection of texts entitled Masses and Prayers for
Various Needs and Occasions, perhaps the most "reformed"
prayers of the entire *Sacramentary* because most clearly
expressive of the concrete human concerns of the twentieth
century: for the unity of Christians, the spread of the Gospel, the progress of peoples, for freedom, security and peace
through the wisdom of civil leadership and the integrity of
the citizenry. Urgency to establish the kingdom of peace and
to bring the message of salvation to all people is evident
throughout this collection of texts. The community of these
prayers is not quietist, asking or expecting God's miracu-
lous direct intervention in human affairs, but rather it recognizes and affirms itself as God's agent of reconciliation for
all peoples. The community, through the performative language of its prayer, embraces its task, asking only that its
heart be changed to act according to God's will: to distribute
goods more equitably, to bring an end to divisions, to work
actively for justice, to be the living presence of Christ in and
for the world.

There is no longer a sense of "we" or "they," whether "they" referred to non-Catholic or non-Christian outsiders or enemies of the faith. Rather, as one new text underscores, the community understands itself in solidarity with the entire human community:

> Father, you have given all peoples one common origin, and your will is to gather them as one family in yourself. Fill the hearts of all men (and women) with the fire of your love and the desire to ensure justice for all their brothers and sisters. By sharing the good things you have given us may we secure justice and equality for every human being, an end to all division, and a human society built on love and peace.

Indeed, the examples could be multiplied and a fruitful comparison of the older and the contemporary corpus of prayers would yield a rich theology of peace, non-violence, solidarity as one human community collaborating in the work of reconciliation. While striking and obvious in the texts *ad diversa*, the same spirit pervades other areas of the church's new voice of prayer.

An examination of the alternative opening prayers, composed to be more concrete and existential renderings of the Latin originals, shows frequent mention of the community's participation in working and praying for peace. Several prefaces, newly composed for the *Missal of Paul VI*, speak of peace as the task of today and the promise of tomorrow for those seeking to live in the image of Jesus, the witness of justice and truth. Two eucharistic prayers of reconciliation whose use has now been extended indefinitely because of their strong popularity, demonstrate the community's concern for conversion. And the content of these prayers expresses a realism about our situation today "in the midst of conflict and division," as well as the hope that friendship, understanding, mercy and forgiveness will put an end to estrangement, strife, hated and vengeance. In addition, both the Rite of Christian Initiation of Adults and the Rite of Reconciliation stress, in their Introductions, a life in solidarity with others, the shaping of new moral consciousness, and the necessity of collaboration with others in the Christian community in the work of peace, justice and reconciliation.

In each of these instances, the liturgy gives new voice to the church at prayer. As event, the liturgy transcends speculative theology. The symbolic language of worship gives expression to an immediate, radical and intersubjective experience of the faith of the church — an elemental expression which, in a sense, comes to full term in theoretical elaboration. *The Challenge of Peace* perfectly complements the new consciousness of the church at prayer as expressed in the language of its rites.

## Liturgy as Underestimated Means

In the first section of this essay we examined a select number of liturgical texts and noted, in a comparison with earlier texts, that our renewed language of prayer contains a new vision of peace and justice, and a challenge to a new way of being in the world in the face of its violence and injustice. Such an examination was based on the methodological presupposition that liturgy (*theologia prima*) functions as a locus of theology, and that theological reflection (*theologia secunda*) might well incorporate the tradition of the church's prayer in its synthesis.

Such work, however, deals only with texts on a printed page, and one might well question what real difference the celebration of liturgy makes in the daily life of believers. Does the language of the rite possess any power to place a claim on participants? Is there any way that the church's liturgy functions critically within the community? Is there any way that the language of our prayer effects what it signifies, gradually transforming the minds and hearts of the community?

In this second section we will first examine the way language functions in worship, including its potentially transformative power, and then we will return to the Pastoral in order to indicate that the power of the liturgy appears to be underestimated as a means of cultivating a Gospel vision of peace in our time.

In speaking about liturgical language two opposite over-simplifications must be avoided if the real power of the language of prayer to transform our minds and hearts is to be released. The first mistaken notion of the way language functions in liturgy is that language in liturgy takes the form of assent to doctrine that a certain fact took place in some empirically verifiable way. So, for example on Easter Sunday, when the church makes the statement "God our Father, by raising Christ your Son you conquered the power of death and opened for us the way to eternal life...," the level of the surface grammar is misleading. It seems to be a simple declarative sentence. It might appear as a straightforward description of a factual state of affairs that in some observable way the Father raised Jesus, that in some verifiable way death is vanquished and eternal life available for the community. Such is not the way language functions to produce meaning in the liturgical assembly.

When the community gathers for its prayer it is not engaged in flat statements of fact. Above all, in its liturgical language, the community recites the saving acts of God in human history in order to engage itself in the telling of its own story and to elicit a response in faith. In the very moment when we profess: "God our Father, by raising Christ your Son..." the community is engaged in a speech-act: an expression of joy, an exclamation of God's power and sovereignty, a proclamation of divine vindication, and a pledge of loyalty to the one we dare to name Father. Each time we address God in prayer we use a metaphor which places us in a relationship with God and commits us to a way of being in the world while we wait in joyful hope for the coming of the Kingdom. The language of our prayer, no matter what its surface grammar may be, is always self-involving and commissive. Our liturgical language summons us to engage in *acts*, in acts of praise and thanksgiving, in acts of acceptance, in promises and pledges and commitments.

The second misconception about liturgical language is that it is not really making statements at all but is the product of our halting attempts to express our inner attitudes. Again, an example will be helpful. In a prayer cited earlier, "For our Oppressors," there is a phrase: "we wish to love sincerely all who oppress us." To speak of a desire to love "all who oppress us" certainly implies that the community experiences such a desire, a wish. Or does it? If we claim that liturgical language is an expression of our state of mind we would also have to acknowledge that sometimes such language does not express what is going on in us. We may feel no such desire (or sorrow, or contrition or peace or whatever), and may even feel just the contrary. Would it not be hypocritical to say Amen to such a prayer?

Such a conception of language in worship makes of it a kind of progress report on our internal state of mind and heart — an accurate report obviously impossible to achieve when language in worship is, of its nature, public and universal and could not possibly capture the state of mind and heart of each one present. In addition, it would have to be presumed that God is already aware of what is going on in our inner selves and that prayer would be simply a means of repeating information to God which God already knows. One is forced to ask the question: why bother to pray at all? Why tell God what God already knows, especially if, in the process, we may be caught in uttering only half-truths?

The point of liturgical language, the point of liturgy, is not for God's sake, as St. Thomas Aquinas pointed out, but for the sake of the community. We come together in the presence of the Holy One and we respond to God's presence in word and deed to bring us to reverence, to allow God, through the liturgy to make a claim upon us, to place ourselves under the consolation and the challenge of the Word, to be transformed, gradually, almost imperceptibly, over time.

In liturgical prayer we are neither primarily assenting to doctrinal statements nor reporting our subjective state of mind. We are engaged in acts; we are doing something, not merely saying something. When we say "Amen" as the communion minister says to us "The Body of Christ," we are, at one and the same time saying: "Yes, it is true," and "Yes, I will be, with God's grace." Every "Amen" spoken in the liturgical assembly makes demands upon us because every "Amen" commits us to live in a new relationship with God through the mediation of Jesus Christ. Such is the potentially transformative power of the church's public ecclesial prayer. Has this power been recognized in the Pastoral as a chief means of cultivating that vision of justice and peace which the letter proposes?

Towards the end of the Pastoral there is a section entitled: "The Pastoral Challenge and Response," a section addressed to the church as a community of "conscience, prayer and penance." In this section of the letter, the community is urged to serious study and reflection on the issues it raises, accompanied by prayer and penance. Perhaps the role of prayer is minimized in this presentation, most specifically, the role of public, ecclesial prayer to nurture a Gospel vision of peace as a way of life and a leaven in society.

At this juncture of our history, faced with the horrors of war and yet confused by the numerous voices and the spectrum of possible legitimate moral options, educational programs undertaken for the formation of conscience are urgently needed. The formation of conscience envisioned by the bishops through the study of their Pastoral letter will clarify issues and lead to intelligent ethical reflection on the many serious questions raised. In many instances it will lead to change of mind in the adopting of the conscious structures of thought presented in the letter. Yet, in the final analysis, what the Christian community needs more, at this moment, is a change of heart. Perhaps the challenge which needs to be addressed to the community is not to become a community of "conscience, prayer and penance," but to become a community of *"prayer, penance and conversion."*

It is not rational to be a peace church; it is not rational to love our enemies; it is not rational to turn the other cheek. At root, the Pastoral letter is calling for a change of heart which is effected by the Lord. Little we can do will make us either just or peaceful, short of opening ourselves to the God of perfect peace and to the Spirit who changes hearts.

This suggestion is made not in an attempt to disparage an intellectual approach to the issues of war and peace, nor to set up a dichotomy between conscience and conversion, nor to imply that peace is really only a matter of sentiment rather than of rigorous and thoughtful reflection. It is offered to underscore the biblical understanding of conversion as human response to the initiative and gracious intervention of God in human life, a biblical position which the letter itself does state: "All of the values we are promoting in this letter rest ultimately in the disarmament of the human heart and the conversion of the human spirit to God, who alone can give authentic peace." (# 284)

If the challenge we now face is that of authentic conversion, then the Pastoral letter would seem to minimize the role of prayer. It is true that the letter urges us to recognize the power of the communion rite, to take the exchange of peace very seriously, and to add an intention for peace to the prayer of the faithful. Such suggestions seem to intimate that the eucharist is made up of a series of elements, some of them more easily adapted to a theme of peace. What may be more helpful to the community is to recognize that when we gather for worship we celebrate not ideas (peace, justice, non-violence, for example) but a Person who alone will make us people of peace. We gather not to express what we can, should, or will do for God but what God has done and continues to do for us in the death and rising of Jesus. The effect of sharing in the eucharist is to allow a claim upon one's whole being and to surrender to the transforming power of the sacrament. Such is true of the Rite of Reconciliation as well. The power of sacramental participation, of gathering as a community for public, ecclesial prayer might well be developed as the Pastoral is being disseminated in communities across the country.

The final draft of the Pastoral included a strong challenge to the community to do penance. The bishops personally assumed the leadership in this area: "As a tangible sign of our need and desire to do penance we, for the cause of peace, commit ourselves to fast and abstinence on each Friday of the year. We call upon our people voluntarily to do penance on Friday by eating less food and by abstaining from meat .... Every Friday should be a day significantly devoted to prayer, penance and almsgiving for peace." (# 298) The bishops noted the relationship of penance to conversion in this context.

The witness of tradition suggests other possibilities as well. It has not been uncommon in the history of the Church to set aside days of public prayer and penance. The origins of the rogation days, for example, are found in a city threatened by disaster and in the actions of a bishop who called for prayer and penance that disaster might be averted. The origins of ember days, while partly a response to pagan festivals, are linked to the community's specific needs for which public penance and intercession seemed apt response. Could we not have a contemporary version of these ancient disciplines, days of public prayer and penance not legislated but as invitation, attractive not because of jurisdiction but because of the moral authority of the leaders of our community calling us to our knees. The Commentary on Instruction on the Liturgical Year seems to propose this course of action: "In our time, when all human beings are fully aware of the serious problems of peace, justice and hunger, the exercises of penance and Christian charity that recur with each of the four seasons need to be given back their original value and power." All decisions regarding ember and rogation day reinstitution have been left to the episcopal conferences.

It would seem a fitting follow-up to the Pastoral letter if the episcopal conference of the United States did seize this opportunity for public fasting and public prayer in cathedrals and churches across the country at specified times during the year. In addition, the episcopal conference might specify that Votive Masses be offered on these days of special public prayer, utilizing some of the very best of the Sacramentary's new prayers, particularly "For Peace and Justice."

"We are called to move from discussion to witness and action." (# 281) Such are the words the bishops used to justify their right to prepare a letter which has political as well as moral dimensions. The same words might well be the response of each Christian who reads this letter and begins the process of discussion and assimilation of its content. The process of study is complex. The issues are profound and not easily assimilated. Nevertheless, even during the process of study, even while our consciences are being formed, we are called to move to witness and action, the witness and action which a community of conversion, prayer and penance might choose. The value of prayer and penance must never be underestimated in the conversion process. They will be a most authentic means of cultivating a Gospel vision of peace among us and a most effective witness to society of the sincerity of our words.

## For Further Reading

John A. Gurrieri, "Catholic Liturgical Sources of Social Commitment," in *Liturgical Foundations of Social Policy in the Catholic and Jewish Traditions*, eds. Daniel Polish and Eugene Fisher (Notre Dame: University of Notre Dame Press, 1983) 19-38.

Stephen Happel, "The Bent World: Sacrament as Orthopraxis," in *The Catholic Theological Society of America Proceedings* 35 (1980) 88-101.

David Hollenbach, "A Prophetic Church and the Catholic Sacramental Imagination," in *The Faith that Does Justice*, ed. John C. Haughey (New York: Paulist Press, 1977) 234-263.

Kathleen Hughes, "Liturgy, Justice, and Peace," in *Education for Peace and Justice*, ed. Padraic O'Hare (San Francisco: Harper and Row, 1983) 189-201.

Mark Searle, ed., *Liturgy and Social Justice* (Collegeville: The Liturgical Press, 1980).

# 10

## Bearing Witness to the Truth in This Moment of History
### Archimedes Fornasari, M.C.C.J.

### The Real Challenge:
### Redeeming the Present Historical Moment

There is a danger that under the urgency of the debate about what *The Challenge of Peace* says about the nuclear arms race, nuclear war and deterrence, the main significance of the letter may go unnoticed. Important as the no's and yes's are, they are only part of a wider and more fundamental topic: peace is challenging us in the present historical moment. This challenge is embodied in a humanity that is struggling to forge a new language, to affirm itself as a truly historical subject by daring to think new thoughts, to imagine and will a more human world. The bishops' letter is another instance (along with Puebla and Medellin) of the church, once accustomed to speak in the manner of eternity, learning how to speak *from* and *with* history.[1] For only as a

[1] The author uses the term history not in the chronological sense of a series of past events but in the sense of an ongoing, dynamic interaction of people and their decisions, progressively shaping the human identity.

148

subject caught up in the common crisis can the church speak to and for history and thereby help regenerate faith in and hope for the life with which our moment of history is pregnant. In this struggling is revealed the full meaning of *aggiornamento* or "renewal." The renewal of structures and methodologies alone could be deceptive. It could be merely a variation of the old rather than the generation of new life. Instead, *aggiornamento* means the process of being once again enabled to speak with power and truth through a novel experience of discipleship to Christ encountered in the present crisis.

The context of this learning is participation in critical events called "the signs of the time":

> The people of God believes that it is led by the Spirit of the Lord, who fills the earth. Motivated by this faith it labors to decipher authentic signs of God's presence and purpose in the happenings, needs and desires in which this people has a part along with other men of our age. For faith throws a new light on everything, manifests God's design for man's total vocation and thus directs the mind to solutions which are fully human.[2]

Thus, the church signifies that it is willing to share the essential historicity of human existence, to live our crises because God also shares them and educates from them. The church is experiencing that true and effective teaching is not done by handing over answers formulated in heaven. Answers are arrived at on earth through dialogue and coop-eration, and the subsequent solutions remain fully human ones.

## Reading the Signs of the Time

The signs of the times refer to possible transformations through which history shows its fruitfulness. The encyclicals

[2]Vatican II. *The Church in the Modern World*, #11.

*Pacem in Terris* and *Octogesima Adviens* and the Pastoral constitution *On the Church in the Modern World* name the most significant ones: the worker movement, the feminist movement, the youth movement and the movement towards independence and self-determination by dominated peoples. These are the places where history is being made and a new language is being born. The presence of ambiguity, contradictions and sin in their strategies and tactics does not remove such movements from being authentic signs of the time. Nor does the fact that the ideologies which originated them or which are used to interpret them may be faulty. John XXIII made these distinctions, and they have become important hermeneutical principles in the church's social teaching. The underlying theology is as old as Paul the apostle and John the evangelist. It is precisely this sinful world that God loves and has assumed in order to defeat the power of sin in it and liberate the new human being, one created in freedom, truth, justice, love and dignity. For John XXIII and the bishops' Pastoral, these are the foundations of a peaceful society. In the effort to speak in a new way, the church is remembering that God walks with humanity and speaks to humanity, including the church, from within the journey.

The bishops refer to three signs of the time as "having particular influence in writing this letter." They are 1) the *cry* "the world needs peace, the world wants peace," 2) the *realization* that "The arms race is one of the greatest curses on the human race," and 3) the *admission* that traditional moral principles are incapable of dealing effectively with the new situation. (#13) These signs of the time converge in a further sign mentioned later in the letter:

> A prominent "sign of the times" today is a sharply increased awareness of the danger of the nuclear arms race. Such an awareness has produced a public discussion about nuclear policy here and in other countries which is unprecedented in its scope and depth. What has been accepted for years with almost no question is now being subjected to the sharpest criticism. . . Many forces are at

work in this new evaluation and we believe one of the crucial elements is the Gospel vision of peace which guides our work in this Pastoral letter. (#125)

To put it a little brashly, the bishops have joined the peace movement! They have recognized in this concrete instance of a cry for peace that what is being offered to us is "the challenge of peace." Today we are called to bear witness to the possibility of peace through a radical renewal of humanity demanded and made possible by God in today's world crisis and which alone can guarantee the survival of our world. This is the main significance of the letter.

## 1984: Will Humanity Find the Will to Survive?

1984 is here. For the "old world," that historic unit which goes beyond the false dichotomy of East-West and which comprises practically the whole of the white race, 1984 is more than a calendar year. It is our moment of truth, taking the form of a question: "Why does the ideological conflict between East and West keep the whole world under its captivity?" The arrogance of the principals of the East-West conflict in assuming an unquestioned right to determine the present and the future of the rest of humanity is but one indication of the nature of the crisis.

Is Orwell's negative utopia the necessary destiny of humanity? His novel *1984* poses the question, as Eric Fromm delineates in the "Afterword":

> Can human nature be changed in such a way that man will forget his longing for freedom, for dignity, for integrity, for love. . . that is to say can man forget that he is human? Or does human nature have a dynamism which will react to the violation of these basis human needs by attempting to change an inhuman society into a human one.[3]

[3]Eric Fromm, "Afterword" to George Orwell's *1984* (New York: New American Library, 1961).

Fromm goes on to state that "The question is a philosophical, anthropological and psychological one and perhaps
also a religious one."

The "perhaps" of Fromm indicates the extent to which
the crisis was affecting the existentialist experiment to save
the meaning of human life, if not its hope, by basing it on the
radically solitary struggle. But hope cannot be dissociated
from meaning. And despair with regard also to meaning
characteristizes the new objectivity of the structuralists.
They see the world as a functional whole of interrelated yet
impersonal forces. The humanist vision assigning to people
a special place in the universe with a unique dignity deserving of immortality is but an allusion. As Claude Lévy-
Strauss concluded in his *Tristes Tropiques*:

> The world began without humanity and will end without
> it. The institutions and the customs in the study and
> cataloguing of which I have spent my life, are only a
> passing efflorescence of a creative process in relation to
> which they have no meaning. Or, perhaps, they have the
> meaning to allow humanity its part.[4]

The same loss of confidence is evidenced on a psychological
level described by Rollo May in *Love and Will*.

> The old myths and symbols by which we oriented our-
> selves are gone, anxiety is rampant; we cling to each other
> and try to persuade ourselves that what we feel is love.[5]

> The inherited basis of our capacity for will and decision
> has been irrevocably destroyed. And, ironically if not
> tragically, it is exactly in this portentous age, when power
> has grown so tremendously and decisions are so neces-
> sary and so fateful, that we find ourselves lacking any new
> basis for will.[6]

[4]Claude Lévy-Strauss, *Tristes Tropiques* (Paris: Plon, 1955), pp. 477-478.
[5]Rollo May, *Love and Will*, (New York: W. W. Norton and Co., 1969), pp.
14-15.
[6]*Ibid.*, p. 182.

## The Crisis of Today

Today's crisis is both structural and global. It is structural, affecting all the structures that sustain human existence and human identity: social, political, economic, psychological, religious and cultural. It is global in the macrocosmic sense of investing the whole human family, as well as the microcosmic sense of affecting the whole individual self. There is a telling symbolism in the marriage of the power harnessed by the splitting of the atom to the power gained through the information-communication network of micro-technology. The fundamental unit of nature, the atom, and the basic social bond of speaking directly and listening have been made irrelevant. They are no longer considered as context and origin of truth. They are related only to power: they become its instruments and channels. A negative transcendence and a negative equality are emerging.

For millions of years, nature has labored to form an ordered cosmos. For a shorter time, a time rich with drama and pathos, humanity has labored to shape the human city as a community of discourse. Both are threatened with extinction. What appears to be symbolized, apparent contradictions notwithstanding, is a purely voluntaristic world without a real human will and without a real human voice. The world of *1984* is a world without speakers and listeners. There are only loudspeakers and receptors. Even Big Brother is not a real person but merely an image on the screen.

The crisis facing us is historical in the sense that it questions whether there can be a real history. Can human beings together make the difference that defeats the power of so-called "necessity"? Can power be married again to truth and thus create a space for freedom? *The Challenge of Peace* addresses this very crisis in the first paragraph: "The human race faces a moment of supreme crisis in its advance towards maturity." (#1) The bishops, contrary to the charges of some critics, do not call for passive resignation. Their letter aims at regenerating hope in and commitment to the human historical project. What is envisioned, however, is not the preservation of the present world order, an order for the defense of which both Western democracies and socialist popular democracies are willing to risk the destruction of the entire world. Instead, the bishops provide a biblical-theological justification for the vision of an alternative world order with a changed humanity, one capable of and committed to waging peace. In the *Summary* we read:

> The letter is intended as an expression of Christian faith, affirming the confidence we have that the risen Lord remains with us precisely in moments of crisis. It is our belief in his presence and power among us which sustains us in confronting the awesome challenge of the nuclear age. We speak from faith to provide hope for all who recognize the challenge and are working to confront it with the resources of faith and reason.

The bishops do not stand on a generic faith in humanity. Rather, they articulate a particular faith that has been formed throughout history by a line of historical events which derive final confirmation and clarification through connectedness with Christ. They stand on the unbreakable relationship constituted between Jesus and history in virtue of Jesus' victory on Good Friday. It is this relationship and its consequences for humanity and our world which are affirmed in the profession that Jesus is the Christ.

## Inauthentic Language

On his messianic entry into Jerusalem, Jesus answered the objections of the authorities regarding what his disciples were shouting by saying: "If they were to keep silence, I tell you the very stones would cry out"(Luke 19:40). The saying raises the question of historically authentic and inauthentic language. Authentic language has to do with the kind of speaking which puts one in contact with reality, which reveals, frees and empowers as opposed to inauthentic speaking which loses one in alienation.

Inauthentic language is not born from active participation in surrounding reality, is not solicited by it, does not respond to it. Inauthentic language is lost in solipsism and unreality. It is the "vain speaking" which Scripture tells us has neither truth nor power.

William Faulkner described the consequences of inauthentic language in the lives of people. Whether idealists like Quentin or materialists like Benji, Faulkner's characters are

> . . . oddly faithful to their ideas rather than to life which they strain to see as they think it is. . . . They are unable to directly comment on events, although they too manage to communicate the details of events.[7]

People are robbed of their capacity to experience the surrounding world, to name their experience and to share it with others. They are excluded from the humanizing power of a real participation in an ongoing dialogue, becoming prisoners of an inauthentic language which has acquired a life of its own much like the "Newspeak" of *1984*. In inauthentic language, subconscious and unconscious forces coopt the speaker for their own agenda, reducing the speaker from a creative self to a mere instance of a balance of non-humanized forces.

## Political Freedom and Dictatorialism

Political freedom derives from a more fundamental freedom of the spirit. The loss of the former is the necessary consequence of the disappearance of the latter, even though the formalities of democracy survive for a time. This is the case when private and national feelings of impotence are not challenged by a call to active and critical participation in policy making. As soon as delegation of office is understood and fostered as delegation of responsibility, the substance of democracy has begun to evaporate. Citizens are reduced to

[7]M. Nochimson, "Faulkner and the Crisis of Inauthentic Language," *Cross-Currents*, Spring (1982), p. 40.

"characters" much as in a play whose words, gestures and actions are already in a script written by someone else.

"Our culture pushes people toward becoming more detached and mechanical,"[8] wrote Rollo May some 15 years ago when *normal anxiety* became the accepted term to describe "the general state affecting technological man." This term is an apt name for existential despair, that feeling of the powerlessness of the powerful symbolized by the temples of iron which have been built throughout the East and West to reassure us that everything is well.

May goes on to note that "We find new words because something of importance is happening in unconscious, unarticulated levels and is pushing for expression."[9] Is there, then, another level of reality which is more fundamental than nature and its structures and which can survive the breakdown of structures, including the language one has been accustomed to speak? Can we put faith in this reality? Will we learn from this faith to once again speak authentically? Only if we dare to risk the challenge of the present moment.

## Does Christ Make a Difference?

Historical language is born in the struggle to make a difference. It is born in the effort to bring into existence a new set of relations between people with nature and with the divinity in which the truth of each and of the whole is more adequately realized. Here is where the bishops part company with some of their critics, such as the authors of the counter-letter *Moral Clarity in a Nuclear Age.*[10] The divergent conclusions are logical consequences of the parting of the ways regarding the interpretation of the Christ event relative to history. For the bishops, sin is a real threat in the world but it is perceived as a threat submitted to the power

[8]R. May, *Love and Will.*

[9]*Ibid.*, p. 26.

[10]M. Novak, et al. "Moral Clarity in the Nuclear Age," *Catholicism in Crisis*, 1983, 1 (4).

that Christ won on the cross. This victory makes peace in history an objective possibility, even if its realization will always be progressive and imperfect. Thus the search for peace becomes a faith imperative.

For the authors of *Moral Clarity*, the world and history are irredeemably under the domination of sin. Whatever Jesus achieved on the cross does not impact on history in any decisive way. Peace is objectively not possible in this world. "In this world Jesus does not promise peace."(*Moral Clarity*, #21) Consequently the only lessons these authors draw from "faith" are:

> ...the precariousness of all human life, the approaching end of history, the perennial wickedness and obdurateness of the human race, and the total sovereignty of God.
> (*Moral Clarity*, #31)

In this vision, sin is abstracted from grace. The radical reconstitution of created reality which took place on the cross (*consummatum est*) whereby humanity is reconciled with God, is not operative.

> Christian optimism based on the glorious cross of Christ and the outpouring of the Holy Spirit is no excuse for self-deception. For Christians, peace on earth is always a challenge because of the presence of sin in man's heart.
> (*Moral Clarity*, #23)

This challenge, however, is in line with Sisyfus' challenge. If Jesus has not achieved a victory for history, then history does indeed remain an impotent struggle.

An historical event can no more be broken up into autonomous parts without the fragments losing the clarity they gained from the relationship of one to another and to the whole anymore than can the fundamental units of nature be so broken up without similar consequences. A fission bomb is as destructive as a fusion bomb. The cross is part of a total event:  death-resurrection-ascension-pentecost-church-world-eschatology. It is only in the interrelations within the whole that what has been accomplished "once and for all" on the cross stands revealed. When related to this accomplishment, sin's real nature also stands revealed: falsehood. Sin's claims to dominion, far from being regrettable historical necessities, are disclosed as expressions of the same falsehood.

The real continued presence of sin in history cannot be accepted as having the kind of unavoidability sin would like us to believe. When we accept the "unavoidability," we also forget the central mystery of the Christian faith. Especially after Auschwitz, this must be said with a vast amount of humility. Those of us who were living at the time of Auschwitz and those who were born later must negate this claim to unavoidability with firmness and passion lest Auschwitz be accepted as an historical necessity. For Auschwitz speaks directly to us as Christians. It questions the central claim of our faith that Jesus is God's Messiah for humanity, the one in whom we can put an undoubtable faith and hope to obtain liberation from the "inevitability" of holocaust. There is in this a theological and soteriological question: "What evidence can we give that the One who has promised humanity liberation and fulfilment has brought to pass in the Jesus event this promise in a way that is both definitive and without repentance?" Can we put an undoubtable faith in the continued presence of this liberating and caring power?

I am reminded of the question of John the Baptist to Jesus: "Are you 'He who is to come' or do we look for another?" (Matt 11:3) The question is legitimate and needs an answer. The same question is being placed to the church today. The church's answer cannot be different from Jesus' answer. If the church is to be what it is called to be, i.e. the visible, concrete symbol of Christ's continued presence in history, the answer lies not in the metaphysics of God or of nature but in the actual occurring of events that make the difference and constitute historical consciousness and practice. There *are* people with another vision, who feel, think and will a life and world in which the central and all-consuming concern is the fostering of the dignity of all human beings. It is these people who bear witness to the fact that something of radical importance has happened in and to history. History is not neutral. There is inscribed in it a truth and a power regarding the destiny of humanity and it expresses God's concern for us, the story of God's faithfulness.

It is important, however, that we reflect also on the nature of this conjunction between the God of the promise, Jesus and the church. The conjunction does not operate apart from historical consciousness and practice. When Christians have decided that the Christ event and the church have no significant relevance for the concreteness of history, that is to say for society, culture, politics and economics, then they have already accepted in principle not only the possibility of the reoccurrence of Auschwitz but also its inevitability. For them, history has no moral imperative since it offers no moral possibility. It does not deal with transformation, and transcendence or with humanity's coming into its own truth and power. Instead history gives place to a *real politik* which is only concerned with the management of presumed "iron-laws," the ethic-free demands of a security state.

The inevitability of a new Auschwitz is inscribed not only in the policy of deterrence, but in all policies that decree that people must die of hunger at a time of over-production, and that curable sick people must die for lack of means to cure them. To insinuate that after the *consummatum est* the destruction of humanity can be contemplated by God strikes me as a blasphemy against God, a damnable lie about Jesus Christ and an obscene offense against humanity.

## Bearing Witness to the Truth

"My task is to bear witness to the truth. For this I was born." (John 18:37) Historical truth can only be brought to light by an act of witnessing. But witnessing does not take place in a vacuum. Rather, it exists in relation to a listening, especially the listening of and by authorities whose task it is to foster the gestation of a truth which they do not own as a private property. The context of Jesus' words reveals that witnessing to an historical truth implies the possibility of witnessing in the face of death. In the term *martyr*, Christianity has recognized this sober fact by associating the two meanings, so that the martyr is one who witnesses to the power of life in the face of the threat of death. Unlike death, life needs witnessing; it needs to be affirmed by someone who wills to become its sponsor. A martyr is one who has chosen to sponsor life that is threatened by death. Thus, martyrdom is the radical expression of faith. In martyrdom one hands over her/his life to the primordial, reliable and assured Yes of the original source and sponsor of life. In doing so, the martyr unmasks the false claims to power by death which are present in the various uses of power. The nuclear arms race and deterrence are instances of the contemporary claims by death to have the power to determine the present and future of humanity.

"It is neither tolerable nor necessary that human beings live under this threat." By these words the bishops perform an act of witnessing rather than merely uttering an abstract truth. Furthermore, they state "Peace-making is not an optional commitment. It is a requirement of our faith." (*Summary*) Faith is not so much concerned with the abstract existence of God, but more with the revelation in history of God's presence as the foundation of human possibility. It is this latter truth that is threatened by sin and blindness and it is the corresponding life that is denied. We are committed by our faith and by our humanity to sponsor this threatened truth and in so doing to witness to the possibility of new life. The challenge of peace today demands nothing short of this kind of witness.

> There is no satisfactory answer to the human problems of the nuclear age which fails to consider the moral and religious dimensions of the questions we face. (*Summary*)

This means that we must be prepared to be brought in front

of the authorities by our faith.

Pilate and Jesus, however, did not communicate. They could not communicate. Their words did not create the human space wherein one speaker could encounter the other and provoke his faith. The obstacle lay in the different perspectives from which they spoke. Pilate spoke "fatalistically," from the position that history had already been decided by fate which was Rome's real god. The myth of Romulus and Remus had covered the real history of Rome with the mantle of "manifest destiny." Consequently historical action, at least present historical action, could open no new possibilities. Historical experience was thus made obsolete. In contrast, Jesus was speaking historically; everything was still in flux, everything was still open to decision. The future hinged on what or whom one was open to in her/his experience. Thus it was not only possible to make a difference, it was demanded. In the making of the difference, one encountered the primordial source and foundation of life. Historical situations *could* be changed and death *could* be defeated.

## The Religious Vision of Peace

The central part of the bishops' Pastoral discusses the "religious vision of peace," which has "an objective basis and is capable of progressive realization." (#20) Discussion can be a form of historical speaking. It depends on whether the religious vision of peace constitutes a real historical possibility.

> Building peace in and among the nations is the work of many individuals and institutions; it is the fruit of ideas and decisions taken in the political, cultural, economic, social, military, and legal sectors of life. We believe that the Church as a community of faith and a social institution, has a proper, necessary, and distinctive part to play in the pursuit of peace. (#21)

Peace is not seen as the direct work of God alone, or of the church alone as God's representative. It is seen as a cooperative effort between all sectors of humanity. The church joins a number of participants, each one claiming to speak from a realistic position. The church has its own concrete stand from which it can show that it is speaking realistically.

> Christ is our peace, "for he has made us both one, and has broken down the dividing wall of hostility. . .that he might create in himself a new man in the place of two, so making peace, and might reconcile both to God." (#21)

What is significant in this vision is that enemies both need and are offered reconciliation with God. Neither party can justify in the name of God the defense of its partial and false vision of peace. And the reconciliation with God cannot be obtained by separate treaties but in the reconciliation of all parties. The event of a new human being capable of peace takes place in this making of one out of two.

An historical event, however, can still be reduced to the status of a myth. This can be avoided only if the stand from which the church speaks constitutes a true presence for our moment of history: of that which makes history possible. The church must stand in unison with the original event of reconciliation, speaking from the cross in a real historical sense. This means that the church must stand in solidarity with all those who are despised, silenced or executed in our moment of history. The cross cannot be allowed to be reduced to a mere ascetical or mystical meaning. It must be recovered as the discriminating event in and for history, scandalous as this statement may be for a worldly wisdom.

## He Makes the Deaf and the Dumb Speak

> The nuclear age is an era of moral as well as of physical danger. We are the first generation since Genesis with the power to threaten the created order. We cannot remain

silent in the face of this danger. . . We fear that our world and our nation are headed in the wrong direction.

(*Summary*)

These words of *The Challenge of Peace* remind me of Jesus' words as reported by Luke.

> If only you had known the path to peace this day; but you have completely lost it from view. Days will come upon you when your enemies encircle you with a rampart. . . . They will wipe you out and your children within the walls . . . because you failed to recognize the time of your visitation. (Luke 19:41-44)

Are Jesus and the bishops indulging in hyperboles of pessimism, much like the "flight of reason into panic" that must be "quietly resisted," itself a consequence of the flight of the same reason "into illusion" that "must be curbed?" (*Moral Clarity*, #8) Jesus was speaking historically, as Luke came to realize some years later. The question is: what kind of speaking bears witness to the truth of a given historical moment? And what are the results of missed opportunities? Jesus was expressing a passionate concern born of another passionate concern that stood at the "origin" of the Jewish people's existence. Before anything else, history is passionate. Yes, there was blindness, but not of "fate." The blindness was, then as now, in people who have forgotten about the passionate concern that brought them to life.

"To whom has the power of God been revealed"? (Is 53:1) The prophet speaks of a sure sign that tells when the time has come for God to remember and not to leave undone the things s/he has promised. (Cf. Is 42:16) The time of God's remembering is at the same time the opportunity offered to people to overcome their foolishness, to turn away from what they had planned to do in their foolishness. The sign of this remembering is a new and strange way of speaking which appeared in the land.

Such speaking is strange because it does not fit the estab-

lished rules of discourse. The very fact of its existence proves
that the existing rules have lost their truth and power; they
have been outlived. The speaking governed by the old rules
hinders rather than facilitates participation in and communion with surrounding reality, becoming an impotent incan-
tation without life-giving action. The speaking is strange
and new because of *what* it says and *who* says it. Everything
happens in contrast to the established rules. "Who could
have believed what we have heard"? (Is 53:1) But the
prophet also tells us how to discern the right speaking: look
for who believes in it and who is perturbed by it and rejects it
(cf. Matt 2:3-4; John 11:2-19).

One of the reasons the new language seems strange, especially to pietistic people, is that it appears to set a criterion
for God's action in a reality other than in God, and in a
sinful reality at that. The scandal, however, is only the result
of forgetting that history originates first of all in the primordial act of transcendence on the part of God who calls
humanity into existence not from afar but by walking along
with it. Irenaeus was referring to this truth in his saying that
"The glory of God is a living humanity."

While there are psychological and sociological reasons
for the different reactions to the new language, the more
fundamental one is theological. The new language is more
than an expression of a mere protest or revolt against the
injustice and oppression which is embodied, allowed or
justified by the old rules. The new language proclaims a new
beginning that has been experienced and seen. It is a radical
call to action, carrying with it a bold conviction about its
own truth and power coming from what one has seen and
heard. If questions are asked, they are not expressions of
doubt but requests for enlightenment needed for rightful
acknowledgement. They deal with what is possible, appear-
ances to the contrary. "How can this be since I do not know
man?" (Luke 1:36) Or the questioning can deal with whose
power one accepts as the determinant of one's life. "Where is
the newborn king of the Jews"? (Matt 2:2) Contrasted with
these questions characterized by complete sincerity, there is
Herod's question "Where is it that the Messiah is to be

born?" (Matt 2:4) The purpose of Herod's question is to hide his real intentions, unlike the purpose of Mary and the wise men.

> Long have I lain still, I have kept silence and held myself
> in check; now I will cry like a woman in labor. (Is 42:14)

Thus the new language originates from the experience of God's labor in history. The signs of the time are the events through which God's sovereignty and purposes are transformed from divine intentions into historical realities.

If we look at the main signs of the times mentioned in the church's documents — the workers' movement, the feminist movement, youth and peace movements and the movement towards self-determination by dominated peoples — we can grasp the last characteristic of the new language. The speakers are those who have been ignored, unrecognized, deprived of voice. This is why the new language generates surprise, astonishment, consternation or the skeptical smile. The new language embodies the occurrence of the unexpected. Thus, it carries with it resistance to being believed for it involves the coming to pass of what had been decreed "impossible." By its very occurrence, however, the new language carries a testimonial of the force that it brings to existence, becoming the test of faith and the proof of the faithfulness. It constitutes the difference between the two laughs of Sarah: the skeptical laugh in front of God's promise of the impossible and the laugh of recognition of what has come to pass: "God has given me cause to laugh" (Gen 18:11-15; 21:6). It is the astonishment of Easter which begins with the intention of completing a burial and ends with the celebration of the One who is living "to die no more." This new language refers to two related words which Western culture has difficulty with: surprise and miracle. But W. H. Auden is right:

> That which is merely possible does not save.
> For we who are dying demand a miracle.
>
> *(In The Meantime)*

The greatest miracle Jesus ever performed is to have people believe in him and become his disciples. This miracle is taking place today. Popes and bishops are perceiving that in the voice of the forgotten ones of history, that is workers, women, youth and dominated peoples, God is giving notice that s/he is remembering the things s/he intends to do and will not leave undone. So popes and bishops become disciples again. In this event hope is confirmed. 1984 is here, but "Newspeak" has met the unexpected in the re-emergence of the Good News witnessing to the truth that history is still possible. There is hope indeed.

## For Further Reading

Thomas Clarke, ed., *Above Every Name* (New York: Paulist Press, 1980).

Rollo May, *Love and Will* (New York: W. W. Norton and Co., 1969).

David O'Brien and Thomas Shannon, eds., *Renewing the Earth: Catholic Documents on Peace, Justice, and Liberation* (Garden City, N.J.: Doubleday, 1980).

Dorothee Soelle, *The Arms Race Kills Even Without War* (Philadelphia: Fortress Press, 1983).

Luigi Sturzo, *The International Community and the Right of War* (Philadelphia: Fortress Press, 1983).

# 11

## Perspectives on Church in the "Challenge of Peace"

### John E. Linnan, C.S.V.

The primary purpose of the bishops of the United States in their pastoral letter, *The Challenge of Peace*, is to address the religious and moral issues raised by nuclear weapons and war. However, in the process of preparing the Pastoral, the bishops have spoken and acted in ways which give some insight into the way they envision church. The ecclesiology which is at the foundation of the Pastoral is not a finely wrought theological construction. It is not the product of conscious elaboration. It does not seem to have been the object of the concentrated attention of the bishops. Rather, the ecclesiology to be found in the Pastoral is a practical one. It is an understanding of the church which is implicit in the way the bishops prepared the Pastoral. This ecclesiology is implied in the way the bishops understand the role of the church in relation to civil society. It approaches explicit expression only occasionally, such as when the bishops seek to clarify their right to teach on issues of war and peace or when they seek to define the ecclesial authority of their teaching. There is much that is tentative about this ecclesiology. It is neither a definitive nor a complete statement of the bishops' theological understanding of the church. It is a theology of church which is in flux, which is still developing. What can be glimpsed through the explicit theological and ethical affirmations of the Pastoral are the sketchily traced outlines of a developing local theology of church.

The purpose of these few pages is to attempt to point out certain aspects of this ecclesiology, some of its major characteristics, and a few of the advances and retreats that characterize a cautiously developing local theology of church. While it would certainly be useful to do a careful history of the various stages of the text, that history must await a more exhaustive study. This brief study will focus on the final text approved by the bishops, with only occasional references to the widely publicized second draft in order to highlight significant shifts in perspective. Particular attention will be given to three areas: 1) the fundamental vision of the church operative in the Pastoral; 2) particular aspects of the church as these relate to peace and 3) the bishops' approach to their magisterium and its mode of exercise. Where references are made to the second draft of the Pastoral, they are to its publication in *Origins*, vol. 12, #20 (Oct. 28, 1982).

## 1. The Vision of the Church

In the Pastoral, the church is seen as a dynamic missionary, minority community. It is a dynamic community, a living community of men and women, disciples of Jesus, grappling with the issues of the day and engaged effectively with the world of which the church is a part. (# 274-278) It is more than a passive witness to the coming kingdom; it is an instrument of that kingdom. (# 22) It is not an unchanging, monolithic society, but a community constantly reshaping itself under the inspiration and guidance of the Spirit. It is a people searching in prayer and dialogue to bring the light of the Gospel to bear on the issues of the day. (# 280-300)

This church of which the bishops speak is missionary. It does not see itself as a shelter, a home, or a refuge from the world, but as a people "called to live the tension between the vision of the reign of God and its concrete realization in history." (#58) The language is "task," "mission," and "instrument." The church is looked at primarily in terms of her mission in the world to bear instrumental witness to the reign of God already present but also yet to come. (#22) The call is for "convinced Christians," for "disciples." (#276) "To be a Christian, according to the New Testament, is not simply to believe with one's mind, but also to become a doer of the word, a wayfarer with and a witness to Jesus." (#276) Clearly the emphasis is on action as the acid test of the church's commitment to Jesus.

The bishops acknowledge clearly that the church no longer conceives itself in "Constantinian" terms. There is no pretense that the church is co-extensive with civil society, no matter how numerous Catholics might be. The church is a minority community living in a secularistic world.

> "It is clear today, perhaps more than in previous genera-
> tions, that convinced Christians are a minority in nearly
> every country in the world — including nominally Chris-
> tian and Catholic nations. . . . As believers we can iden-
> tify rather easily with the early Church as a company of
> witnesses engaged in a difficult mission." (#276)

The realism of this assessment is refreshing. It constitutes a call to seriously reconsider how the church might reshape its institutional presence to make its mission more effective in this new situation. This self-understanding on the part of the church also seems to engender a greater openness to searching with other institutions, both civil and religious, for more effective ways to promote justice and peace in the world. (cf. #16-24, 319-329)

The vision of the church proposed in the final text of the Pastoral is substantially the same as that proposed in the second draft. And yet, there has been a change in tone. While the final text affirms in the same language the missionary and minority status of the church, its affirmation of the internal dynamism of the church is somewhat attenuated. A comparison of the two versions (Second draft, p. 325, cols. 2 and 3; Final text, #326-329) suggests that in the approved text there is greater hesitancy in acknowledging pluralism within the church and the consequent need for a more dialogical approach. The second draft of the Pastoral describes the church as a community of conscience, that is a community which, in virtue of the faith it holds, is obliged to engage in that moral discourse which leads it to decision. The church is a community required to "shape an internal consensus on key issues." But as a community of conscience, the church is also obliged to engage civil society: "The church's function as a community of conscience is not to remain separate from civil debate, but to inform, shape and influence it." They are well aware of how difficult it is for both church and state to shape a consensus when the issues are as complex and emotional as those of war and peace. But it is for this very reason that the church has a special call "to demonstrate how a community can acknowledge a pluralism of views, but not be divided by them." It is because the church is both a community of conscience and a community of pluralistic views, that its effort to achieve an internal consensus enables it to be a witness and model for the civic community. The bishops acknowledge that in preparing this Pastoral they have already encountered strongly divergent views within the Catholic community. They expect "respectful consideration" of their views, but also "vigorous debate." At the same time, they remain convinced "that in the midst of pluralism within the church, we can forge a limited but still substantial consensus of thought leading to action." They do not look for some kind of monolithic uniformity, but for a limited consensus of thought, substantial enough to lead to action.

This emphasis on the church as a community of conscience, on the pluralism existing in the church, and on the need for dialogue and debate is something new. It suggests a more realistic conception of the church as a human community, effectively engaged with the larger civic community of which it is a part. It suggests also that its witness of unity both to its own members and to the world is effective precisely because it is willing to grapple with the pluralism of views within itself. Its own pluralism becomes the foil for the unity it achieves in and through the assistance of the Spirit.

However, in the final text of the Pastoral, the references to the church itself as a community of conscience are dropped. Instead the church "helps to create a community of conscience in the wider civil community." (#328) The church does this first of all "by teaching clearly within the church the moral principles which bind and shape the Catholic conscience." (#328) It does this secondly by "striving to share the moral wisdom of the Catholic tradition with the larger society." (# 328) There seems to be a conception of church here very different from that in the second draft. Here the assumption is that the church already possesses the moral principles necessary to guide its action. There is no need to shape internal consensus. The principles need only be taught by the church (hierarchy?) to the church (members?) and obeyed. This establishes the church as a fit teacher for the civil society, helping it to become a community of conscience. This view of church seems to assume a static understanding of moral principles as absolutes, that once having been shaped never need to be re-thought in terms of contemporary needs or situations. Further this view suggests that the church passes untouched through history, and is not itself subject to the historical condition. Finally, this view of church suggests that there are really two churches; one which possesses "the moral principles which bind and shape the Catholic conscience" and another church which must be taught these moral principles; one church that is active, one that is passive; one church that teaches, one that is taught. The notion that the "teaching church" must also be at one and the same time "the learning church" may be lost sight of here.

Also, in the final text, all references to pluralism within the church, to the need to form a limited consensus of thought leading to action, and to the need for dialogue within the church are dropped. Rather the discussion is limited to the role of the church in public debate of civil issues.

This shift in the conception of the church is startling. What it shows most clearly is an ecclesiology in the process of development. The second draft represents a bold foray into a thorough-going rethinking of the church as a pluralistic community of conscience and dialogue. It is a very realistic vision of the church as a human community, that is historically conditioned, pluralistic, and needing always to constitute again and again its unity in order to function effectively as a moral agent in the larger human community. The final text, however, is marked by a cautious retreat to a more familiar understanding of the church, an understanding in which the roles of hierarchy and magisterium are emphasized, and in which the church adopts a more paternal/ maternal relationship to civil society. It is unfortunate that in the approved text one vision replaces the other; what is really needed is a synthesis of the two, since each complements the other.

## 2. Particular Aspects of Church Related to Peace

The Pastoral also calls attention to other aspects of the church which, while not new, have nevertheless often been ignored or neglected. Some of the more important notions either presented or alluded to by the bishops are the nature of the church as instrumental witness, the role of peace in the church, the significance of catholicity, and what it means to be a Christian.

The bishops explicitly affirm that the church's task is to be a witness in the world to the kingdom of God — and more than that — to be an "instrument of the kingdom of God in history." (#22) This instrumental witness requires that the church be actively engaged not only with its own members but also with the whole human community in order to make real in human history, even if only in a limited and partial way, the basic elements of God's promise, namely peace, justice and love. (#20, 23-24) It is, therefore, not enough for the church simply to be a community in the world which by its existence alone functions as a sign of God's reign yet to come in its fullness. This is a theological truth: "the unity of the human family, rooted in common creation, destined for the kingdom and united by moral bonds of rights and duties." (#236) The church by who she is and by what she does must bear witness to this truth — and must constantly call her members beyond narrow-minded patriotism to a vision that embraces the whole human community. (#327)

Finally, the bishops made a remark that suggests more than it states. "To become true disciples, we must undergo a demanding course of induction into the adult Christian community." (#277) This seems more than an endorsement of the new Rite for the Christian Initiation of Adults. It emphasizes the intrinsically adult character of the Christian community. It may indeed also be calling us to reshape our whole approach to the formal and informal processes of initiating children and adolescents into the Christian community. This together with the Pastoral's general emphasis on mission, action and discipleship suggests a more realistic understanding of Christian life and the need to give pastoral and sacramental shape to that understanding. Furthermore, it calls upon all in the church to prize adult faith, a reality that needs to be defined anew and celebrated in ways not yet discovered.

## 3. The Magisterial Style of the Bishops

The second draft of the Pastoral bore witness to a style of magisterial teaching that was new and exciting. The way the drafting committee had composed this Pastoral and presented it to the church for critique, its language and tone, its reiterated invitation to dialogue, strongly suggested, if not a different conception of the episcopal magisterium, at least a different style. The Pastoral was the product of much study and consultation with experts in theology, scripture, ethics, public policy, defense, nuclear arms and strategy. It was written with a clear awareness that the two publics it addressed, the church and the civic community, are deeply divided on the issues. It recognized that even among the angels there is division.

Furthermore, the second draft did not pretend to offer a final answer. It carefully defined the bishops' task: "As bishops we seek to fulfill a pastoral responsibility by drawing upon the teaching of the Roman Catholic tradition, using it to address the nuclear arms race and inviting Catholics and all members of our political community to dialogue and decision about this awesome question." (p. 307, col. 1) The same theme was repeated again and again. The bishops "feel a special obligation to call our community of faith to shape this conscious choice." (p. 307, col. 1) "This pastoral letter is more an invitation to continue the new appraisal of war and peace than a final synthesis of such an appraisal." (p. 308, col. 3) "We must learn together how to make correct and responsible moral judgments." (p. 322, col. 3) "To fulfill its role as a community of conscience, the church as a community must shape an internal consensus of key issues." (p. 325, col. 2)

The second draft seems to see it to be the duty and task of bishops, as leaders in the church, to do three things:

1) to bring to bear on issues of the day the teaching of the Roman Catholic tradition;
2) to challenge the whole Christian community to shape in the light of the tradition an internal consensus on these issues, "a limited but still a substantial consensus of thought leading to action"; (p. 325, col. 3) and
3) to lead the Catholic community in this dialogical process in which the whole church, as a community, learns together how to make correct and responsible moral judgments. (p. 322, col. 3)

In addition, the second draft asserts that the task of the bishops is to challenge not only the members of the church, but all men and women of good will to "form a consensus in our community" on the issue of the pursuit of peace in our day. (p. 308) By inviting all people of good will, church members or not, to participate in the study, dialogue, and debate, the second draft also is implicitly acknowledging that in different ways the Spirit is at work both within the church and outside of it.

The second draft of the Pastoral also presented us with a conception of the magisterium which was collaborative and dialogical. It was an approach to the exercise of the church's teaching mission which explicitly recognized that bishops, experts, church members and other people, each had unique, essential, and irreplaceable roles to fulfill in order for the church to be able to formulate its teaching on the moral and religious dimensions of public policy. The role of the *sensus fidelium* and the role of the Spirit in church and world are clearly recognized in this process of developing an ethical consensus. It seemed to define the episcopal magisterium as an act of ecclesial leadership which proclaims the gospel, identifies the urgent issues of the day, and calls the community of believers to penance, prayer, reflection and dialogue, precisely in order to enable the church to learn what it is the Spirit now calls the church to be and to do. In this way, the episcopal magisterium would function *in persona Christi* by calling together his disciples to receive the Spirit of Truth, in effect, sacramentalizing the action of Jesus in the Spirit congregating again and again the people of God.

In the final text of the Pastoral, the bishops hesitate to affirm without reservation this more collaborative and dialogical approach to their teaching office. In the second draft the bishops understand their role in these terms: "As Catholic bishops in the United States we feel a special obligation to call our community of faith to shape this conscious choice to save humanity." (p. 307, col. 1) The role of the bishops is to call the community of faith to this task; it belongs to the whole community, including the bishops, to shape the conscious choice. This description of the relationship of bishops to the community of faith and of their respective functions is omitted in the final text. Instead, the final text of the Pastoral describes the role of the bishops in these terms:

> "We also speak as bishops of the church in the United States, who have both the obligation and opportunity to share and interpret the moral and religious wisdom of the Catholic tradition by applying it to the problems of war and peace today." (#6)

The emphasis is on the authority of the bishops as teacher. No mention is made of the role of the community of faith in this context. While the differences are not enormous, the tone and style of the final text seem more authoritarian than in the second draft, less inviting and collaborative, and seem to leave less room for significant participation by the community of faith in the process by which the church shapes her own doctrinal and moral positions relative to the issue of war and peace.

The second draft (p. 325, cols. 2 and 3) recognizes the rightful pluralism that exists in the church concerning the moral evaluation of the ways and means to peace. But in the final text the three paragraphs discussing this pluralism and the need for mutual respect, civility and charity in the dialogue that this pluralism makes necessary are omitted. The final draft replaces these paragraphs with a reference to democratic pluralism in the United States and the opportunities this affords the church to influence public policy. The references in the second draft to pluralism in the church and the need for the church as a community to "forge a limited but still substantial consensus of thought leading to action" (p. 325, col. 3) is replaced by this statement: "It [the church] does this [helps to create a community of conscience in the wider civil community] by teaching clearly within the church the moral principles which bind and shape the Catholic conscience." (#328) A magisterium which conceives of the church as "teaching clearly within the church the moral principles which bind and shape the Catholic conscience" is a very different magisterium from one in which bishops "call our community of faith to shape this conscious choice," (p. 307, col. 1) different too from one in which "To fulfill its role as a community of conscience, the church as a community must shape an internal consensus on key issues." (p. 325, col. 2)

There is also a shift in the way the bishops describe how the church participates in the public debate on these issues. The second draft says that it is "Through this consensus [the limited but still substantial consensus of thought leading to action forged by the community in the midst of its pluralism] we can share in the wider public debate...." (p. 325, col. 3) In the final text, it would seem that the church enters the public debate as a teacher: "The church also fulfills a teaching role, however, in striving to share the moral wisdom of the Catholic tradition with the larger society."(#328)

The changes made in the way the bishops present their magisterium from the second draft to the final text are disappointing. The second draft seems to represent a serious effort to distinguish between the essentially secular and autocratic character of a pyramidal conception of church order, and the essentially religious and organic character of an hierarchical church order. In the latter, it is the community of faith that is endowed with the power of the Spirit, and each member is thereby enabled to serve in accord with the particular gift he or she has received from the Spirit.

The second draft also suggested an effort on the part of the bishops to understand the church of the "Dogmatic Constitution on the Church"(*Lumen Gentium*) in the light of the "Pastoral Constitution on the Church in the Modern World" (*Gaudium et Spes*). This interpretation suggests that the church in her engagement to serve the world as an instrumental witness must also undergo transformation by the world she serves.

Too little is still known of the debate and discussions of the American bishops among themselves and with representatives of other hierarchies and the Holy See to determine what led them to draw back from the directions taken in the second draft. However, it does seem that the "Rome Consultation on Peace and Disarmament" in which at the invitation of the Holy See representatives of the bishops of the United States met with representatives of the European bishops and the Holy See had a significant impact on the development of the Pastoral between the second draft and the final text (cf. *Origins*, vol. 12, #43 [April 7, 1983], pp. 691-695). The way the second draft expressed the teaching role of the bishops was subject to significant criticism. Particular attention was focused on the final pages of the draft, which were criticized in these terms:

> "The concluding pages of the draft seem ambiguous when they refer to pluralism of opinions on the matters touched upon in the Pastoral and at the same time urge substantial consensus. Substantial consensus must be based on doctrine and does not flow from debate. It is wrong to propose the teaching of the bishops merely as a basis for debate; the teaching ministry of the bishops means that they lead the people of God and therefore their teaching should not be obscured or reduced to one element among several in a free debate." (p. 693, cols. 1-2)

The concern of the European bishops and of the Holy See seems to have been to prevent confusion of different levels of authority in episcopal teaching.

> "The draft mixes different levels of authority and it will be difficult for the reader to make the necessary distinctions. Hence grave questions of conscience will arise for Catholics. A clear line must be drawn between the statement of principles and practical choices based on prudential judgment. When bishops offer elements for reflection or when they wish to stimulate debate — something that for pastoral reasons they might be called upon to do in present-day situations — they must do it in such a way that they clearly differentiate this from what they are found to propose as *doctores fidei*." (p. 693)

There is no question that the way the second draft deals with the episcopal magisterium and its exercise is very different from the expectations of the Europeans and Romans at the Consultation. Whether the difference is at the level of doctrine or culture is difficult to discern. It seems to be more cultural than doctrinal. The American bishops stated their understanding of their role as authoritative teachers in the church in terms of the American experience of participation and process in leadership, learning, and decision-making. The second draft seems to give expression to a *local* theology of magisterium, whether or not this was clearly recognized or intended by all parties concerned. That it met with opposition and criticism when it encountered another local theology of the magisterium (shaped by the very different European experience of authority, teaching, decision-making) is not surprising. And since the role of the magisterium was not the principal concern of the U.S. bishops of this Pastoral, it is understandable that the offending passages were dropped. Even with the changes made in the final text to respond to the criticism of the second draft, the bishops continue to demonstrate a conception of the magisterium which includes dialogue and consultation. And if their words are not all that explicit, their actions are clear. The very methodology followed by the bishops in the writing of this Pastoral is a remarkable testimony to their respect for consultation, participation, shared information, and dialogue. This is a happy portent for the church in America.

## Conclusion

This review of the ecclesiological perspectives in the bishops' Pastoral, *The Challenge of Peace*, is too brief to afford grand conclusions. However, to understand the ecclesiology which undergirds the bishops' approach to their ministry and to the mission of the church in the world is not only important but deserves more effort and careful study than it has thus far received. As the number of national pastorals and statements increase, so does the data for the ecclesiology implicit in these statements. In this instance, the Pastoral presents evidence for an emerging *local* theology of church. This theology is understood and expressed in the idiom of American experience. The theology itself is tentative, cautious, and at times uncertain, because it is still a theology in the process of becoming —only gradually becoming aware of the uniqueness of its own perspective, and not yet having acquired the language needed to express that perspective in terms that meet the expectations of other cultures. For all that it is a theology in flux, it presents the church as a dynamic, missionary community of the disciples of Jesus. It is a church which challenges us to commitment, to become part of corporate, instrumental witness of God's reign. The Pastoral emphasizes the role of the church as an instrument of the Kingdom. It focuses on peace and catholicity as constitutive elements of that witness. Finally, with caution and a certain tentativeness it promotes a new style of episcopal teaching that illumines more clearly than ever the richness of Roman Catholic tradition.

## For Further Reading

Avery Dulles, *A Church to Believe In* (New York: Crossroad, 1982).

Frederick Herzog, *Justice Church* (Maryknoll, New York: Orbis, 1980).

Johann B. Metz, *Faith in History and Society* (New York: Seabury Press, 1980).

K. Rahner, *Concern for the Church* (New York: Crossroad, 1981).

*Appendix*

# THE CHALLENGE OF PEACE: GOD'S PROMISE AND OUR RESPONSE

## A Pastoral Letter on War and Peace

May 3, 1983
National Conference of Catholic Bishops

# CONTENTS

# Summary

The Second Vatican Council opened its evaluation of modern warfare with the statement: "The whole human race faces a moment of supreme crisis in its advance toward maturity." We agree with the council's assessment; the crisis of the moment is embodied in the threat which nuclear weapons pose for the world and much that we hold dear in the world. We have seen and felt the effects of the crisis of the nuclear age in the lives of people we serve. Nuclear weaponry has drastically changed the nature of warfare, and the arms race poses a threat to human life and human civilization which is without precedent.

We write this letter from the perspective of Catholic faith. Faith does not insulate us from the daily challenges of life but intensifies our desire to address them precisely in light of the gospel which has come to us in the person of the risen Christ. Through the resources of faith and reason we desire in this letter to provide hope for people in our day and direction toward a world freed of the nuclear threat.

As Catholic bishops we write this letter as an exercise of our teaching ministry. The Catholic tradition on war and peace is a long and complex one; it stretches from the Sermon on the Mount to the statements of Pope John Paul II. We wish to explore and explain the resources of the moral-religious teaching and to apply it to specific questions of our day. In doing this we realize, and we want readers of this letter to recognize, that not all statements in this letter have the same moral authority. At times we state universally binding moral principles found in the teaching of the Church; at other times the pastoral letter makes specific applications, observations and recommendations which allow for diversity of opinion on the part of those who assess the factual data of a situations differently. However, we expect Catholics to give our moral judgments serious consideration when they are forming their own views on specific problems.

The experience of preparing this letter has manifested to us the range of strongly held opinion in the Catholic community on questions of fact and judgment concerning issues of war and peace. We urge mutual respect among individuals and groups in the Church as this letter is analyzed and discussed. Obviously, as bishops, we believe that such differences should be expressed within the framework of Catholic moral teaching. We need in the Church not only conviction and commitment but also civility and charity.

While this letter is addressed principally to the Catholic community, we want it to make a contribution to the wider public debate in our country on the dangers and dilemmas of the nuclear age. Our contribution will not be primarily technical or political, but we are convinced that there is no satisfactory answer to the human problems of the nuclear age which fails to consider the moral and religious dimensions of the questions we face.

Although we speak in our own name, as Catholic bishops of the Church in the United States, we have been conscious in the preparation of this letter of the consequences our teaching will have not only for the United States but for other nations as well. One important expression of this awareness has been the consultation we have had, by correspondence and in an important meeting held at the Vatican (January 18–19, 1983), with representatives of European bishops' conferences. This consultation with bishops of other countries, and, of course, with the Holy See, has been very helpful to us.

Catholic teaching has always understood peace in positive terms. In the words of Pope John Paul II: "Peace is not just the absence of war. . . . Like a cathedral, peace must be constructed patiently and with unshakable faith." (Coventry, England, 1982) Peace is the fruit of order. Order in human society must be shaped on the basis of respect for the transcendence of God and the unique dignity of each person, understood in terms of freedom, justice, truth and love. To avoid war in our day we must be intent on building peace in an increasingly interdependent world. In Part III of this letter we set forth a positive vision of peace and the demands such a vision makes on diplomacy, national policy, and personal choices.

While pursuing peace incessantly, it is also necessary to limit the use of force in a world comprised of nation states, faced with common problems but devoid of an adequate international political authority. Keeping the peace in the nuclear age is a moral and political imperative. In Parts I and II of this letter we set forth both the principles of Catholic teaching on war and a series of judgments, based on these principles, about concrete policies. In making these judgments we speak as moral teachers, not as technical experts.

# I. Some Principles, Norms and Premises of Catholic Teaching

## A. ON WAR

1. Catholic teaching begins in every case with a presumption against war and for peaceful settlement of disputes. In exceptional cases, determined by the moral principles of the just-war tradition, some uses of force are permitted.

2. Every nation has a right and duty to defend itself against unjust aggression.

3. Offensive war of any kind is not morally justifiable.

4. It is never permitted to direct nuclear or conventional weapons to "the indiscriminate destruction of whole cities or vast areas with their populations. . . ." (*Pastoral Constitution*, #80.) The intentional killing of innocent civilians or non-combatants is always wrong.

5. Even defensive response to unjust attack can cause destruction which violates the principle of proportionality, going far beyond the limits of legitimate defense. This judgment is particularly important when assessing planned use of nuclear weapons. No defensive strategy, nuclear or conventional, which exceeds the limits of proportionality is morally permissible.

## B. ON DETERRENCE

1. "In current conditions 'deterrence' based on balance, certainly not as an end in itself but as a step on the way toward a progressive disarmament, may still be judged morally acceptable. Nonetheless, in order to ensure peace, it is indispensable not to be satisfied with this minimum which is always susceptible to the real danger of explosion." (Pope John Paul II, "Message to U.N. Special Session on Disarmament," #8, June 1982.)

2. No *use* of nuclear weapons which would violate the principles of discrimination or proportionality may be *intended* in a strategy of deterrence. The moral demands of Catholic teaching re-

quire resolute willingness not to intend or to do moral evil even to save our own lives or the lives of those we love.

3. Deterrence is not an adequate strategy as a long-term basis for peace; it is a transitional strategy justifiable only in conjunction with resolute determination to pursue arms control and disarmament. We are convinced that "the fundamental principle on which our present peace depends must be replaced by another, which declares that the true and solid peace of nations consists not in equality of arms but in mutual trust alone." (Pope John XXIII, *Peace on Earth*, #113.)

## C. THE ARMS RACE AND DISARMAMENT

1. The arms race is one of the greatest curses on the human race; it is to be condemned as a danger, an act of aggression against the poor, and a folly which does not provide the security it promises. (Cf: *Pastoral Constitution*, #81, *Statement of the Holy See to the United Nations*, 1976.)

2. Negotiations must be pursued in every reasonable form possible; they should be governed by the "demand that the arms race should cease; that the stockpiles which exist in various countries should be reduced equally and simultaneously by the parties concerned; that nuclear weapons should be banned; and that a general agreement should eventually be reached about progressive disarmament and an effective method of control." (Pope John XXIII, *Peace On Earth*, #112.)

## D. ON PERSONAL CONSCIENCE

1. *Military Service:* "All those who enter the military service in loyalty to their country should look upon themselves as the custodians of the security and freedom of their fellow countrymen; and when they carry out their duty properly, they are contributing to the maintenance of peace." (*Pastoral Constitution*, #79.)

2. *Conscientious Objection:* "Moreover, it seems just that laws should make humane provision for the case of conscientious objectors who refuse to carry arms, provided they accept some other form of community service." (*Pastoral Constitution*, #79.)

3. *Non-violence:* "In this same spirit we cannot but express our admiration for all who forego the use of violence to vindicate their rights and resort to other means of defense which are available to weaker parties, provided it can be done without harm to the rights

and duties of others and of the community." (*Pastoral Constitution,* #78.)

4. *Citizens and Conscience:* "Once again we deem it opportune to remind our children of their duty to take an active part in public life, and to contribute towards the attainment of the common good of the entire human family as well as to that of their own political community. . . . In other words, it is necessary that human beings, in the intimacy of their own consciences, should so live and act in their temporal lives as to create a synthesis between scientific, technical and professional elements on the one hand, and spiritual values on the other." (Pope John XXIII, *Peace On Earth,* #146, 150.)

## II. Moral Principles and Policy Choices

As bishops in the United States, assessing the concrete circumstances of our society, we have made a number of observations and recommendations in the process of applying moral principles to specific policy choices.

## A. ON THE USE OF NUCLEAR WEAPONS

1. *Counter Population Use:* Under no circumstances may nuclear weapons or other instruments of mass slaughter be used for the purpose of destroying population centers or other predominantly civilian targets. Retaliatory action which would indiscriminately and disproportionately take many wholly innocent lives, lives of people who are in no way responsible for reckless actions of their government, must also be condemned.

2. *The Initiation of Nuclear War:* We do not perceive any situation in which the deliberate initiation of nuclear war, on however restricted a scale, can be morally justified. Non-nuclear attacks by another state must be resisted by other than nuclear means. Therefore, a serious moral obligation exists to develop non-nuclear defensive strategies as rapidly as possible. In this letter we urge NATO to move rapidly toward the adoption of a "no first use" policy, but we recognize this will take time to implement and will require the development of an adequate alternative defense posture.

3. *Limited Nuclear War:* Our examination of the various arguments on this question makes us highly skeptical about the real

meaning of "limited." One of the criteria of the just-war teaching is that there must be a reasonable hope of success in bringing about justice and peace. We must ask whether such a reasonable hope can exist once nuclear weapons have been exchanged. The burden of proof remains on those who assert that meaningful limitation is possible. In our view the first imperative is to prevent any use of nuclear weapons and we hope that leaders will resist the notion that nuclear conflict can be limited, contained or won in any traditional sense.

## B. ON DETERRENCE

In concert with the evaluation provided by Pope John Paul II, we have arrived at a strictly conditional moral acceptance of deterrence. In this letter we have outlined criteria and recommendations which indicate the meaning of conditional acceptance of deterrence policy. We cannot consider such a policy adequate as a long-term basis for peace.

## C. ON PROMOTING PEACE

1. We support immediate, bilateral verifiable agreements to halt the testing, production and deployment of new nuclear weapons systems. This recommendation is not to be identified with any specific political initiative.
2. We support efforts to achieve deep cuts in the arsenals of both superpowers; efforts should concentrate first on systems which threaten the retaliatory forces of either major power.
3. We support early and successful conclusion of negotiations of a comprehensive test ban treaty.
4. We urge new efforts to prevent the spread of nuclear weapons in the world, and to control the conventional arms race, particularly the conventional arms trade.
5. We support, in an increasingly interdependent world, political and economic policies designed to protect human dignity and to promote the human rights of every person, especially the least among us. In this regard, we call for the establishment of some form of global authority adequate to the needs of the international common good.

This letter includes many judgments from the perspective of ethics, politics and strategy needed to speak concretely and correctly to the "moment of supreme crisis" identified by Vatican II. We stress again that readers should be aware, as we have been, of the distinction between our statement of moral principles and of official Church teaching and our application of these to concrete issues. We urge that special care be taken not to use passages out of context; neither should brief portions of this document be cited to support positions it does not intend to convey or which are not truly in accord with the spirit of its teaching.

In concluding this summary we respond to two key questions often asked about this pastoral letter:

Why do we address these matters fraught with such complexity, controversy and passion? We speak as pastors, not politicians. We are teachers, not technicians. We cannot avoid our responsibility to lift up the moral dimensions of the choices before our world and nation. The nuclear age is an era of moral as well as physical danger. We are the first generation since Genesis with the power to threaten the created order. We cannot remain silent in the face of such danger. Why do we address these issues? We are simply trying to live up to the call of Jesus to be peacemakers in our own time and situation.

What are we saying? Fundamentally, we are saying that the decisions about nuclear weapons are among the most pressing moral questions of our age. While these decisions have obvious military and political aspects, they involve fundamental moral choices. In simple terms, we are saying that good ends (defending one's country, protecting freedom, etc.) cannot justify immoral means (the use of weapons which kill indiscriminately and threaten whole societies). We fear that our world and nation are headed in the wrong direction. More weapons with greater destructive potential are produced every day. More and more nations are seeking to become nuclear powers. In our quest for more and more security we fear we are actually becoming less and less secure.

In the words of our Holy Father, we need a "moral about-face." The whole world must summon the moral courage and technical means to say no to nuclear conflict; no to weapons of mass destruction; no to an arms race which robs the poor and the vulnerable; and no to the moral danger of a nuclear age which places before humankind indefensible choices of constant terror or surrender. Peacemaking is not an optional commitment. It is a requirement of our faith. We are called to be peacemakers, not by some movement of the moment, but by our Lord Jesus. The content and context of our peacemaking is set not by some political agenda or ideological program, but by the teaching of his Church.

Ultimately, this letter is intended as an expression of Christian faith, affirming the confidence we have that the risen Lord remains with us precisely in moments of crisis. It is our belief in his presence and power among us which sustain us in confronting the awesome challenge of the nuclear age. We speak from faith to provide hope for all who recognize the challenge and are working to confront it with the resources of faith and reason.

To approach the nuclear issue in faith is to recognize our absolute need for prayer: we urge and invite all to unceasing prayer for peace with justice for all people. In a spirit of prayerful hope we present this message of peace.

# Introduction

*1.*     "The whole human race faces a moment of supreme crisis in its advance toward maturity." Thus the Second Vatican Council opened its treatment of modern warfare.[1] Since the council, the dynamic of the nuclear arms race has intensified. Apprehension about nuclear war is almost tangible and visible today. As Pope John Paul II said in his message to the United Nations concerning disarmament: "Currently, the fear and preoccupation of so many groups in various parts of the world reveals that people are more frightened about what would happen if irresponsible parties unleash some nuclear war."[2]

*2.*     As bishops and pastors ministering in one of the major nuclear nations, we have encountered this terror in the minds and hearts of our people—indeed, we share it. We write this letter because we agree that the world is at a moment of crisis, the effects of which are evident in people's lives. It is not our intent to play on fears, however, but to speak words of hope and encouragement in time of fear. Faith does not insulate us from the challenges of life; rather, it

---

1. Vatican II, the *Pastoral Constitution on the Church in the Modern World* (hereafter cited: *Pastoral Constitution*), #77. Papal and conciliar texts will be referred to by title with paragraph number. Several collections of these texts exist although no single collection is comprehensive; see the following: *Peace and Disarmament: Documents of the World Council of Churches and the Roman Catholic Church* (Geneva and Rome: 1982) (hereafter cited: *Documents*, with page number); J. Gremillion, *The Gospel of Peace and Justice: Catholic Social Teaching Since Pope John* (Maryknoll, N.Y.: 1976); D. J. O'Brien and T. A. Shannon, eds., *Renewing the Earth: Catholic Documents on Peace, Justice and Liberation* (New York: 1977); A. Flannery, O.P., ed., *Vatican Council II: The Conciliar and Post Conciliar Documents* (Collegeville, Minn.: 1975); W. Abbot, ed., *The Documents of Vatican II* (New York: 1966). Both the Flannery and Abbot translations of the *Pastoral Constitution* are used in this letter.

2. John Paul II, "Message to the Second Special Session of the United Nations General Assembly Devoted to Disarmament" (June 1982) (hereafter cited: "Message U.N. Special Session 1982"), #7.

intensifies our desire to help solve them precisely in light of the good news which has come to us in the person of Jesus, the Lord of history. From the resources of our faith we wish to provide hope and strength to all who seek a world free of the nuclear threat. Hope sustains one's capacity to live with danger without being overwhelmed by it; hope is the will to struggle against obstacles even when they appear insuperable. Ultimately our hope rests in the God who gave us life, sustains the world by his power, and has called us to revere the lives of every person and all peoples.

3.    The crisis of which we speak arises from this fact: nuclear war threatens the existence of our planet; this is a more menacing threat than any the world has known. It is neither tolerable nor necessary that human beings live under this threat. But removing it will require a major effort of intelligence, courage, and faith. As Pope John Paul II said at Hiroshima: "From now on it is only through a conscious choice and through a deliberate policy that humanity can survive."[3]

4.    As Americans, citizens of the nation which was first to produce atomic weapons, which has been the only one to use them and which today is one of the handful of nations capable of decisively influencing the course of the nuclear age, we have grave human, moral and political responsibilities to see that a "conscious choice" is made to save humanity. This letter is therefore both an invitation and a challenge to Catholics in the United States to join with others in shaping the conscious choices and deliberate policies required in this "moment of supreme crisis."

---

3. John Paul II, "Address to Scientists and Scholars," #4, *Origins* 10 (1981):621.

# I

# Peace in the Modern World: Religious Perspectives and Principles

5.      The global threat of nuclear war is a central concern of the universal Church, as the words and deeds of recent popes and the Second Vatican Council vividly demonstrate. In this pastoral letter we speak as bishops of the universal Church, heirs of the religious and moral teaching on modern warfare of the last four decades. We also speak as bishops of the Church in the United States, who have both the obligation and the opportunity to share and interpret the moral and religious wisdom of the Catholic tradition by applying it to the problems of war and peace today.

6.      The nuclear threat transcends religious, cultural, and national boundaries. To confront its danger requires all the resources reason and faith can muster. This letter is a contribution to a wider common effort, meant to call Catholics and all members of our political community to dialogue and specific decisions about this awesome question.

7.      The Catholic tradition on war and peace is a long and complex one, reaching from the Sermon on the Mount to the statements of Pope John Paul II. Its development cannot be sketched in a straight line and it seldom gives a simple answer to complex questions. It speaks through many voices and has produced multiple forms of religious witness. As we locate ourselves in this tradition, seeking to draw from it and to develop it, the document which provides profound inspiration and guidance for us is the *Pastoral Constitution on the Church in the Modern World* of Vatican II, for it is based on doctrinal

principles and addresses the relationship of the Church to the world with respect to the most urgent issues of our day.[4]

8.    A rule of interpretation crucial for the *Pastoral Constitution* is equally important for this pastoral letter although the authority inherent in these two documents is quite distinct. Both documents use principles of Catholic moral teaching and apply them to specific contemporary issues. The bishops at Vatican II opened the *Pastoral Constitution* with the following guideline on how to relate principles to concrete issues:

> In the first part, the Church develops her teaching on man, on the world which is the enveloping context of man's existence, and on man's relations to his fellow men. In Part II, the Church gives closer consideration to various aspects of modern life and human society; special consideration is given to those questions and problems which, in this general area, seem to have a greater urgency in our day. As a result, in Part II the subject matter which is viewed in the light of doctrinal principles is made up of diverse elements. Some elements have a permanent value; others, only a transitory one. Consequently, the constitution must be interpreted according to the general norms of theological interpretion. Interpreters must bear in mind—especially in Part II—the changeable circumstances which the subject matter, by its very nature, involves.[5]

9.    In this pastoral letter, too, we address many concrete questions concerning the arms race, contemporary warfare, weapons systems, and negotiating strategies. We do not intend that our treatment of each of these issues carry the same moral authority as our statement of universal moral principles and formal Church teaching. Indeed, we stress here at the beginning that not every statement in this letter has the same moral authority. At times we reassert universally binding moral principles (e.g., non-combatant immunity and proportionality). At still other times we reaffirm statements of recent popes and the teaching of Vatican II. Again, at other times we apply moral principles to specific cases.

10.    When making applications of these principles we realize— and we wish readers to recognize—that prudential judgments are involved based on specific circumstances which can change or which can be interpreted differently by people of good will (e.g., the treat-

---

4. The *Pastoral Constitution* is made up of two parts; yet it constitutes an organic unity. By way of explanation: the constitution is called "pastoral" because, while resting on doctrinal principles, it seeks to express the relation of the Church to the world and modern mankind. The result is that, on the one hand, a pastoral slant is present in the first part and, on the other hand, a doctrinal slant is present in the second part. *Pastoral Constitution*, note 1 above.

5. Ibid.

ment of "no first use"). However, the moral judgments that we make in specific cases, while not binding in conscience, are to be given serious attention and consideration by Catholics as they determine whether their moral judgments are consistent with the Gospel.

*11.*     We shall do our best to indicate, stylistically and substantively, whenever we make such applications. We believe such specific judgments are an important part of this letter, but they should be interpreted in light of another passage from the *Pastoral Constitution*:

> Often enough the Christian view of things will itself suggest some specific solution in certain circumstances. Yet it happens rather frequently, and legitimately so, that with equal sincerity some of the faithful will disagree with others on a given matter. Even against the intention of their proponents, however, solutions proposed on one side or another may be easily confused by many people with the Gospel message. Hence it is necessary for people to remember that no one is allowed in the aforementioned situations to appropriate the Church's authority for his opinion. They should always try to enlighten one another through honest discussion, preserving mutual charity and caring above all for the common good.[6]

*12.*     This passage acknowledges that, on some complex social questions, the Church expects a certain diversity of views even though all hold the same universal moral principles. The experience of preparing this pastoral letter has shown us the range of strongly held opinion in the Catholic community on questions of war and peace. Obviously, as bishops we believe that such differences should be expressed within the framework of Catholic moral teaching. We urge mutual respect among different groups in the Church as they analyze this letter and the issues it addresses. Not only conviction and commitment are needed in the Church, but also civility and charity.

*13.*     The *Pastoral Constitution* calls us to bring the light of the gospel to bear upon "the signs of the times." Three signs of the times have particularly influenced the writing of this letter. The first, to quote Pope John Paul II at the United Nations, is that "the world wants peace, the world needs peace."[7] The second is the judgment of Vatican II about the arms race: "The arms race is one of the greatest curses on the human race and the harm it inflicts upon the poor is more than can be endured."[8] The third is the way in which the unique dangers and dynamics of the nuclear arms race present qualitatively new problems which must be addressed by fresh appli-

---

6. Ibid., #43.

7. John Paul II, "Message U.N. Special Session 1982," #2.

8. *Pastoral Constitution*, #81.

cations of traditional moral principles. In light of these three characteristics, we wish to examine Catholic teaching on peace and war.

14.    The Catholic social tradition, as exemplified in the *Pastoral Constitution* and recent papal teachings, is a mix of biblical, theological, and philosophical elements which are brought to bear upon the concrete problems of the day. The biblical vision of the world, created and sustained by God, scarred by sin, redeemed in Christ and destined for the kingdom, is at the heart of our religious heritage. This vision requires elaboration, explanation, and application in each age; the important task of theology is to penetrate ever more adequately the nature of the biblical vision of peace and relate it to a world not yet at peace. Consequently, the teaching about peace examines both how to construct a more peaceful world and how to assess the phenomenon of war.

15.    At the center of the Church's teaching on peace and at the center of all Catholic social teaching are the transcendence of God and the dignity of the human person. The human person is the clearest reflection of God's presence in the world; all of the Church's work in pursuit of both justice and peace is designed to protect and promote the dignity of every person. For each person not only reflects God, but is the expression of God's creative work and the meaning of Christ's redemptive ministry. Christians approach the problem of war and peace with fear and reverence. God is the Lord of life, and so each human life is sacred; modern warfare threatens the obliteration of human life on a previously unimaginable scale. The sense of awe and "fear of the Lord" which former generations felt in approaching these issues weighs upon us with new urgency. In the words of the *Pastoral Constitution*:

> Men of this generation should realize that they will have to render an account of their warlike behavior; the destiny of generations to come depends largely on the decisions they make today.[9]

16.    Catholic teaching on peace and war has had two purposes: to help Catholics form their consciences and to contribute to the public policy debate about the morality of war. These two purposes have led Catholic teaching to address two distinct but overlapping audiences. The first is the Catholic faithful, formed by the premises of the gospel and the principles of Catholic moral teaching. The second is the wider civil community, a more pluralistic audience, in which our brothers and sisters with whom we share the name Christian, Jews, Moslems, other religious communities, and all people of

---

9. Ibid., #80.

good will also make up our polity. Since Catholic teaching has traditionally sought to address both audiences, we intend to speak to both in this letter, recognizing that Catholics are also members of the wider political community.

*17.*     The conviction, rooted in Catholic ecclesiology, that both the community of the faithful and the civil community should be addressed on peace and war has produced two complementary but distinct styles of teaching. The religious community shares a specific perspective of faith and can be called to live out its implications. The wider civil community, although it does not share the same vision of faith, is equally bound by certain key moral principles. For all men and women find in the depth of their consciences a law written on the human heart by God.[10] From this law reason draws moral norms. These norms do not exhaust the gospel vision, but they speak to critical questions affecting the welfare of the human community, the role of states in international relations, and the limits of acceptable action by individuals and nations on issues of war and peace.

*18.*     Examples of these two styles can be found in recent Catholic teaching. At times the emphasis is upon the problems and requirements for a just public policy (e.g., Pope John Paul II at the U.N. Special Session 1982); at other times the emphasis is on the specific role Christians should play (e.g., Pope John Paul II at Coventry, England, 1982). The same difference of emphasis and orientation can be found in Pope John XXIII's *Peace on Earth* and Vatican II's *Pastoral Constitution.*

*19.*     As bishops we believe that the nature of Catholic moral teaching, the principles of Catholic ecclesiology, and the demands of our pastoral ministry require that this letter speak both to Catholics in a specific way and to the wider political community regarding public policy. Neither audience and neither mode of address can be neglected when the issue has the cosmic dimensions of the nuclear arms race.

*20.*     We propose, therefore, to discuss both the religious vision of peace among peoples and nations and the problems associated with realizing this vision in a world of sovereign states, devoid of any central authority and divided by ideology, geography, and competing claims. We believe the religious vision has an objective basis and is capable of progressive realization. Christ is our peace, for he has "made us both one, and has broken down the dividing wall of hostility . . . that he might create in himself one new man in place of the

---

10. Ibid., #16.

two, so making peace, and might reconcile us both to God" (Eph. 2:14-16). We also know that this peace will be achieved fully only in the kingdom of God. The realization of the kingdom, therefore, is a continuing work, progressively accomplished, precariously maintained, and needing constant effort to preserve the peace achieved and expand its scope in personal and political life.

*21.*    Building peace within and among nations is the work of many individuals and institutions; it is the fruit of ideas and decisions taken in the political, cultural, economic, social, military, and legal sectors of life. We believe that the Church, as a community of faith and social institution, has a proper, necessary, and distinctive part to play in the pursuit of peace.

*22.*    The distinctive contribution of the Church flows from her religious nature and ministry. The Church is called to be, in a unique way, the instrument of the kingdom of God in history. Since peace is one of the signs of that kingdom present in the world, the Church fulfills part of her essential mission by making the peace of the kingdom more visible in our time.

*23.*    Because peace, like the kingdom of God itself, is both a divine gift and a human work, the Church should continually pray for the gift and share in the work. We are called to be a Church at the service of peace, precisely because peace is one manifestation of God's word and work in our midst. Recognition of the Church's responsibility to join with others in the work of peace is a major force behind the call today to develop a theology of peace. Much of the history of Catholic theology on war and peace has focused on limiting the resort to force in human affairs; this task is still necessary, and is reflected later in this pastoral letter, but it is not a sufficient response to Vatican II's challenge "to undertake a completely fresh reappraisal of war."[11]

*24.*    A fresh reappraisal which includes a developed theology of peace will require contributions from several sectors of the Church's life: biblical studies, systematic and moral theology, ecclesiology, and the experience and insights of members of the Church who have struggled in various ways to make and keep the peace in this often violent age. This pastoral letter is more an invitation to continue the new appraisal of war and peace than a final synthesis of the results of such an appraisal. We have some sense of the characteristics of a theology of peace, but not a systematic statement of their relationships.

---

11. Ibid., #80.

25.   A theology of peace should ground the task of peacemaking solidly in the biblical vision of the kingdom of God, then place it centrally in the ministry of the Church. It should specify the obstacles in the way of peace, as these are understood theologically and in the social and political sciences. It should both identify the specific contributions a community of faith can make to the work of peace and relate these to the wider work of peace pursued by other groups and institutions in society. Finally, a theology of peace must include a message of hope. The vision of hope must be available to all, but one source of its content should be found in a Church at the service of peace.

26.   We offer now a first step toward a message of peace and hope. It consists of a sketch of the biblical conception of peace; a theological understanding of how peace can be pursued in a world marked by sin; a moral assessment of key issues facing us in the pursuit of peace today; and an assessment of the political and personal tasks required of all people of good will in this most crucial period of history.

## A. Peace and the Kingdom

27.   For us as believers, the sacred scriptures provide the foundation for confronting war and peace today. Any use of scripture in this area is conditioned by three factors. *First*, the term "peace" has been understood in different ways at various times and in various contexts. For example, peace can refer to an individual's sense of well-being or security, or it can mean the cessation of armed hostility, producing an atmosphere in which nations can relate to each other and settle conflicts without resorting to the use of arms. For men and women of faith, peace will imply a right relationship with God, which entails forgiveness, reconciliation, and union. Finally, the scriptures point to eschatological peace, a final, full realization of God's salvation when all creation will be made whole. Among these various meanings, the last two predominate in the scriptures and provide direction to the first two.

28.   *Second*, the scriptures as we have them today were written over a long period of time and reflect many varied historical situations, all different from our own. Our understanding of them is both complicated and enhanced by these differences, but not in any way obscured or diminished by them. *Third*, since the scriptures speak

primarily of God's intervention in history, they contain no specific treatise on war and peace. Peace and war must always be seen in light of God's intervention in human affairs and our response to that intervention. Both are elements within the ongoing revelation of God's will for creation.

29.    Acknowledging this complexity, we still recognize in the scriptures a unique source of revelation, a word of God which is addressed to us as surely as it has been to all preceding generations. We call upon the spirit of God who speaks in that word and in our hearts to aid us in our listening. The sacred texts have much to say to us about the ways in which God calls us to live in union with and in fidelity to the divine will. They provide us with direction for our lives and hold out to us an object of hope, a final promise, which guides and directs our actions here and now.

## 1. OLD TESTAMENT

30.    War and peace are significant and highly complex elements within the multilayered accounts of the creation and development of God's people in the Old Testament.

*a. War*

31.    Violence and war are very much present in the history of the people of God, particularly from the Exodus period to the monarchy. God is often seen as the one who leads the Hebrews in battle, protects them from their enemies, makes them victorious over other armies (see, for example, Deut. 1:30; 20:4; Jos. 2:24; Jgs. 3:28). The metaphor of warrior carried multifaceted connotations for a people who knew themselves to be smaller and weaker than the nations which surrounded them. It also enabled them to express their conviction about God's involvement in their lives and his desire for their growth and development. This metaphor provided the people with a sense of security; they had a God who would protect them even in the face of overwhelming obstacles. It was also a call to faith and to trust; the mighty God was to be obeyed and followed. No one can deny the presence of such images in the Old Testament nor their powerful influence upon the articulation of this people's understanding of the involvement of God in their history. The warrior God was highly significant during long periods of Israel's understanding of its faith. But this image was not the only image, and it was gradually transformed, particularly after the experience of the exile, when God was no longer identified with military victory and might. Other

images and other understandings of God's activity became predominant in expressing the faith of God's people.

## b. Peace

*32.*   Several points must be taken into account in considering the image of peace in the Old Testament. First, all notions of peace must be understood in light of Israel's relation to God. Peace is always seen as a gift from God and as fruit of God's saving activity. Secondly, the individual's personal peace is not greatly stressed. The well-being and freedom from fear which result from God's love are viewed primarily as they pertain to the community and its unity and harmony. Furthermore, this unity and harmony extend to all of creation; true peace implied a restoration of the right order not just among peoples, but within all of creation. Third, while the images of war and the warrior God become less dominant as a more profound and complex understanding of God is presented in the texts, the images of peace and the demands upon the people for covenantal fidelity to true peace grow more urgent and more developed.

## c. Peace and Fidelity to the Covenant

*33.*   If Israel obeyed God's laws, God would dwell among them. "I will walk among you and will be your God and you shall be my people" (Lv. 26:12). God would strengthen the people against those who opposed them and would give peace in the land. The description of life in these circumstances witnesses to unity among peoples and creation, to freedom from fear and to security (Lv. 26:3-16). The right relationship between the people and God was grounded in and expressed by a covenantal union. The covenant bound the people to God in fidelity and obedience; God was also committed in the covenant, to be present with the people, to save them, to lead them to freedom. Peace is a special characteristic of this covenant; when the prophet Ezekiel looked to the establishment of the new, truer covenant, he declared that God would establish an everlasting covenant of peace with the people (Ez. 37:26).

*34.*   Living in covenantal fidelity with God had ramifications in the lives of the people. It was part of fidelity to care for the needy and helpless; a society living with fidelity was one marked by justice and integrity. Furthermore, covenantal fidelity demanded that Israel put its trust in God alone and look only to him for its security. When Israel tended to forget the obligations of the covenant, prophets arose to remind the people and call them to return to God. True peace is an image which they stressed.

*35.*    Ezekiel, who promised a covenant of peace, condemned in no uncertain terms the false prophets who said there was peace in the land while idolatry and injustice continued (Ez. 13:16). Jeremiah followed in this tradition and berated those who "healed the wounds of the people lightly" and proclaimed peace while injustice and infidelity prevailed (Jer. 6:14; 8:10-12). Jeremiah and Isaiah both condemned the leaders when, against true security, they depended upon their own strength or alliances with other nations rather than trusting in God (Is. 7:1-9; 30:1-4; Jer. 37:10). The lament of Isaiah 48:18 makes clear the connection between justice, fidelity to God's law, and peace; he cries out: "O that you had hearkened to my commandments! Then your peace would have been like a river, and your righteousness like the waves of the sea."

### d. Hope for Eschatological Peace

*36.*    Experience made it clear to the people of God that the covenant of peace and the fullness of salvation had not been realized in their midst. War and enmity were still present, injustices thrived, sin still manifested itself. These same experiences also convinced the people of God's fidelity to a covenant which they often neglected. Because of this fidelity, God's promise of a final salvation involving all peoples and all creation and of an ultimate reign of peace became an integral part of the hope of the Old Testament. In the midst of their failures and sin, God's people strove for greater fidelity to him and closer relationship with him; they did so because, believing in the future they had been promised, they directed their lives and energies toward an eschatological vision for which they longed. Peace is an integral component of that vision.

*37.*    The final age, the Messianic time, is described as one in which the "Spirit is poured on us from on high." In this age, creation will be made whole, "justice will dwell in the wilderness," the effect of righteousness will be peace, and the people will "abide in a peaceful habitation and in secure dwellings and in quiet resting places" (Is. 32:15-20). There will be no need for instruments of war (Is. 2:4; Mi. 4:3),[12] God will speak directly to the people and "righteousness and peace will embrace each other" (Ps. 85:10-11). A messiah will appear, a servant of God upon whom God has placed his spirit and who will faithfully bring forth justice to the nations: "He will not cry or lift

---

12. The exact opposite of this vision is presented in Joel 3:10 where the foreign nations are told that their weapons will do them no good in the face of God's coming wrath.

up his voice, or make it heard in the street; a bruised reed he will not break and a dimly burning wick he will not quench; he will faithfully bring forth justice." (Is. 42:2-3).

38.    The Old Testament provides us with the history of a people who portrayed their God as one who intervened in their lives, who protected them and led them to freedom, often as a mighty leader in battle. They also appear as a people who longed constantly for peace. Such peace was always seen as a result of God's gift which came about in fidelity to the covenantal union. Furthermore, in the midst of their unfulfilled longing, God's people clung tenaciously to hope in the promise of an eschatological time when, in the fullness of salvation, peace and justice would embrace and all creation would be secure from harm. The people looked for a messiah, one whose coming would signal the beginning of that time. In their waiting, they heard the prophets call them to love according to the covenantal vision, to repent, and to be ready for God's reign.

## 2. NEW TESTAMENT

39.    As Christians we believe that Jesus is the messiah or Christ so long awaited. God's servant (Mt. 12:18-21), prophet and more than prophet (Jn. 4:19-26), the one in whom the fullness of God was pleased to dwell, through whom all things in heaven and on earth were reconciled to God, Jesus made peace by the blood of the cross (Col. 1:19-20). While the characteristics of the *shalom* of the Old Testament (gift from God, inclusive of all creation, grounded in salvation and covenantal fidelity, inextricably bound up with justice) are present in the New Testament traditions, all discussion of war and peace in the New Testament must be seen within the context of the unique revelation of God that is Jesus Christ and of the reign of God which Jesus proclaimed and inaugurated.

### a. War

40.    There is no notion of a warrior God who will lead the people in an historical victory over its enemies in the New Testament. The only war spoken of is found in apocalyptic images of the final moments, especially as they are depicted in the Book of Revelation. Here war stands as image of the eschatological struggle between God and Satan. It is a war in which the Lamb is victorious (Rv. 17:14).

41.    Military images appear in terms of the preparedness which one must have for the coming trials (Lk. 14:31; 22:35-38). Swords appear in the New Testament as an image of division (Mt. 12:34;

Heb. 4:12); they are present at the arrest of Jesus, and he rejects their use (Lk. 22:51 and parallel texts); weapons are transformed in Ephesians, when the Christians are urged to put on the whole armor of God which includes the breastplate of righteousness, the helmet of salvation, the sword of the Spirit, "having shod your feet in the equipment of the gospel of peace" (Eph. 6:10-17; cf. I Thes. 5:8-9). Soldiers, too, are present in the New Testament. They are at the crucifixion of Jesus, of course, but they are also recipients of the baptism of John, and one centurion receives the healing of his servant (Mt. 8:5-13 and parallel texts; cf. Jn. 4:46-53).

*42.*    Jesus challenged everyone to recognize in him the presence of the reign of God and to give themselves over to that reign. Such a radical change of allegiance was difficult for many to accept and families found themselves divided, as if by a sword. Hence, the gospels tell us that Jesus said he came not to bring peace but rather the sword (Mt. 10:34). The peace which Jesus did not bring was the false peace which the prophets had warned against. The sword which he did bring was that of the division caused by the word of God which, like a two-edged sword, "pierces to the division of soul and spirit, of joints and marrow, and discerns the thoughts and intentions of the heart" (Heb. 4:12).

*43.*    All are invited into the reign of God. Faith in Jesus and trust in God's mercy are the criteria. Living in accord with the demands of the kingdom rather than those of one's specific profession is decisive. [13]

## b. Jesus and Reign of God

*44.*    Jesus proclaimed the reign of God in his words and made it present in his actions. His words begin with a call to conversion and a proclamation of the arrival of the kingdom. "The time is fulfilled, and the kingdom of God is at hand; repent, and believe in the gospel" (Mk. 1:15, Mt. 4:17). The call to conversion was at the same time an invitation to enter God's reign. Jesus went beyond the prophets'

---

13. An omission in the New Testament is significant in this context. Scholars have made us aware of the presence of revolutionary groups in Israel during the time of Jesus. Barabbas, for example, was "among the rebels in prison who had committed murder in the insurrection" (Mk. 15:7). Although Jesus had come to proclaim and to bring about the true reign of God which often stood in opposition to the existing order, he makes no reference to nor does he join in any attempts such as those of the Zealots to overthrow authority by violent means. See M. Smith, "Zealots and Sicarii, Their Origins and Relations," *Harvard Theological Review* 64 (1971):1-19.

cries for conversion when he declared that, in him, the reign of God had begun and was in fact among the people (Lk. 17:20-21; 12:32).
*45.*    His words, especially as they are preserved for us in the Sermon on the Mount, describe a new reality in which God's power is manifested and the longing of the people is fulfilled. In God's reign the poor are given the kingdom, the mourners are comforted, the meek inherit the earth, those hungry for righteousness are satisfied, the merciful know mercy, the pure see God, the persecuted know the kingdom, and peacemakers are called the children of God (Mt. 5:3-10).
*46.*    Jesus' words also depict for us the conduct of one who lives under God's reign. His words call for a new way of life which fulfills and goes beyond the law. One of the most striking characteristics of this new way is forgiveness. All who hear Jesus are repeatedly called to forgive one another, and to do so not just once, but many, many times (Mt. 6:14-15; Lk. 6:37; Mt. 18:21-22; Mk. 11:25; Lk. 11:4; 17:3-4). The forgiveness of God, which is the beginning of salvation, is manifested in communal forgiveness and mercy.
*47.*    Jesus also described God's reign as one in which love is an active, life-giving, inclusive force. He called for a love which went beyond family ties and bonds of friendship to reach even those who were enemies (Mt. 5:44-48; Lk. 6:27-28). Such a love does not seek revenge but rather is merciful in the face of threat and opposition (Mt. 5:39-42; Lk. 6:29-31). Disciples are to love one another as Jesus has loved them (Jn. 15:12).
*48.*    The words of Jesus would remain an impossible, abstract ideal were it not for two things: the actions of Jesus and his gift of the spirit. In his actions, Jesus showed the way of living in God's reign; he manifested the forgiveness which he called for when he accepted all who came to him, forgave their sins, healed them, released them from the demons who possessed them. In doing these things, he made the tender mercy of God present in a world which knew violence, oppression, and injustice. Jesus pointed out the injustices of his time and opposed those who laid burdens upon the people or defiled true worship. He acted aggressively and dramatically at times, as when he cleansed the temple of those who had made God's house into a "den of robbers" (Mt. 21:12-17 and parallel texts; Jn. 3:13-25).
*49.*    Most characteristic of Jesus' actions are those in which he showed his love. As he had commanded others, his love led him even to the giving of his own life to effect redemption. Jesus' message and his actions were dangerous ones in his time, and they led to his death—a cruel and viciously inflicted death, a criminal's death (Gal.

3:13). In all of his suffering, as in all of his life and ministry, Jesus refused to defend himself with force or with violence. He endured violence and cruelty so that God's love might be fully manifest and the world might be reconciled to the One from whom it had become estranged. Even at his death, Jesus cried out for forgiveness for those who were his executioners: "Father, forgive them . . . " (Lk. 23:34).

50.    The resurrection of Jesus is the sign to the world that God indeed does reign, does give life in death, and that the love of God is stronger even than death (Rom. 8:36-39).

51.    Only in light of this, the fullest demonstration of the power of God's reign, can Jesus' gift of peace—a peace which the world cannot give (Jn. 14:27)—be understood. Jesus gives that peace to his disciples, to those who had witnessed the helplessness of the crucifixion and the power of the resurrection (Jn. 20:19, 20, 26). The peace which he gives to them as he greets them as their risen Lord is the fullness of salvation. It is the reconciliation of the world and God (Rom. 5:1-2; Col. 1:20); the restoration of the unity and harmony of all creation which the Old Testament spoke of with such longing. Because the walls of hostility between God and humankind were broken down in the life and death of the true, perfect servant, union and well-being between God and the world were finally fully possible (Eph. 2:13-22; Gal. 3:28).

## c. Jesus and the Community of Believers

52.    As his first gift to his followers, the risen Jesus gave his gift of peace. This gift permeated the meetings between the risen Jesus and his followers (Jn. 20:19-29). So intense was that gift and so abiding was its power that the remembrance of that gift and the daily living of it became the hallmark of the community of faith. Simultaneously, Jesus gave his spirit to those who followed him. These two personal and communal gifts are inseparable. In the spirit of Jesus the community of believers was enabled to recognize and to proclaim the savior of the world.

53.    Gifted with Jesus' own spirit, they could recognize what God had done and know in their own lives the power of the One who creates from nothing. The early Christian communities knew that this power and the reconciliation and peace which marked it were not yet fully operative in their world. They struggled with external persecution and with interior sin, as do all people. But their experience of the spirit of God and their memory of the Christ who was with them nevertheless enabled them to look forward with unshakable confidence to the time when the fullness of God's reign would make

itself known in the world. At the same time, they knew that they were called to be ministers of reconciliation (2 Cor. 5:19-20), people who would make the peace which God had established visible through the love and the unity within their own communities.

*54.*     Jesus Christ, then, is our peace, and in his death-resurrection he gives God's peace to our world. In him God has indeed reconciled the world, made it one, and has manifested definitively that his will is this reconciliation, this unity between God and all peoples, and among the peoples themselves. The way to union has been opened, the covenant of peace established. The risen Lord's gift of peace is inextricably bound to the call to follow Jesus and to continue the proclamation of God's reign. Matthew's gospel (Mt. 28:16-20; cf. Lk. 24:44-53) tells us that Jesus' last words to his disciples were a sending forth and a promise: "I shall be with you all days." In the continuing presence of Jesus, disciples of all ages find the courage to follow him. To follow Jesus Christ implies continual conversion in one's own life as one seeks to act in ways which are consonant with the justice, forgiveness, and love of God's reign. Discipleship reaches out to the ends of the earth and calls for reconciliation among all peoples so that God's purpose, "a plan for the fullness of time, to unite all things in him" (Eph. 1:10), will be fulfilled.

## 3. CONCLUSION

*55.*     Even a brief examination of war and peace in the scriptures makes it clear that they do not provide us with detailed answers to the specifics of the questions which we face today. They do not speak specifically of nuclear war or nuclear weapons, for these were beyond the imagination of the communities in which the scriptures were formed. The sacred texts do, however, provide us with urgent direction when we look at today's concrete realities. The fullness of eschatological peace remains before us in hope and yet the gift of peace is already ours in the reconciliation effected in Jesus Christ. These two profoundly religious meanings of peace inform and influence all other meanings for Christians. Because we have been gifted with God's peace in the risen Christ, we are called to our own peace and to the making of peace in our world. As disciples and as children of God, it is our task to seek for ways in which to make the forgiveness, justice and mercy and love of God visible in a world where violence and enmity are too often the norm. When we listen to God's word, we hear again and always the call to repentance and to belief: to repentance because although we are redeemed we continue to need redemption; to belief, because although the reign of God is near, it is still seeking its fullness.

## B. Kingdom and History

56.    The Christian understanding of history is hopeful and confident but also sober and realistic. "Christian optimism based on the glorious cross of Christ and the outpouring of the Holy Spirit is no excuse for self-deception. For Christians, peace on earth is always a challenge because of the presence of sin in man's heart."[14] Peace must be built on the basis of justice in a world where the personal and social consequences of sin are evident.

57.    Christian hope about history is rooted in our belief in God as creator and sustainer of our existence and our conviction that the kingdom of God will come in spite of sin, human weakness, and failure. It is precisely because sin is part of history that the realization of the peace of the kingdom is never permanent or total. This is the continuing refrain from the patristic period to Pope John Paul II:

> For it was sin and hatred that were an obstacle to peace with God and with others: he destroyed them by the offering of life on the cross; he reconciled in one body those who were hostile (cf. Eph. 2:16; Rom. 12:5) . . . Although Christians put all their best energies into preventing war or stopping it, they do not deceive themselves about their ability to cause peace to triumph, nor about the effect of their efforts to this end. They therefore concern themselves with all human initiatives in favor of peace and very often take part in them. But they regard them with realism and humility. One could almost say that they relativize them in two senses: they relate them both to the self-deception of humanity and to God's saving plan.[15]

58.    Christians are called to live the tension between the vision of the reign of God and its concrete realization in history. The tension is often described in terms of "already but not yet": i.e., we already live in the grace of the kingdom, but it is not yet the completed kingdom. Hence, we are a pilgrim people in a world marked by conflict and injustice. Christ's grace is at work in the world; his command of love and his call to reconciliation are not purely future ideals but call us to obedience today.

---

14. John Paul II, "World Day of Peace Message 1982," #12, *Origins* 11 (1982): 477.

15. Ibid., #11-12, pp. 477-78.

59.    ⸢With Pope Paul VI and Pope John Paul II we are convinced that "peace is possible."[16] At the same time, experience convinces us that "in this world a totally and permanently peaceful human society is unfortunately a utopia, and that ideologies that hold up that prospect as easily attainable are based on hopes that cannot be realized, whatever the reason behind them."[17]

60.    This recognition—that peace is possible but never assured and that its possibility must be continually protected and preserved in the face of obstacles and attacks upon it—accounts in large measure for the complexity of Catholic teaching on warfare. In the kingdom of God, peace and justice will be fully realized. Justice is always the foundation of peace. In history, efforts to pursue both peace and justice are at times in tension, and the struggle for justice may threaten certain forms of peace.

61.    It is within this tension of kingdom and history that Catholic teaching has addressed the problem of war. Wars mark the fabric of human history, distort the life of nations today, and, in the form of nuclear weapons, threaten the destruction of the world as we know it and the civilization which has been patiently constructed over centuries. The causes of war are multiple and not easily identified. Christians will find in any violent situation the consequences of sin: not only sinful patterns of domination, oppression or aggression, but the conflict of values and interests which illustrate the limitations of a sinful world. The threat of nuclear war which affects the world today reflects such sinful patterns and conflicts.

62.    In the "already but not yet" of Christian existence, members of the Church choose different paths to move toward the realization of the kingdom in history. As we examine both the positions open to individuals for forming their consciences on war and peace and the Catholic teaching on the obligation of the state to defend society, we draw extensively on the *Pastoral Constitution* for two reasons.

63.    First, we find its treatment of the nature of peace and the avoidance of war compelling, for it represents the prayerful thinking of bishops of the entire world and calls vigorously for fresh new attitudes, while faithfully reflecting traditional Church teaching. Secondly, the council fathers were familiar with more than the horrors of World Wars I and II. They saw conflicts continuing "to produce

---

16. John Paul II, "Message U.N. Special Session 1982," #13; Pope Paul VI, "World Day of Peace Message 1973."

17. John Paul II, "World Day of Peace Message 1982," #12, cited, p. 478.

their devastating effect day by day somewhere in the world," the
increasing ferocity of warfare made possible by modern scientific
weapons, guerrilla warfare "drawn out by new methods of deceit and
subversion," and terrorism regarded as a new way to wage war.[18]
The same phenomena mark our day.

64.    For similar reasons we draw heavily upon the popes of the
nuclear age, from Pope Pius XII through Pope John Paul II. The
teaching of popes and councils must be incarnated by each local
church in a manner understandable to its culture. This allows each
local church to bring its unique insights and experience to bear on
the issues shaping our world. From 1966 to the present, American
bishops, individually and collectively, have issued numerous statements on the issues of peace and war, ranging from the Vietnam War
to conscientious objection and the use of nuclear weapons. These
statements reflect not only the concerns of the hierarchy but also the
voices of our people who have increasingly expressed to us their alarm
over the threat of war. In this letter we wish to continue and develop
the teaching on peace and war which we have previously made, and
which reflects both the teaching of the universal Church and the
insights and experience of the Catholic community of the United
States.

65.    It is significant that explicit treatment of war and peace is
reserved for the final chapter of the *Pastoral Constitution*. Only after
exploring the nature and destiny of the human person does the council
take up the nature of peace, which it sees not as an end in itself, but
as an *indispensable condition* for the task "of constructing for all
men everywhere a world more genuinely human."[19] An understanding
of this task is crucial to understanding the Church's view of the moral
choices open to us as Christians.


## C. The Moral Choices for the Kingdom

66.    In one of its most frequently quoted passages, the *Pastoral
Constitution* declares that it is necessary "to undertake a completely
fresh reappraisal of war."[20] The council's teaching situates this call
for a "fresh reappraisal" within the context of a broad analysis of

---

18. *Pastoral Constitution*, #79.

19. Ibid., #77.

20. Ibid., #80.

the dignity of the human person and the state of the world today. If we lose sight of this broader discussion we cannot grasp the council's wisdom. For the issue of war and peace confronts everyone with a basic question: what contributes to, and what impedes, the construction of a more genuinely human world? If we are to evaluate war with an entirely new attitude, we must be serious about approaching the human person with an entirely new attitude. The obligation for all of humanity to work toward universal respect for human rights and human dignity is a fundamental imperative of the social, economic, and political order.

67.    It is clear, then, that to evaluate war with a new attitude, we must go far beyond an examination of weapons systems or military strategies. We must probe the meaning of the moral choices which are ours as Christians. In accord with the vision of Vatican II, we need to be sensitive to both the danger of war and the conditions of true freedom within which moral choices can be made.[21] Peace is the setting in which moral choice can be most effectively exercised. How can we move toward that peace which is indispensable for true human freedom? How do we define such peace?

## 1. THE NATURE OF PEACE

68.    [ The Catholic tradition has always understood the meaning of peace in positive terms. Peace is both a gift of God and a human work. It must be constructed on the basis of central human values: truth, justice, freedom, and love.] The *Pastoral Constitution* states the traditional conception of peace:

> Peace is not merely the absence of war. Nor can it be reduced solely to the maintenance of a balance of power between enemies. Nor is it brought about by dictatorship. Instead, it is rightly and appropriately called "an enterprise of justice" (Is. 32:17). Peace results from that harmony built into human society by its divine founder and actualized by men as they thirst after ever greater justice.[22]

69.    Pope John Paul II has enhanced this positive conception of peace by relating it with new philosophical depth to the Church's teaching on human dignity and human rights. The relationship was articulated in his 1979 Address to the General Assembly of the United Nations and also in his "World Day of Peace Message 1982":

---

21. Ibid., #17.

22. Ibid., #78.

Unconditional and effective respect for each one's unprescriptable and inalienable rights is the necessary condition in order that peace may reign in a society. Vis-a-vis these basic rights all others are in a way derivatory and secondary. In a society in which these rights are not protected, the very idea of universality is dead, as soon as a small group of individuals set up for their own exclusive advantage a principle of discrimination whereby the rights and even the lives of others are made dependent on the whim of the stronger.[23]

70.     As we have already noted, however, the protection of human rights and the preservation of peace are tasks to be accomplished in a world marked by sin and conflict of various kinds. The Church's teaching on war and peace establishes a strong presumption against war which is binding on all; it then examines when this presumption may be overriden, precisely in the name of preserving the kind of peace which protects human dignity and human rights.

## 2. THE PRESUMPTION AGAINST WAR AND THE PRINCIPLE OF LEGITIMATE SELF-DEFENCE

71.     Under the rubric, "curbing the savagery of war," the council contemplates the "melancholy state of humanity." It looks at this world as it is, not simply as we would want it to be. The view is stark: ferocious new means of warfare threatening savagery surpassing that of the past, deceit, subversion, terrorism, genocide. This last crime, in particular, is vehemently condemned as horrendous, but all activities which deliberately conflict with the all-embracing principles of universal natural law, which is permanently binding, are criminal, as are all orders commanding such action. Supreme commendation is due the courage of those who openly and fearlessly resist those who issue such commands. All individuals, especially government officials and experts, are bound to honor and improve upon agreements which are "aimed at making military activity and its consequences less inhuman" and which "better and more workably lead to restraining the frightfulness of war."[24]

72.     This remains a realistic appraisal of the world today. Later in this section the council calls for us "to strain every muscle as we work for the time when all war can be completely outlawed by in-

---

23. John Paul II, "World Day of Peace Message 1982," #9, cited. The *Pastoral Constitution* stresses that peace is not only the fruit of justice, but also love, which commits us to engage in "the studied practice of brotherhood" (#78).

24. *Pastoral Constitution,* #79.

ternational consent." We are told, however, that this goal requires the establishment of some universally recognized public authority with effective power "to safeguard, on the behalf of all, security, regard for justice, and respect for rights."[25] *But what of the present?* The council is exceedingly clear, as are the popes:

> Certainly, war has not been rooted out of human affairs. As long as the danger of war remains and there is no competent and sufficiently powerful authority at the international level, governments cannot be denied the right to legitimate defense once every means of peaceful settlement has been exhausted. Therefore, government authorities and others who share public responsibility have the duty to protect the welfare of the people entrusted to their care and to conduct such grave matters soberly.
>
> But it is one thing to undertake military action for the just defense of the people, and something else again to seek the subjugation of other nations. Nor does the possession of war potential make every military or political use of it lawful. Neither does the mere fact that war has unhappily begun mean that all is fair between the warring parties.[26]

73.    The Christian has no choice but to defend peace, properly understood, against aggression. This is an inalienable obligation. It is the *how* of defending peace which offers moral options. We stress this principle again because we observe so much misunderstanding about both those who resist bearing arms and those who bear them. Great numbers from both traditions provide examples of exceptional courage, examples the world continues to need. Of the millions of men and women who have served with integrity in the armed forces, many have laid down their lives. Many others serve today throughout the world in the difficult and demanding task of helping to preserve that "peace of a sort" of which the council speaks. We see many deeply sincere individuals who, far from being indifferent or apathetic to world evils, believe strongly in conscience that they are best defending true peace by refusing to bear arms. In some cases they are motivated by their understanding of the gospel and the life and death of Jesus as forbidding all violence. In others, their motivation is simply to give personal example of Christian forbearance as a positive, constructive approach toward loving reconciliation with enemies. In still other cases, they propose or engage in "active non-violence" as programmed resistance to thwart aggression, or to render ineffective any oppression attempted by force of arms. No government, and

---

25. Ibid., #82.
26. Ibid., #79.

certainly no Christian, may simply assume that such individuals are mere pawns of conspiratorial forces or guilty of cowardice.]

*74.*    Catholic teaching sees these two distinct moral responses as having a complementary relationship, in the sense that both seek to serve the common good. They differ in their perception of how the common good is to be defended most effectively, but both responses testify to the Christian conviction that peace must be pursued and rights defended within moral restraints and in the context of defining other basic human values.

*75.*    [In all of this discussion of distinct choices, of course, we are referring to options open to individuals. The council and the popes have stated clearly that governments threatened by armed, unjust aggression must defend their people. This includes defense by armed force if necessary as a last resort.] We shall discuss below the conditions and limits imposed on such defense. Even when speaking of individuals, however, the council is careful to preserve the fundamental *right* of defense.] Some choose not to vindicate their rights by armed force and adopt other methods of defense, but they do not lose the right of defense nor may they renounce their obligations to others. They are praised by the council, as long as the rights and duties of others or of the community itself are not injured.

*76.*    Pope Pius XII is especially strong in his conviction about the responsibility of the Christian to resist unjust aggression:

> *A people threatened with an unjust aggression, or already its victim, may not remain passively indifferent, if it would think and act as befits a Christian.* All the more does the solidarity of the family of nations forbid others to behave as mere spectators, in any attitude of apathetic neutrality. Who will ever measure the harm already caused in the past by such indifference to war of aggression, which is quite alien to the Christian instinct? How much more keenly has it brought any advantage in recompense? On the contrary, it has only reassured and encouraged the authors and fomentors of aggression, while it obliges the several peoples, left to themselves, to increase their armaments indefinitely . . . Among (the) goods (of humanity) some are of such importance for society, that it is perfectly lawful to defend them against unjust aggression. *Their defense is even an obligation for the nations as a whole, who have a duty not to abandon a nation that is attacked.*[27]

---

27. Pius XII, "Christmas Message," 1948; The same theme is reiterated in Pius XII's "Message" of October 3, 1953: "The community of nations must reckon with unprincipled criminals who, in order to realize their ambitious plans, are not afraid to unleash total war. This is the reason why other countries if they wish to preserve their very existence and their most precious possessions, and unless they are prepared to accord free action to international criminals, have no alternative but to get ready for the day when they must defend themselves. *This right to be prepared for self-defense cannot be denied, even in these days, to any state.*"

77.    None of the above is to suggest, however, that armed force is the only defense against unjust aggression, regardless of circumstances. Well does the council require that grave matters concerning the protection of peoples be conducted *soberly*. The council fathers were well aware that in today's world, the "horror and perversity of war are immensely magnified by the multiplication of scientific weapons. For acts of war involving these weapons can inflict massive and indiscriminate destruction far exceeding the bounds of legitimate defense."[28] Hence, we are warned: "Men of our time must realize that they will have to give a somber reckoning for their deeds of war. For the course of the future will depend largely on the decisions they make today."[29] There must be serious and continuing study and efforts to develop programmed methods for both individuals and nations to defend against unjust aggression without using violence.

78.    [We believe work to develop non-violent means of fending off aggression and resolving conflict best reflects the call of Jesus both to love and to justice. Indeed, each increase in the potential destructiveness of weapons and therefore of war serves to underline the rightness of the way that Jesus mandated to his followers. But, on the other hand, the fact of aggression, oppression and injustice in our world also serves to legitimate the resort to weapons and armed force in defense of justice. We must recognize the reality of the paradox we face as Christians living in the context of the world as it presently exists; we must continue to articulate our belief that love is possible and the only real hope for all human relations, and yet accept that force, even deadly force, is sometimes justified and that nations must provide for their defense. It is the mandate of Christians, in the face of this paradox, to strive to resolve it through an even greater commitment to Christ and his message. As Pope John Paul II said:

> Christians are aware that plans based on aggression, domination and the manipulation of others lurk in human hearts, and sometimes even secretly nourish human intentions, in spite of certain declarations or manifestations of a pacifist nature. For Christians know that in this world a totally and permanently peaceful human society is unfortunately a utopia, and that ideologies that hold up that prospect as easily attainable are based on hopes that cannot be realized, whatever the reason behind them. It is a question of a mistaken view of the human condition, a lack of application in considering the question as a whole; or it may be a case of evasion in order to calm fear, or in still other cases a matter of calculated self-interest.

---

28. *Pastoral Constitution*, #80.

29. Ibid.

Christians are convinced, if only because they have learned from personal experience, that these deceptive hopes lead straight to the false peace of totalitarian regimes. But this realistic view in no way prevents Christians from working for peace; instead, it stirs up their ardor, for they also know that Christ's victory over deception, hate and death gives those in love with peace a more decisive motive for action than what the most generous theories about man have to offer; Christ's victory likewise gives a hope more surely based than any hope held out by the most audacious dreams.

This is why Christians, even as they strive to resist and prevent every form of warfare, have no hesitation in recalling that, in the name of an elementary requirement of justice, peoples have a right and even a duty to protect their existence and freedom by proportionate means against an unjust aggressor.[30]

*79.*    In light of the framework of Catholic teaching on the nature of peace, the avoidance of war, and the state's right of legitimate defense, we can now spell out certain moral principles within the Catholic tradition which provide guidance for public policy and individual choice.

## 3. THE JUST-WAR CRITERIA

*80.*    The moral theory of the "just-war" or "limited-war" doctrine begins with the presumption which binds all Christians: we should do no harm to our neighbors; how we treat our enemy is the key test of whether we love our neighbor; and the possibility of taking even one human life is a prospect we should consider in fear and trembling. How is it possible to move from these presumptions to the idea of a justifiable use of lethal force?

*81.*    Historically and theologically the clearest answer to the question is found in St. Augustine. Augustine was impressed by the fact and the consequences of sin in history—the "not yet" dimension of the kingdom. In his view war was both the result of sin and a tragic remedy for sin in the life of political societies. War arose from disordered ambitions, but it could also be used, in some cases at least, to restrain evil and protect the innocent. The classic case which illustrated his view was the use of lethal force to prevent aggression against innocent victims. Faced with the fact of attack on the innocent, the presumption that we do no harm, even to our enemy, yielded to the command of love understood as the need to restrain an enemy who would injure the innocent.

---

30. John Paul II, "World Day of Peace Message 1982," #12, cited, p. 478.

*82.*    The just-war argument has taken several forms in the history of Catholic theology, but this Augustinian insight is its central premise.[31] In the twentieth century, papal teaching has used the logic of Augustine and Aquinas[32] to articulate a right of self-defense for states in a decentralized international order and to state the criteria for exercising that right. The essential position was stated by Vatican II: "As long as the danger of war persists and there is no international authority with the necessary competence and power, governments cannot be denied the right of lawful self-defense, once all peace efforts have failed."[33] We have already indicated the centrality of this principle for understanding Catholic teaching about the state and its duties.

*83.*    Just-war teaching has evolved, however, as an effort to prevent war; only if war cannot be rationally avoided, does the teaching then seek to restrict and reduce its horrors. It does this by establishing a set of rigorous conditions which must be met if the decision to go to war is to be morally permissible. Such a decision, especially today, requires extraordinarily strong reasons for overriding the presumption *in favor of peace* and *against* war. This is one significant reason why valid just-war teaching makes provision for conscientious dissent. It is presumed that all sane people prefer peace, never *want* to initiate war, and accept even the most justifiable defensive war only as a sad necessity. Only the most powerful reasons may be permitted to override such objection. In the words of Pope Pius XII:

> The Christian will for peace . . . is very careful to avoid recourse to the force of arms in the defense of rights which, however legitimate, do not offset the risk of kindling a blaze with all its spiritual and material consequences.[34]

---

31. Augustine called it a Manichaean heresy to assert that war is intrinsically evil and contrary to Christian charity, and stated: "War and conquest are a sad necessity in the eyes of men of principle, yet it would be still more unfortunate if wrongdoers should dominate just men." (*The City of God*, Book IV, C. 15)

Representative surveys of the history and theology of the just-war tradition include: F. H. Russell, *The Just War in the Middle Ages* (New York: 1975); P. Ramsey, *War and the Christian Conscience* (Durham, N.C.: 1961); P. Ramsey, *The Just War: Force and Political Responsibility* (New York: 1968), James T. Johnson, *Ideology, Reason and the Limitation of War* (Princeton: 1975), *Just War Tradition and the Restraint of War: A Moral and Historical Inquiry* (Princeton: 1981); L. B. Walters, *Five Classic Just-War Theories* (Ph.D. Dissertation, Yale University, 1971); W. O'Brien, *War and/or Survival* (New York: 1969), *The Conduct of Just and Limited War* (New York: 1981); J. C. Murray, "Remarks on the Moral Problem of War," *Theological Studies* 20 (1959):40-61.

32. Aquinas treats the question of war in the *Summa Theologica*, II-IIae, q. 40; also cf. II-IIae, q. 64.

33. *Pastoral Constitution*, #79.

34. Pius XII, "Christmas Message," 1948.

*84.*    The determination of *when* conditions exist which allow the resort to force in spite of the strong presumption against it is made in light of *jus ad bellum* criteria. The determination of *how* even a justified resort to force must be conducted is made in light of the *jus in bello* criteria. We shall briefly explore the meaning of both.[35]

## Jus ad Bellum

*85.*    Why and when recourse to war is permissible.

*86.*    *a) Just Cause:* War is permissible only to confront "a real and certain danger," i.e., to protect innocent life, to preserve conditions necessary for decent human existence, and to secure basic human rights. As both Pope Pius XII and Pope John XXIII made clear, if war of retribution was ever justifiable, the risks of modern war negate such a claim today.

*87.*    *b) Competent Authority:* In the Catholic tradition the right to use force has always been joined to the common good; war must be declared by those with responsibility for public order, not by private groups or individuals.

*88.*    The requirement that a decision to go to war must be made by competent authority is particularly important in a democratic society. It needs detailed treatment here since it involves a broad spectrum of related issues. Some of the bitterest divisions of society in our own nation's history, for example, have been provoked over the question of whether or not a president of the United States has acted constitutionally and legally in involving our country in a *de facto* war, even if—indeed, especially if—war was never formally declared. Equally perplexing problems of conscience can be raised for individuals expected or legally required to go to war even though our duly elected representatives in Congress have, in fact, voted for war.

*89.*    The criterion of competent authority is of further importance in a day when revolutionary war has become commonplace. Historically, the just-war tradition has been open to a "just revolution" position, recognizing that an oppressive government may lose its claim to legitimacy. Insufficient analytical attention has been given to the moral issues of revolutionary warfare. The mere possession of sufficient weaponry, for example, does not legitimize the initiation of war by "insurgents" against an established government, any more

---

35. For an analysis of the content and relationship of these principles cf.: R. Potter, "The Moral Logic of War," *McCormick Quarterly* 23 (1970):203-33; J. Childress, "Just War Criteria," in T. Shannon, ed., *War or Peace: The Search for New Answers* (N.Y.: 1980).

than the government's systematic oppression of its people can be carried out under the doctrine of "national security."

90.    While the legitimacy of revolution in some circumstances cannot be denied, just-war teachings must be applied as rigorously to revolutionary-counterrevolutionary conflicts as to others. The issue of who constitutes competent authority and how such authority is exercised is essential.

91.    When we consider in this letter the issues of conscientious objection (C.O.) and selective conscientious objection (S.C.O.), the issue of competent authority will arise again.

92.    c) *Comparative Justice:* Questions concerning the *means* of waging war today, particularly in view of the destructive potential of weapons, have tended to override questions concerning the comparative justice of the positions of respective adversaries or enemies. In essence: which side is sufficiently "right" in a dispute, and are the values at stake critical enough to override the presumption against war? The question in its most basic form is this: do the rights and values involved justify killing? For whatever the means used, war, by definition, involves violence, destruction, suffering, and death.

93.    The category of comparative justice is designed to emphasize the presumption against war which stands at the beginning of just-war teaching. In a world of sovereign states recognizing neither a common moral authority nor a central political authority, comparative justice stresses that no state should act on the basis that it has "absolute justice" on its side. Every party to a conflict should acknowledge the limits of its "just cause" and the consequent requirement to use *only* limited means in pursuit of its objectives. Far from legitimizing a crusade mentality, comparative justice is designed to relativize absolute claims and to restrain the use of force even in a "justified" conflict.[36]

94.    Given techniques of propaganda and the ease with which nations and individuals either assume or delude themselves into believing that God or right is clearly on their side, the test of comparative justice may be extremely difficult to apply. Clearly, however, this is not the case in every instance of war. Blatant aggression from without

---

36. James T. Johnson, *Ideology, Reason and the Limitation of War*, cited; W. O'Brien, *The Conduct of Just and Limited War*, cited, pp. 13-30; W. Vanderpol, *La doctrine scolastique du droit de guerre*, p. 387ff; J. C. Murray, "Theology and Modern Warfare," in W. J. Nagel, ed., *Morality and Modern Warfare*, p. 80ff.

and subversion from within are often enough readily identifiable by all reasonably fair-minded people.

95.    *d) Right Intention:* Right intention is related to just cause—war can be legitimately intended only for the reasons set forth above as a just cause. During the conflict, right intention means pursuit of peace and reconciliation, including avoiding unnecessarily destructive acts or imposing unreasonable conditions (e.g., unconditional surrender).

96.    *e) Last Resort:* For resort to war to be justified, all peaceful alternatives must have been exhausted. There are formidable problems in this requirement. No international organization currently in existence has exercised sufficient internationally recognized authority to be able either to mediate effectively in most cases or to prevent conflict by the intervention of United Nations or other peacekeeping forces. Furthermore, there is a tendency for nations or peoples which perceive conflict between or among other nations as advantageous to themselves to attempt to prevent a peaceful settlement rather than advance it.

97.    We regret the apparent unwillingness of some to see in the United Nations organization the potential for world order which exists and to encourage its development. Pope Paul VI called the United Nations the last hope for peace. The loss of this hope cannot be allowed to happen. Pope John Paul II is again instructive on this point:

> I wish above all to repeat my confidence in you, the leaders and members of the International Organizations, and in you, the international officials! In the course of the last ten years, your organizations have too often been the object of attempts at manipulation on the part of nations wishing to exploit such bodies. However it remains true that the present multiplicity of violent clashes, divisions and blocks on which bilateral relations founder, offer the great International Organizations the opportunity to engage upon the qualitative change in their activities, even to reform on certain points their own structures in order to take into account new realities and to enjoy effective power.[37]

98.    *f) Probability of Success:* This is a difficult criterion to apply, but its purpose is to prevent irrational resort to force or hopeless resistance when the outcome of either will clearly be disproportionate or futile. The determination includes a recognition that at times defense of key values, even against great odds, may be a "proportionate" witness.

---

37.  John Paul II, "World Day of Peace Message 1983," #11.

*99.*     *g) Proportionality:* In terms of the *jus ad bellum* criteria, proportionality means that the damage to be inflicted and the costs incurred by war must be proportionate to the good expected by taking up arms. Nor should judgments concerning proportionality be limited to the temporal order without regard to a spiritual dimension in terms of "damage," "cost," and "the good expected." In today's interdependent world even a local conflict can affect people everywhere; this is particularly the case when the nuclear powers are involved. Hence a nation cannot justly go to war today without considering the effect of its action on others and on the international community.

*100.*     This principle of proportionality applies throughout the conduct of the war as well as to the decision to begin warfare. During the Vietnam war our bishops' conference ultimately concluded that the conflict had reached such a level of devastation to the adversary and damage to our own society that continuing it could not be justified.[38]

## Jus in Bello

*101.*     Even when the stringent conditions which justify resort to war are met, the conduct of war (i.e., strategy, tactics, and individual actions) remains subject to continuous scrutiny in light of two principles which have special significance today precisely because of the destructive capability of modern technological warfare. These principles are proportionality and discrimination. In discussing them here, we shall apply them to the question of *jus ad bellum* as well as *jus in bello*; for today it becomes increasingly difficult to make a decision to use any kind of armed force, however limited initially in intention and in the destructive power of the weapons employed, without facing at least the possibility of escalation to broader, or even total, war and to the use of weapons of horrendous destructive potential. This is especially the case when adversaries are "superpowers," as the council clearly envisioned:

> Indeed, if the kind of weapons now stocked in the arsenals of the great powers were to be employed to the fullest, the result would be the almost complete reciprocal slaughter of one side by the other, not to speak of the widespread devastation that would follow in the world and the deadly aftereffects resulting from the use of such weapons.[39]

---

38. National Conference of Catholic Bishops, *Resolution on Southeast Asia* (Washington, D.C.: 1971).

39. *Pastoral Constitution*, #80.

*102*.    It should not be thought, of course, that massive slaughter and destruction would result only from the extensive use of nuclear weapons. We recall with horror the carpet and incendiary bombings of World War II, the deaths of hundreds of thousands in various regions of the world through "conventional" arms, the unspeakable use of gas and other forms of chemical warfare, the destruction of homes and of crops, the utter suffering war has wrought during the centuries before and the decades since the use of the "atom bomb." Nevertheless, every honest person must recognize that, especially given the proliferation of modern scientific weapons, we now face possibilities which are appalling to contemplate. Today, as never before, we must ask not merely what *will* happen, but what *may* happen, especially if major powers embark on war. Pope John Paul II has repeatedly pleaded that world leaders confront this reality:

> [I]n view of the difference between classical warfare and nuclear or bac-
> teriological war—a difference so to speak of nature—and in view of the
> scandal of the arms race seen against the background of the needs of the
> Third World, this right [of defense], which is very real in principle, only
> underlines the urgency of world society to equip itself with effective means
> of negotiation. In this way the nuclear terror that haunts our time can
> encourage us to enrich our common heritage with a very simple discovery
> that is within our reach, namely that war is the most barbarous and least
> effective way of resolving conflicts.[40]

*103*.    The Pontifical Academy of Sciences reaffirmed the Holy Father's theme, in its November 1981 "Statement on the Consequences of Nuclear War." Then, in a meeting convoked by the Pontifical Academy, representatives of national academies of science from throughout the world issued a "Declaration on the Prevention of Nuclear War" which specified the meaning of Pope John Paul II's statement that modern warfare differs by nature from previous forms of war. The scientists said:

> Throughout its history humanity has been confronted with war, but since
> 1945 the nature of warfare has changed so profoundly that the future of
> the human race, of generations yet unborn, is imperiled. . . . For the first
> time it is possible to cause damage on such a catastrophic scale as to wipe
> out a large part of civilization and to endanger its very survival. The large-
> scale use of such weapons could trigger major and irreversible ecological
> and genetic changes whose limits cannot be predicted.[41]

And earlier, with such thoughts plainly in mind, the council had

---

40. John Paul II, "World Day of Peace Message 1982," #12, cited.

41. "Declaration on Prevention of Nuclear War" (Sept. 24, 1982).

made its own "the condemnation of total war already pronounced by recent popes."[42] This condemnation is demanded by the principles of proportionality and discrimination. Response to aggression must not exceed the nature of the aggression. To destroy civilization as we know it by waging a "total war" as today it *could* be waged would be a monstrously disproportionate response to aggression on the part of any nation.

*104.* Moreover, the lives of innocent persons may never be taken directly, regardless of the purpose alleged for doing so. To wage truly "total" war is by definition to take huge numbers of innocent lives. Just response to aggression must be discriminate; it must be directed against unjust aggressors, not against innocent people caught up in a war not of their making. The council therefore issued its memorable declaration:

> Any act of war aimed indiscriminately at the destruction of entire cities or of extensive areas along with their population is a crime against God and man himself. It merits unequivocal and unhesitating condemnation.[43]

*105.* When confronting choices among specific military options, the question asked by proportionality is: once we take into account not only the military advantages that will be achieved by using this means but also all the harms reasonably expected to follow from using it, can its use still be justified? We know, of course, that no end can justify means evil in themselves, such as the executing of hostages or the targeting of non-combatants. Nonetheless, even if the means adopted is not evil in itself, it is necessary to take into account the probable harms that will result from using it and the justice of accepting those harms. It is of utmost importance, in assessing harms and the justice of accepting them, to think about the poor and the helpless, for they are usually the ones who have the least to gain and the most to lose when war's violence touches their lives.

*106.* In terms of the arms race, if the *real* end in view is legitimate defense against unjust aggression, and the means to this end are not evil in themselves, we must still examine the question of proportionality concerning attendant evils. Do the exorbitant costs, the general climate of insecurity generated, the possibility of accidental detonation of highly destructive weapons, the danger of error and miscalculation that could provoke retaliation and war—do such evils or others attendant upon and indirectly deriving from the arms race

---

42. *Pastoral Constitution*, #80.

43. Ibid.

make the arms race itself a disproportionate response to aggression? Pope John Paul II is very clear in his insistence that the exercise of the right and duty of a people to protect their existence and freedom is contingent on the use of proportionate means.[44]

*107.*    Finally, another set of questions concerns the interpretation of the principle of discrimination. The principle prohibits directly intended attacks on non-combatants and non-military targets. It raises a series of questions about the term "intentional," the category of "non-combatant," and the meaning of "military."

*108.*    These questions merit the debate occurring with increasing frequency today. We encourage such debate, for concise and definitive answers still appear to be wanting. Mobilization of forces in modern war includes not only the military, but to a significant degree the political, economic, and social sectors. It is not always easy to determine who is directly involved in a "war effort" or to what degree. Plainly, though, not even by the broadest definition can one rationally consider combatants entire classes of human beings such as schoolchildren, hospital patients, the elderly, the ill, the average industrial worker producing goods not directly related to military purposes, farmers, and many others. They may never be directly attacked.

*109.*    Direct attacks on military targets involve similar complexities. Which targets are "military" ones and which are not? To what degree, for instance, does the use (by either revolutionaries or regular military forces) of a village or housing in a civilian populated area invite attack? What of a munitions factory in the heart of a city? Who is directly responsible for the deaths of noncombatants should the attack be carried out? To revert to the question raised earlier, how many deaths of non-combatants are "tolerable" as a result of indirect attacks—attacks directed against combat forces and military targets, which nevertheless kill non-combatants at the same time?

*110.*    These two principles, in all their complexity, must be applied to the range of weapons—conventional, nuclear, biological, and chemical—with which nations are armed today.


## 4. THE VALUE OF NON-VIOLENCE


*111.*    Moved by the example of Jesus' life and by his teaching, some Christians have from the earliest days of the Church committed

---

44. John Paul II, "World Day of Peace Message 1982," #12, cited.

themselves to a non-violent lifestyle.[45] Some understood the gospel of Jesus to prohibit all killing. Some affirmed the use of prayer and other spiritual methods as means of responding to enmity and hostility.

*112.*    In the middle of the second century, St. Justin proclaimed to his pagan readers that Isaiah's prophecy about turning swords into ploughshares and spears into sickles had been fulfilled as a consequence of Christ's coming:

> And we who delighted in war, in the slaughter of one another, and in every other kind of iniquity have in every part of the world converted our weapons into implements of peace—our swords into ploughshares, our spears into farmers' tools—and we cultivate piety, justice, brotherly charity, faith and hope, which we derive from the Father through the crucified Savior . . .[46]

*113.*    Writing in the third century, St. Cyprian of Carthage struck a similar note when he indicated that the Christians of his day did not fight against their enemies. He himself regarded their conduct as proper:

> They do not even fight against those who are attacking since it is not granted to the innocent to kill even the aggressor, but promptly to deliver up their souls and blood that, since so much malice and cruelty are rampant in the world, they may more quickly withdraw from the malicious and the cruel.[47]

*114.*    Some of the early Christian opposition to military service was a response to the idolatrous practices which prevailed in the Roman army. Another powerful motive was the fact that army service involved preparation for fighting and killing. We see this in the case of St. Martin of Tours during the fourth century, who renounced his soldierly profession with the explanation: "Hitherto I have served you as a soldier. Allow me now to become a soldier of God . . . I am a soldier of Christ. It is not lawful for me to fight."[48]

---

45. Representative authors in the tradition of Christian pacifism and non-violence include: R. Bainton, *Christian Attitudes Toward War and Peace* (Abington: 1960), chs. 4, 5, 10; J. Yoder, *The Politics of Jesus* (Grand Rapids: 1972), *Nevertheless: Varieties of Religious Pacifism* (Scottsdale: 1971); T. Merton, *Faith and Violence: Christian Teaching and Christian Practice* (Notre Dame: 1968); G. Zahn, *War, Conscience and Dissent* (New York: 1967); E. Egan, "The Beatitudes: Works of Mercy and Pacifism," in T. Shannon, ed., *War or Peace: The Search for New Answers* (New York: 1980), pp. 169-187; J. Fahey, "The Catholic Church and the Arms Race," *Worldview* 22 (1979):38-41; J. Douglass, *The Nonviolent Cross: A Theology of Revolution and Peace* (New York: 1966).

46. Justin, *Dialogue with Trypho*, ch. 110; cf. also *The First Apology*, chs. 14, 39.

47. Cyprian, *Collected Letters*; Letters to Cornelius.

48. Sulpicius Severus, *The Life of Martin*, 4.3.

*115.*    In the centuries between the fourth century and our own day, the theme of Christian non-violence and Christian pacifism has echoed and re-echoed, sometimes more strongly, sometimes more faintly. One of the great non-violent figures in those centuries was St. Francis of Assisi. Besides making personal efforts on behalf of reconciliation and peace, Francis stipulated that laypersons who became members of his Third Order were not "to take up lethal weapons, or bear them about, against anybody."

*116.*    The vision of Christian non-violence is not passive about injustice and the defense of the rights of others; it rather affirms and exemplifies what it means to resist injustice through non-violent methods.

*117.*    In the twentieth century, prescinding from the non-Christian witness of a Mahatma Ghandi and its worldwide impact, the non-violent witness of such figures as Dorothy Day and Martin Luther King has had a profound impact upon the life of the Church in the United States. The witness of numerous Christians who had preceded them over the centuries was affirmed in a remarkable way at the Second Vatican Council.

*118.*    Two of the passages which were included in the final version of the *Pastoral Constitution* gave particular encouragement for Catholics in all walks of life to assess their attitudes toward war and military service in the light of Christian pacifism. In paragraph 79 the council fathers called upon governments to enact laws protecting the rights of those who adopted the position of conscientious objection to all war: "Moreover, it seems right that laws make humane provisions for the case of those who for reasons of conscience refuse to bear arms, provided, however, that they accept some other form of service to the human community."[49] This was the first time a call for legal protection of conscientious objection had appeared in a document of such prominence. In addition to its own profound meaning this statement took on even more significance in the light of the praise that the council fathers had given in the preceding section "to those who renounce the use of violence and the vindication of their rights."[50] In *Human Life in Our Day* (1968) we called for legislative provision to recognize selective conscientious objectors as well.[51]

---

49. *Pastoral Constitution*, #79.

50. Ibid., #78.

51. United States Catholic Conference, *Human Life in Our Day* (Washington, D.C.: 1968), p. 44.

*119.*     As Catholic bishops it is incumbent upon us to stress to our own community and to the wider society the significance of this support for a pacifist option for individuals in the teaching of Vatican II and the reaffirmation that the popes have given to nonviolent witness since the time of the council.

*120.*     In the development of a theology of peace and the growth of the Christian pacifist position among Catholics, these words of the *Pastoral Constitution* have special significance: "All these factors force us to undertake a completely fresh reappraisal of war."[52] The council fathers had reference to "the development of armaments by modern science (which) has immeasurably magified the horrors and wickedness of war."[53] While the just-war teaching has clearly been in possession for the past 1,500 years of Catholic thought, the "new moment" in which we find ourselves sees the just-war teaching and non-violence as distinct but interdependent methods of evaluating warfare. They diverge on some specific conclusions, but they share a common presumption against the use of force as a means of settling disputes.

*121.*     Both find their roots in the Christian theological tradition; each contributes to the full moral vision we need in pursuit of a human peace. We believe the two perspectives support and complement one another, each preserving the other from distortion. Finally, in an age of technological warfare, analysis from the viewpoint of non-violence and analysis from the viewpoint of the just-war teaching often converge and agree in their opposition to methods of warfare which are in fact indistinguishable from total warfare.

---

52. *Pastoral Constitution,* #80.

53. Ibid.

# II

# War and Peace in the
# Modern World:
# Problems and Principles

*122.* Both the just-war teaching and non-violence are confronted with a unique challenge by nuclear warfare. This must be the starting point of any further moral reflection: nuclear weapons particularly and nuclear warfare as it is planned today, raise new moral questions. No previously conceived moral position escapes the fundamental confrontation posed by contemporary nuclear strategy. Many have noted the similarity of the statements made by eminent scientists and Vatican II's observation that we are forced today "to undertake a completely fresh reappraisal of war." The task before us is not simply to repeat what we have said before; it is first to consider anew whether and how our religious-moral tradition can assess, direct, contain, and, we hope, help to eliminate the threat posed to the human family by the nuclear arsenals of the world. Pope John Paul II captured the essence of the problem during his pilgrimage to Hiroshima:

> In the past it was possible to destroy a village, a town, a region, even a country. Now it is the whole planet that has come under threat.[54]

*123.* The Holy Father's observation illustrates why the moral problem is also a religious question of the most profound significance. In the nuclear arsenals of the United States or the Soviet Union alone, there exists a capacity to do something no other age could imagine: we can threaten the entire planet.[55] For people of faith this means we read the Book of Genesis with a new awareness; the moral issue at stake in nuclear war involves the meaning of sin in its most graphic dimensions. Every sinful act is a confrontation of the creature and

---

54. John Paul II, "Address to Scientists and Scholars," #4, cited, p. 621.

55. Cf. "Declaration on Prevention of Nuclear War."

the creator. Today the destructive potential of the nuclear powers
threatens the human person, the civilization we have slowly constructed, and even the created order itself.

*124.*    We live today, therefore, in the midst of a cosmic drama; we
possess a power which should never be used, but which might be
used if we do not reverse our direction. We live with nuclear weapons
knowing we cannot afford to make one serious mistake. This fact
dramatizes the precariousness of our position, politically, morally,
and spiritually.

*125.*    A prominent "sign of the times" today is a sharply increased
awareness of the danger of the nuclear arms race. Such awareness
has produced a public discussion about nuclear policy here and in
other countries which is unprecedented in its scope and depth. What
has been accepted for years with almost no question is now being
subjected to the sharpest criticism. What previously had been defined
as a safe and stable system of deterrence is today viewed with political
and moral skepticism. Many forces are at work in this new evaluation,
and we believe one of the crucial elements is the gospel vision of
peace which guides our work in this pastoral letter. The nuclear age
has been the theater of our existence for almost four decades; today
it is being evaluated with a new perspective. For many the leaven of
the gospel and the light of the Holy Spirit create the decisive dimension
of this new perspective.

## A. The New Moment

*126.*    At the center of the new evaluation of the nuclear arms race
is a recognition of two elements: the destructive potential of nuclear
weapons, and the stringent choices which the nuclear age poses for
both politics and morals.

*127.*    The fateful passage into the nuclear age as a military reality
began with the bombing of Nagasaki and Hiroshima, events described
by Pope Paul VI as a "butchery of untold magnitude."[56] Since then,
in spite of efforts at control and plans for disarmament (e.g., the
Baruch Plan of 1946), the nuclear arsenals have escalated, particularly
in the two superpowers. The qualitative superiority of these two states,
however, should not overshadow the fact that four other countries

---

56. Paul VI, "World Day of Peace Message 1976," in *Documents*, p. 198.

possess nuclear capacity and a score of states are only steps away from becoming "nuclear nations."

*128.*    This nuclear escalation has been opposed sporadically and selectively but never effectively. The race has continued in spite of carefully expressed doubts by analysts and other citizens and in the face of forcefully expressed opposition by public rallies. Today the opposition to the arms race is no longer selective or sporadic, it is widespread and sustained. The danger and destructiveness of nuclear weapons are understood and resisted with new urgency and intensity. There is in the public debate today an endorsement of the position submitted by the Holy See at the United Nations in 1976: the arms race is to be condemned as a danger, an act of aggression against the poor, and a folly which does not provide the security it promises.[57]

*129.*    Papal teaching has consistently addressed the folly and danger of the arms race; but the new perception of it which is now held by the general public is due in large measure to the work of scientists and physicians who have described for citizens the concrete human consequences of a nuclear war.[58]

*130.*    In a striking demonstration of his personal and pastoral concern for preventing nuclear war, Pope John Paul II commissioned a study by the Pontifical Academy of Sciences which reinforced the findings of other scientific bodies. The Holy Father had the study transmitted by personal representative to the leaders of the United States, the Soviet Union, the United Kingdom, and France, and to the president of the General Assembly of the United Nations. One of its conclusions is especially pertinent to the public debate in the United States:

> Recent talk about winning or even surviving a nuclear war must reflect a failure to appreciate a medical reality: Any nuclear war would inevitably cause death, disease and suffering of pandemonic proportions and without the possibility of effective medical intervention. That reality leads to the same conclusion physicians have reached for life-threatening epidemics throughout history. Prevention is essential for control.[59]

*131.*    This medical conclusion has a moral corollary. Traditionally, the Church's moral teaching sought first to prevent war and then to

---

57. "Statement of the Holy See to the United Nations" (1976), in *The Church and the Arms Race*; Pax Christi-USA (New York: 1976), pp. 23-24.

58. R. Adams and S. Cullen, *The Final Epidemic: Physicians and Scientists on Nuclear War* (Chicago: 1981).

59. Pontifical Academy of Sciences, "Statement on the Consequences of the Use of Nuclear Weapons," in *Documents*, p. 241.

limit its consequences if it occurred. Today the possibilities for placing political and moral limits on nuclear war are so minimal that the moral task, like the medical, is prevention: as a people, we must refuse to legitimate the idea of nuclear war. Such a refusal will require not only new ideas and new vision, but what the gospel calls conversion of the heart.

*132.*   To say "no" to nuclear war is both a necessary and a complex task. We are moral teachers in a tradition which has always been prepared to relate moral principles to concrete problems. Particularly in this letter we could not be content with simply restating general moral principles or repeating well-known requirements about the ethics of war. We have had to examine, with the assistance of a broad spectrum of advisors of varying persuasions, the nature of existing and proposed weapons systems, the doctrines which govern their use, and the consequences of using them. We have consulted people who engage their lives in protest against the existing nuclear strategy of the United States, and we have consulted others who have held or do hold responsibility for this strategy. It has been a sobering and perplexing experience. In light of the evidence which witnesses presented and in light of our study, reflection, and consultation, we must reject nuclear war. But we feel obliged to relate our judgment to the specific elements which comprise the nuclear problem.

*133.*   Though certain that the dangerous and delicate nuclear relationship the superpowers now maintain should not exist, we understand how it came to exist. In a world of sovereign states, devoid of central authority and possessing the knowledge to produce nuclear weapons, many choices were made, some clearly objectionable, others well-intended with mixed results, which brought the world to its present dangerous situation.

*134.*   We see with increasing clarity the political folly of a system which threatens mutual suicide, the psychological damage this does to ordinary people, especially the young, the economic distortion of priorities—billions readily spent for destructive instruments while pitched battles are waged daily in our legislatures over much smaller amounts for the homeless, the hungry, and the helpless here and abroad. But it is much less clear how we translate a "no" to nuclear war into the personal and public choices which can move us in a new direction, toward a national policy and an international system which more adequately reflect the values and vision of the kingdom of God.

*135.*   These tensions in our assessment of the politics and strategy of the nuclear age reflect the conflicting elements of the nuclear dilemma and the balance of terror which it has produced. We have said earlier in this letter that the fact of war reflects the existence of sin in the world. The nuclear threat and the danger it poses to human life and civilization exemplify in a qualitatively new way the perennial struggle of the political community to contain the use of force, particularly among states.

*136.*    Precisely because of the destructive nature of nuclear weapons, strategies have been developed which previous generations would have found unintelligible. Today military preparations are undertaken on a vast and sophisticated scale, but the declared purpose is not to use the weapons produced. Threats are made which would be suicidal to implement. The key to security is no longer only military secrets, for in some instances security may best be served by informing one's adversary publicly what weapons one has and what plans exist for their use. The presumption of the nation-state system, that sovereignty implies an ability to protect a nation's territory and population, is precisely the presumption denied by the nuclear capacities of both superpowers. In a sense each is at the mercy of the other's perception of what strategy is "rational," what kind of damage is "unacceptable," how "convincing" one side's threat is to the other.

*137.*    The political paradox of deterrence has also strained our moral conception. May a nation threaten what it may never do? May it possess what it may never use? Who is involved in the threat each superpower makes: government officials? or military personnel? or the citizenry in whose defense the threat is made?

*138.*    In brief, the danger of the situation is clear; but how to prevent the use of nuclear weapons, how to assess deterrence, and how to delineate moral responsibility in the nuclear age are less clearly seen or stated. Reflecting the complexity of the nuclear problem, our arguments in this pastoral must be detailed and nuanced; but our "no" to nuclear war must, in the end, be definitive and decisive.

## B. *Religious Leadership and the Public Debate*

*139.*    Because prevention of nuclear war appears, from several perspectives, to be not only the surest but only way to limit its destructive potential, we see our role as moral teachers precisely in terms of helping to form public opinion with a clear determination to resist resort to nuclear war as an instrument of national policy. If "prevention is the only cure," then there are diverse tasks to be performed in preventing what should never occur. As bishops we see a specific task defined for us in Pope John Paul II's "World Day of Peace Message 1982":

> Peace cannot be built by the power of rulers alone. Peace can be firmly constructed only if it corresponds to the resolute determination of all people of good will. Rulers must be supported and enlightened by a public opinion that encourages them or, where necessary, expresses disapproval.[60]

*140.*    The pope's appeal to form public opinion is not an abstract task. Especially in a democracy, public opinion can passively acquiesce in policies and strategies or it can, through a series of measures, indicate the limits beyond which a government should not proceed. The "new moment" which exists in the public debate about nuclear weapons provides a creative opportunity and a moral imperative to examine the relationship between public opinion and public policy. We believe it is necessary, for the sake of prevention, to build a barrier against the concept of nuclear war as a viable strategy for defense. There should be a clear public resistance to the rhetoric of "winnable" nuclear wars, or unrealistic expectations of "surviving" nuclear exchanges, and strategies of "protracted nuclear war." We oppose such rhetoric.

*141.*    We seek to encourage a public attitude which sets stringent limits on the kind of actions our own government and other governments will take on nuclear policy. We believe religious leaders have a task in concert with public officials, analysts, private organizations, and the media to set the limits beyond which our military policy should not move in word or action. Charting a moral course in a complex public policy debate involves several steps. We will address four questions, offering our reflections on them as an invitation to a public moral dialogue:

1) the use of nuclear weapons;
2) the policy of deterrence in principle and in practice;
3) specific steps to reduce the danger of war;
4) long-term measures of policy and diplomacy.

## C. The Use of Nuclear Weapons

*142.*    Establishing moral guildelines in the nuclear debate means

---

60. John Paul II, "World Day of Peace Message 1982," #6, cited, p. 476.

addressing first the question of the use of nuclear weapons. That question has several dimensions.

*143.*    It is clear that those in the Church who interpret the gospel teaching as forbidding all use of violence would oppose any use of nuclear weapons under any conditions. In a sense the existence of these weapons simply confirms and reinforces one of the initial insights of the non-violent position, namely, that Christians should not use lethal force since the hope of using it selectively and restrictively is so often an illusion. Nuclear weapons seem to prove this point in a way heretofore unknown.

*144.*    For the tradition which acknowledges some legitimate use of force, some important elements of contemporary nuclear strategies move beyond the limits of moral justification. A justifiable use of force must be both discriminatory and proportionate. Certain aspects of both U.S. and Soviet strategies fail both tests as we shall discuss below. The technical literature and the personal testimony of public officials who have been closely associated with U.S. nuclear strategy have both convinced us of the overwhelming probability that major nuclear exchange would have no limits.[61]

*145.*    On the more complicated issue of "limited" nuclear war, we are aware of the extensive literature and discussion which this topic

---

61. The following quotations are from public officials who have served at the highest policy levels in recent administrations of our government: "It is time to recognize that no one has ever succeeded in advancing any persuasive reason to believe that any use of nuclear weapons, even on the smallest scale, could reliably be expected to remain limited." M. Bundy, G. F. Kennan, R. S. McNamara and G. Smith, "Nuclear Weapons and the Atlantic Alliance," *Foreign Affairs* 60 (1982):757.

"From my experience in combat there is no way that [nuclear escalation] . . . can be controlled because of the lack of information, the pressure of time and the deadly results that are taking place on both sides of the battle line." Gen. A. S. Collins, Jr. (former deputy commander in chief of U.S. Army in Europe), "Theatre Nuclear Warfare: The Battlefield," in J. F. Reichart and S. R. Sturn, eds., *American Defense Policy*, 5th ed., (Baltimore: 1982), pp. 359-60.

"None of this potential flexibility changes my view that a full-scale thermonuclear exchange would be an unprecedented disaster for the Soviet Union as well as for the United States. Nor is it at all clear that an initial use of nuclear weapons—however selectively they might be targeted—could be kept from escalating to a full-scale thermonuclear exchange, especially if command-and-control centers were brought under attack. The odds are high, whether weapons were used against tactical or strategic targets, that control would be lost on both sides and the exchange would become unconstrained." Harold Brown, *Department of Defense Annual Report FY 1979* (Washington, D.C.: 1978).

Cf. also: *The Effects of Nuclear War* (Washington, D.C.: 1979, U.S. Government Printing Office).

has generated.[62] As a general statement, it seems to us that public officials would be unable to refute the following conclusion of the study made by the Pontifical Academy of Sciences:

> Even a nuclear attack directed only at military facilities would be devastating to the country as a whole. This is because military facilities are widespread rather than concentrated at only a few points. Thus, many nuclear weapons would be exploded.
>
> Furthermore, the spread of radiation due to the natural winds and atmospheric mixing would kill vast numbers of people and contaminate large areas. The medical facilities of any nation would be inadequate to care for the survivors. An objective examination of the medical situation that would follow a nuclear war leads to but one conclusion: prevention is our only recourse.[63]

## Moral Principles and Policy Choices

146.    In light of these perspectives we address three questions more explicitly: (1) counter population warfare; (2) initiation of nuclear war; and (3) limited nuclear war.

### 1. Counter Population Warfare

147.    Under no circumstances may nuclear weapons or other instruments of mass slaughter be used for the purpose of destroying population centers or other predominantly civilian targets. Popes have repeatedly condemned "total war" which implies such use. For example, as early as 1954 Pope Pius XII condemned nuclear warfare "when it entirely escapes the control of man," and results in "the pure and simple annihilation of all human life within the radius of action."[64] The condemnation was repeated by the Second Vatican Council:

> Any act of war aimed indiscriminately at the destruction of entire cities or of extensive areas along with their population is a crime against God and man itself. It merits unequivocal and unhesitating condemnation.[65]

---

62. For example, cf.: H. A. Kissinger, *Nuclear Weapons and Foreign Policy* (New York: 1957), *The Necessity for Choice* (New York: 1960); R. Osgood and R. Tucker, *Force, Order and Justice* (Baltimore: 1967); R. Aron, *The Great Debate: Theories of Nuclear Strategy* (New York: 1965); D. Ball, *Can Nuclear War Be Controlled?* Adelphi Paper #161 (London: 1981); M. Howard, "On Fighting a Nuclear War," *International Security* 5 (1981):3-17.

63. "Statement on the Consequences of the Use of Nuclear Weapons," cited, p. 243.

64. Pius XII, "Address to the VIII Congress of the World Medical Association," in *Documents*, p. 131.

65. *Pastoral Constitution*, #80.

*148.*    Retaliatory action whether nuclear or conventional which would indiscriminately take many wholly innocent lives, lives of people who are in no way responsible for reckless actions of their government, must also be condemned. This condemnation, in our judgment, applies even to the retaliatory use of weapons striking enemy cities after our own have already been struck. No Christian can rightfully carry out orders or policies deliberately aimed at killing non-combatants.[66]

*149.*    We make this judgment at the beginning of our treatment of nuclear strategy precisely because the defense of the principle of non-combatant immunity is so important for an ethic of war and because the nuclear age has posed such extreme problems for the principle. Later in this letter we shall discuss specific aspects of U.S. policy in light of this principle and in light of recent U.S. policy statements stressing the determination not to target directly or strike directly against civilian populations. Our concern about protecting the moral value of noncombatant immunity, however, requires that we make a clear reassertion of the principle our first word on this matter.

## 2. The Initiation of Nuclear War

*150.*    We do not perceive any situation in which the deliberate initiation of nuclear warfare, on however restricted a scale, can be morally justified. Non-nuclear attacks by another state must be resisted by other than nuclear means. Therefore, a serious moral obligation exists to develop non-nuclear defensive strategies as rapidly as possible.

*151.*    A serious debate is under way on this issue.[67] It is cast in political terms, but it has a significant moral dimension. Some have argued that at the very beginning of a war nuclear weapons might be used, only against military targets, perhaps in limited numbers. Indeed it has long been American and NATO policy that nuclear weapons, especially so-called tactical nuclear weapons, would likely be used if NATO forces in Europe seemed in danger of losing a conflict that until then had been restricted to conventional weapons. Large numbers of tactical nuclear weapons are now deployed in Europe by the NATO forces and about as many by the Soviet Union. Some are substantially smaller than the bomb used on Hiroshima,

---

66. Ibid.

67. M. Bundy, et al., "Nuclear Weapons," cited; K. Kaiser, G. Leber, A. Mertes, F. J. Schulze, "Nuclear Weapons and the Preservation of Peace," *Foreign Affairs* 60 (1982):1157-70; cf. other responses to Bundy article in the same issue of *Foreign Affairs*.

some are larger. Such weapons, if employed in great numbers, would totally devastate the densely populated countries of Western and Central Europe.

*152.*    Whether under conditions of war in Europe, parts of Asia or the Middle East, or the exchange of strategic weapons directly between the United States and the Soviet Union, the difficulties of limiting the use of nuclear weapons are immense. A number of expert witnesses advise us that commanders operating under conditions of battle probably would not be able to exercise strict control; the number of weapons used would rapidly increase, the targets would be expanded beyond the military, and the level of civilian casualties would rise enormously.[68] No one can be certain that this escalation would not occur, even in the face of political efforts to keep such an exchange "limited." The chances of keeping use limited seem remote, and the consequences of escalation to mass destruction would be appalling. Former public officials have testified that it is improbable that any nuclear war could actually be kept limited. Their testimony and the consequences involved in this problem lead us to conclude that the danger of escalation is so great that it would be morally unjustifiable to initiate nuclear war in any form. The danger is rooted not only in the technology of our weapons systems but in the weakness and sinfulness of human communities. We find the moral responsibility of beginning nuclear war not justified by rational political objectives.

*153.*    This judgment affirms that the willingness to initiate nuclear war entails a distinct, weighty moral responsibility; it involves transgressing a fragile barrier—political, psychological, and moral—which has been constructed since 1945. We express repeatedly in this letter our extreme skepticism about the prospects for controlling a nuclear exchange, however limited the first use might be. Precisely because of this skepticism, we judge resort to nuclear weapons to counter a conventional attack to be morally unjustifiable.[69] Consequently we seek to reinforce the barrier against any use of nuclear weapons. Our support of a "no first use" policy must be seen in this light.

*154.*    At the same time we recognize the responsibility the United States has had and continues to have in assisting allied nations in their defense against either a conventional or a nuclear attack. Es-

---

68. Testimony given to the National Conference of Catholic Bishops Committee during preparation of this pastoral letter. The testimony is reflected in the quotes found in note 61.

69. Our conclusions and judgments in this area although based on careful study and reflection of the application of moral principles do not have, of course, the same force as the principles themselves and therefore allow for different opinions, as the Summary makes clear.

pecially in the European theater, the deterrence of a *nuclear* attack may require nuclear weapons for a time, even though their possession and deployment must be subject to rigid restrictions.

*155.*    The need to defend against a conventional attack in Europe imposes the political and moral burden of developing adequate, alternative modes of defense to present reliance on nuclear weapons. Even with the best coordinated effort—hardly likely in view of contemporary political division on this question—development of an alternative defense position will still take time.

*156.*    In the interim, deterrence against a conventional attack relies upon two factors: the not inconsiderable conventional forces at the disposal of NATO and the recognition by a potential attacker that the outbreak of large scale conventional war could escalate to the nuclear level through accident or miscalculation by either side. We are aware that NATO's refusal to adopt a "no first use" pledge is to some extent linked to the deterrent effect of this inherent ambiguity. Nonetheless, in light of the probable effects of initiating nuclear war, we urge NATO to move rapidly toward the adoption of a "no first use" policy, but doing so in tandem with development of an adequate alternative defense posture.

### 3. Limited Nuclear War

*157.*    It would be possible to agree with our first two conclusions and still not be sure about retaliatory use of nuclear weapons in what is called a "limited exchange." The issue at stake is the *real* as opposed to the *theoretical* possibility of a "limited nuclear exchange."

*158.*    We recognize that the policy debate on this question is inconclusive and that all participants are left with hypothetical projections about probable reactions in a nuclear exchange. While not trying to adjudicate the technical debate, we are aware of it and wish to raise a series of questions which challenge the actual meaning of "limited" in this discussion.

—Would leaders have sufficient information to know what is happening in a nuclear exchange?

—Would they be able under the conditions of stress, time pressures, and fragmentary information to make the extraordinarily precise decision needed to keep the exchange limited if this were technically possible?

—Would military commanders be able, in the midst of the destruction and confusion of a nuclear exchange, to maintain a policy of "discriminate targeting"? Can this be done in modern warfare, waged across great distances by aircraft and missiles?

—Given the accidents we know about in peacetime conditions, what assurances are there that computer errors could be avoided in the midst of a nuclear exchange?

—Would not the casualties, even in a war defined as limited by strategists, still run in the millions?

—How "limited" would be the long-term effects of radiation, famine, social fragmentation, and economic dislocation?

*159.*    Unless these questions can be answered satisfactorily, we will continue to be highly skeptical about the real meaning of "limited." One of the criteria of the just-war tradition is a reasonable hope of success in bringing about justice and peace. We must ask whether such a reasonable hope can exist once nuclear weapons have been exchanged. The burden of proof remains on those who assert that meaningful limitation is possible.

*160.*    A nuclear response to either conventional or nuclear attack can cause destruction which goes far beyond "legitimate defense." Such use of nuclear weapons would not be justified.

*161.*    In the face of this frightening and highly speculative debate on a matter involving millions of human lives, we believe the most effective contribution or moral judgment is to introduce perspectives by which we can assess the empirical debate. Moral perspective should be sensitive not only to the quantitative dimensions of a question but to its psychological, human, and religious characteristics as well. The issue of limited war is not simply the size of weapons contemplated or the strategies projected. The debate should include the psychological and political significance of crossing the boundary from the conventional to the nuclear arena in any form. To cross this divide is to enter a world where we have no experience of control, much testimony against its possibility, and therefore no moral justification for submitting the human community to this risk.[70] We therefore express our view that the first imperative is to prevent any use of nuclear weapons and our hope that leaders will resist the notion that nuclear conflict can be limited, contained, or won in any traditional sense.

---

70. Undoubtedly aware of the long and detailed technical debate on limited war, Pope John Paul II highlighted the unacceptable moral risk of crossing the threshold to nuclear war in his "Angelus Message" of December 13, 1981: "I have, in fact, the deep conviction that, in the light of a nuclear war's effects, which can be scientifically foreseen as certain, the only choice that is morally and humanly valid is represented by the reduction of nuclear armaments, while waiting for their future complete elimination, carried out simultaneously by all the parties, by means of explicit agreements and with the commitment of accepting effective controls." In *Documents*, p. 240.

## D. Deterrence in Principle and Practice

*162.*    The moral challenge posed by nuclear weapons is not exhausted by an analysis of their possible uses. Much of the political and moral debate of the nuclear age has concerned the strategy of deterrence. Deterrence is at the heart of the U.S.-Soviet relationship, currently the most dangerous dimension of the nuclear arms race.

### 1. THE CONCEPT AND DEVELOPMENT OF DETERRENCE POLICY

*163.*    The concept of deterrence existed in military strategy long before the nuclear age, but it has taken on a new meaning and significance since 1945. Essentially, deterrence means "dissuasion of a potential adversary from initiating an attack or conflict, often by the threat of unacceptable retaliatory damage."[71] In the nuclear age, deterrence has become the centerpiece of both U.S. and Soviet policy. Both superpowers have for many years now been able to promise a retaliatory response which can inflict "unacceptable damage." A situation of stable deterrence depends on the ability of each side to deploy its retaliatory forces in ways that are not vulnerable to an attack (i.e., protected against a "first strike"); preserving stability requires a willingness by both sides to refrain from deploying weapons which appear to have a first strike capability.

*164.*    This general definition of deterrence does not explain either the elements of a deterrence strategy or the evolution of deterrence policy since 1945. A detailed description of either of these subjects would require an extensive essay, using materials which can be found in abundance in the technical literature on the subject of deterrence.[72] Particularly significant is the relationship between "declaratory policy" (the public explanation of our strategic intentions and capabilities) and "action policy" (the actual planning and targeting policies to be followed in a nuclear attack).

---

71. W. H. Kincade and J. D. Porro, *Negotiating Security: An Arms Control Reader* (Washington, D.C.: 1979).

72. Several surveys are available, for example cf.: J. H. Kahin, *Security in the Nuclear Age: Developing U.S. Strategic Policy* (Washington, D.C.: 1975); M. Mandelbaum, *The Nuclear Question: The United States and Nuclear Weapons 1946-1976* (Cambridge, England: 1979); B. Brodie, "Development of Nuclear Strategy," *International Security* 2 (1978):65-83.

*165.*    The evolution of deterrence strategy has passed through several stages of declaratory policy. Using the U.S. case as an example, there is a significant difference between "massive retaliation" and "flexible response," and between "mutual assured destruction" and "countervailing strategy." It is also possible to distinguish between "counterforce" and "countervalue" targeting policies; and to contrast a posture of "minimum deterrence" with "extended deterrence." These terms are well known in the technical debate on nuclear policy; they are less well known and sometimes loosely used in the wider public debate. It is important to recognize that there has been substantial continuity in U.S. action policy in spite of real changes in declaratory policy.[73]

*166.*    The recognition of these different elements in the deterrent and the evolution of policy means that moral assessment of deterrence requires a series of distinct judgments. They include: an analysis of the *factual character* of the deterrent (e.g., what is involved in targeting doctrine); analysis of the *historical development* of the policy (e.g., wnether changes have occurred which are significant for moral analysis of the policy): the relationship of deterrence policy and other aspects of *U.S.-Soviet affairs*; and determination of the key *moral questions* involved in deterrence policy.

## 2. THE MORAL ASSESSMENT OF DETERRENCE

*167.*    The distinctively new dimensions of nuclear deterrence were recognized by policymakers and strategists only after much reflection. Similarly, the moral challenge posed by nuclear deterrence was grasped only after careful deliberation. The moral and political paradox posed by deterrence was concisely stated by Vatican II:

> Undoubtedly, armaments are not amassed merely for use in wartime. Since the defensive strength of any nation is thought to depend on its capacity for immediate retaliation, the stockpiling of arms which grows from year to year serves, in a way hitherto unthought of, as a deterrent to potential attackers. Many people look upon this as the most effective way known at the present time for maintaining some sort of peace among nations. Whatever one may think of this form of deterrent, people are convinced that the arms race, which quite a few countries have entered, is no infallible way of maintaining real peace and that the resulting so-called balance of power is no sure genuine path to achieving it. Rather than eliminate the causes of war, the arms race serves only to aggravate the position. As

---

73. The relationship of these two levels of policy is the burden of an article by D. Ball, "U.S. Strategic Forces: How Would They Be Used?" *International Security* 7 (1982/83):31-60

long as extravagent sums of money are poured into the development of new weapons, it is impossible to devote adequate aid in tackling the misery which prevails at the present day in the world. Instead of eradicating international conflict once and for all, the contagion is spreading to other parts of the world. New approaches, based on reformed attitudes, will have to be chosen in order to remove this stumbling block, to free the earth from its pressing anxieties, and give back to the world a genuine peace.[74]

*168.*    Without making a specific moral judgment on deterrence, the council clearly designated the elements of the arms race: the tension between "peace of a sort" preserved by deterrence and "genuine peace" required for a stable international life; the contradiction between what is spent for destructive capacity and what is needed for constructive development.

*169.*    In the post-conciliar assessment of war and peace, and specifically of deterrence, different parties to the political-moral debate within the Church and in civil society have focused on one aspect or another of the problem. For some, the fact that nuclear weapons have not been used since 1945 means that deterrence has worked, and this fact satisfies the demands of both the political and the moral order. Others contest this assessment by highlighting the risk of failure involved in continued reliance on deterrence and pointing out how politically and morally catastrophic even a single failure would be. Still others note that the absence of nuclear war is not necessarily proof that the policy of deterrence has prevented it. Indeed, some would find in the policy of deterrence the driving force in the superpower arms race. Still other observers, many of them Catholic moralists, have stressed that deterrence may not morally include the intention of deliberately attacking civilian populations or non-combatants.

*170.*    The statements of the NCCB/USCC over the past several years have both reflected and contributed to the wider moral debate on deterrence. In the NCCB pastoral letter, *To Live In Christ Jesus* (1976), we focused on the moral limits of declaratory policy while calling for stronger measures of arms control.[75] In 1979 John Cardinal Krol, speaking for the USCC in support of SALT II ratification, brought into focus the other element of the deterrence problem: the actual use of nuclear weapons may have been prevented (a moral good), but the risk of failure and the physical harm and moral evil

---

74. *Pastoral Constitution,* #81.

75. United States Catholic Conference, *To Live in Christ Jesus* (Washington, D.C.: 1976), p. 34.

resulting from possible nuclear war remained. "This explains," Cardinal Krol stated, "the Catholic dissatisfaction with nuclear deterrence and the urgency of the Catholic demand that the nuclear arms race be reversed. It is of the utmost importance that negotiations proceed to meaningful and continuing reductions in nuclear stockpiles, and eventually to the phasing out altogether of nuclear deterrence and the threat of mutual-assured destruction."[76]

*171.*    These two texts, along with the conciliar statement, have influenced much of Catholic opinion expressed recently on the nuclear question.

*172.*    In June 1982, Pope John Paul II provided new impetus and insight to the moral analysis with his statement to the United Nations Second Special Session on Disarmament. The pope first situated the problem of deterrence within the context of world politics. No power, he observes, will admit to wishing to start a war, but each distrusts others and considers it necessary to mount a strong defense against attack. He then discusses the notion of deterrence:

> Many even think that such preparations constitute the way—even the only way—to safeguard peace in some fashion or at least to impede to the utmost in an efficacious way the outbreak of wars, especially major conflicts which might lead to the ultimate holocaust of humanity and the destruction of the civilization that man has constructed so laboriously over the centuries.
>
> In this approach one can see the "philosophy of peace" which was proclaimed in the ancient Roman principle: *Si vis pacem, para bellum.* Put in modern terms, this "philosophy" has the label of "deterrence" and one can find it in various guises of the search for a "balance of forces" which sometimes has been called, and not without reason, the "balance of terror."[77]

*173.*    Having offered this analysis of the general concept of deterrence, the Holy Father introduces his considerations on disarmament, especially, but not only, nuclear disarmament. Pope John Paul II makes this statement about the morality of deterrence:

> In current conditions "deterrence" based on balance, certainly not as an end in itself but as a step on the way toward a progressive disarmament, may still be judged morally acceptable. Nonetheless in order to ensure peace, it is indispensable not to be satisfied with this minimum which is always susceptible to the real danger of explosion.[78]

---

76. John Cardinal Krol, "Testimony on Salt II," *Origins* (1979):197.

77. John Paul II, "Message U.N. Special Session 1982," #3.

78. Ibid., #8.

*174.*    In Pope John Paul II's assessment we perceive two dimensions of the contemporary dilemma of deterrence. One dimension is the danger of nuclear war, with its human and moral costs. The possession of nuclear weapons, the continuing quantitative growth of the arms race, and the danger of nuclear proliferation all point to the grave danger of basing "peace of a sort" on deterrence. The other dimension is the independence and freedom of nations and entire peoples, including the need to protect smaller nations from threats to their independence and integrity. Deterrence reflects the radical distrust which marks international politics, a condition identified as a major problem by Pope John XIII in *Peace on Earth* and reaffirmed by Pope Paul VI and Pope John Paul II. Thus a balance of forces, preventing either side from achieving superiority, can be seen as a means of safeguarding both dimensions.

*175.*    The moral duty today is to prevent nuclear war from ever occurring *and* to protect and preserve those key values of justice, freedom and independence which are necessary for personal dignity and national integrity. In reference to these issues, Pope John Paul II judges that deterrence may still be judged morally acceptable, "certainly not as an end in itself but as a step on the way toward a progressive disarmament."

*176.*    On more than one occasion the Holy Father has demonstrated his awareness of the fragility and complexity of the deterrence relationship among nations. Speaking to UNESCO in June 1980, he said:

> Up to the present, we are told that nuclear arms are a force of dissuasion which have prevented the eruption of a major war. And that is probably true. Still, we must ask if it will always be this way.[79]

In a more recent and more specific assessment Pope John Paul II told an international meeting of scientists on August 23, 1982:

> You can more easily ascertain that the logic of nuclear deterrence cannot be considered a final goal or an appropriate and secure means for safeguarding international peace.[80]

*177.*    Relating Pope John Paul's general statements to the specific policies of the U.S. deterrent requires both judgments of fact and an application of moral principles. In preparing this letter we have tried,

---

79. John Paul II, "Address to UNESCO, 1980," #21.

80. John Paul II, "Letter to International Seminar on the World Implications of a Nuclear Conflict," August 23, 1982, text in *NC News Documentary*, August 24, 1982.

through a number of sources, to determine as precisely as possible the factual character of U.S. deterrence strategy. Two questions have particularly concerned us: 1) the targeting doctrine and strategic plans for the use of the deterrent, particularly their impact on civilian casualties; and 2) the relationship of deterrence strategy and nuclear war-fighting capability to the likelihood that war will in fact be prevented.

## Moral Principles and Policy Choices

*178.* Targeting doctrine raises significant moral questions because it is a significant determinant of what would occur if nuclear weapons were ever to be used. Although we acknowledge the need for deterrent, not all forms of deterrence are morally acceptable. There are moral limits to deterrence policy as well as to policy regarding use. Specifically, it is not morally acceptable to intend to kill the innocent as part of a strategy of deterring nuclear war. The question of whether U.S. policy involves an intention to strike civilian centers (directly targeting civilian populations) has been one of our factual concerns. *179.* This complex question has always produced a variety of responses, official and unofficial in character. The NCCB Committee has received a series of statements of clarification of policy from U.S. government officials.[81] Essentially these statements declare that it is not U.S. strategic policy to target the Soviet civilian population as such or to use nuclear weapons deliberately for the purpose of destroying population centers. These statements respond, in principle at least, to one moral criterion for assessing deterrence policy: the immunity of non-combatants from direct attack either by conventional or nuclear weapons.

---

81. Particularly helpful was the letter of January 15, 1983, of Mr. William Clark, national security adviser, to Cardinal Bernardin. Mr. Clark stated: "For moral, political and military reasons, the United States does not target the Soviet civilian population as such. There is no deliberately opaque meaning conveyed in the last two words. We do not threaten the existence of Soviet civilization by threatening Soviet cities. Rather, we hold at risk the war-making capability of the Soviet Union—its armed forces, and the industrial capacity to sustain war. It would be irresponsible for us to issue policy statements which might suggest to the Soviets that it would be to their advantage to establish privileged sanctuaries within heavily populated areas, thus inducing them to locate much of their war-fighting capability within those urban sanctuaries." A reaffirmation of the administration's policy is also found in Secretary Weinberger's *Annual Report to the Congress* (Caspar Weinberger, *Annual Report to the Congress*, February 1, 1983, p. 55): "The Reagan Administration's policy is that under no circumstances may such weapons be used deliberately for the purpose of destroying populations." Also the letter of Mr. Weinberger to Bishop O'Connor of February 9, 1983, has a similar statement.

*180.*    These statements do not address or resolve another very troublesome moral problem, namely, that an attack on military targets or militarily significant industrial targets could involve "indirect" (i.e., unintended) but massive civilian casualties. We are advised, for example, that the United States strategic nuclear targeting plan (SIOP—Single Integrated Operational Plan) has identified 60 "military" targets within the city of Moscow alone, and that 40,000 "military" targets for nuclear weapons have been identified in the whole of the Soviet Union.[82] It is important to recognize that Soviet policy is subject to the same moral judgment; attacks on several "industrial targets" or politically significant targets in the United States could produce massive civilian casualties. The number of civilians who would necessarily be killed by such strikes is horrendous.[83] This problem is unavoidable because of the way modern military facilities and production centers are so thoroughly interspersed with civilian living and working areas. It is aggravated if one side deliberately positions military targets in the midst of a civilian population. In our consultations, administration officials readily admitted that, while they hoped any nuclear exchange could be kept limited, they were prepared to retaliate in a massive way if necessary. They also agreed that once any substantial numbers of weapons were used, the civilian casualty levels would quickly become truly catastrophic, and that even with attacks limited to "military" targets, the number of deaths in a substantial exchange would be almost indistinguishable from what might occur if civilian centers had been deliberately and directly struck. These possibilities pose a different moral question and are to be judged by a different moral criterion: the principle of proportionality.

*181.*    While any judgment of proportionality is always open to differing evaluations, there are actions which can be decisively judged to be disproportionate. A narrow adherence exclusively to the principle of noncombatant immunity as a criterion for policy is an inadequate moral posture for it ignores some evil and unacceptable consequences. Hence, we cannot be satisfied that the assertion of an intention not to strike civilians directly, or even the most honest effort to implement that intention, by itself constitutes a "moral policy" for the use of nuclear weapons.

---

82. S. Zuckerman, *Nuclear Illusion and Reality* (New York: 1982); D. Ball, cited, p. 36; T. Powers, "Choosing a Strategy for World War III," *The Atlantic Monthly*, November 1982, pp. 82-110.

83. Cf. the comments in Pontifical Academy of Sciences "Statement on the Consequences of the Use of Nuclear Weapons," cited.

*182.*    The location of industrial or militarily significant economic targets within heavily populated areas or in those areas affected by radioactive fallout could well involve such massive civilian casualties that, in our judgment, such a strike would be deemed morally disproportionate, even though not intentionally indiscriminate.

*183.*    The problem is not simply one of producing highly accurate weapons that might minimize civilian casualties in any single explosion, but one of increasing the likelihood of escalation at a level where many, even "discriminating," weapons would cumulatively kill very large numbers of civilians. Those civilian deaths would occur both immediately and from the long-term effects of social and economic devastation.

*184.*    A second issue of concern to us is the relationship of deterrence doctrine to war-fighting strategies. We are aware of the argument that war-fighting capabilities enhance the credibility of the deterrent, particularly the strategy of extended deterrence. But the development of such capabilities raises other strategic and moral questions. The relationship of war-fighting capabilities and targeting doctrine exemplifies the difficult choices in this area of policy. Targeting civilian populations would violate the principle of discrimination—one of the central moral principles of a Christian ethic of war. But "counterforce targeting," while preferable from the perspective of protecting civilians, is often joined with a declaratory policy which conveys the notion that nuclear war is subject to precise rational and moral limits. We have already expressed our severe doubts about such a concept. Furthermore, a purely counterforce strategy may seem to threaten the viability of other nations' retaliatory forces, making deterrence unstable in a crisis and war more likely.

*185.*    While we welcome any effort to protect civilian populations, we do not want to legitimize or encourage moves which extend deterrence beyond the specific objective of preventing the use of nuclear weapons or other actions which could lead directly to a nuclear exchange.

*186.*    These considerations of concrete elements of nuclear deterrence policy, made in light of John Paul II's evaluation, but applying it through our own prudential judgments, lead us to a strictly conditioned moral acceptance of nuclear deterrence. We cannot consider it adequate as a long-term basis for peace.

*187.*    This strictly conditioned judgment yields *criteria* for morally assessing the elements of deterrence strategy. Clearly, these criteria demonstrate that we cannot approve of every weapons system, strategic doctrine, or policy initiative advanced in the name of strengthening deterrence. On the contrary, these criteria require continual public scrutiny of what our government proposes to do with the deterrent.

*188.    On the basis of these criteria we wish now to make some specific evaluations:*

1) If nuclear deterrence exists only to prevent the *use* of nuclear weapons by others, then proposals to go beyond this to planning for prolonged periods of repeated nuclear strikes and counter-strikes, or "prevailing" in nuclear war, are not acceptable. They encourage notions that nuclear war can be engaged in with tolerable human and moral consequences. Rather, we must continually say "no" to the idea of nuclear war.

2) If nuclear deterrence is our goal, "sufficiency" to deter is an adequate strategy; the quest for nuclear superiority must be rejected.

3) Nuclear deterrence should be used as a step on the way toward progressive disarmanent. Each proposed addition to our strategic system or change in strategic doctrine must be assessed precisely in light of whether it will render steps toward "progressive disarmament" more or less likely.

*189.*    Moreover, these criteria provide us with the means to make some judgments and recommendations about the present direction of U.S. strategic policy. Progress toward a world freed of dependence on nuclear deterrence must be carefully carried out. But it must not be delayed. There is an urgent moral and political responsibility to use the "peace of a sort" we have as a framework to move toward authentic peace through nuclear arms control, reductions, and disarmament. Of primary importance in this process is the need to prevent the development and deployment of destabilizing weapons systems on either side; a second requirement is to insure that the more sophisticated command and control systems do not become mere hair triggers for automatic launch on warning; a third is the need to prevent the proliferation of nuclear weapons in the international system.

*190.*    In light of these general judgments *we oppose* some specific proposals in respect to our present deterrence posture:

1) The addition of weapons which are likely to be vulnerable to attack, yet also possess a "prompt hard-target kill" capability that threatens to make the other side's retaliatory forces vulnerable. Such weapons may seem to be useful primarily in a first strike;[84] we resist

---

84. Several experts in strategic theory would place both the MX missile and Pershing II missiles in this category.

such weapons for this reason and we oppose Soviet deployment of such weapons which generate fear of a first strike against U.S. forces.

2) The willingness to foster strategic planning which seeks a nuclear war-fighting capability that goes beyond the limited function of deterrence outlined in this letter.

3) Proposals which have the effect of lowering the nuclear threshold and blurring the difference between nuclear and conventional weapons.

*191.*    In support of the concept of "sufficiency" as an adequate deterrent, and in light of the present size and composition of both the U.S. and Soviet strategic arsenals, *we recommend*:

1) Support for immediate, bilateral, verifiable agreements to halt the testing, production, and deployment of new nuclear weapons systems.[85]

2) Support for negotiated bilateral deep cuts in the arsenals of both superpowers, particularly those weapons systems which have destabilizing characteristics; U.S. proposals like those for START (Strategic Arms Reduction Talks) and INF (Intermediate-range Nuclear Forces) negotiations in Geneva are said to be designed to achieve deep cuts;[86] our hope is that they will be pursued in a manner which will realize these goals.

3) Support for early and successful conclusion of negotiations of a comprehensive test ban treaty.

4) Removal by all parties of short-range nuclear weapons which multiply dangers disproportionate to their deterrent value.

5) Removal by all parties of nuclear weapons from areas where they are likely to be overrun in the early stages of war, thus forcing rapid and uncontrollable decisions on their use.

6) Strengthening of command and control over nuclear weapons to prevent inadvertent and unauthorized use.

*192.*    These judgments are meant to exemplify how a lack of unequivocal condemnation of deterrence is meant only to be an attempt to acknowledge the role attributed to deterrence, but not to support its extension beyond the limited purpose discussed above. Some have

---

85. In each of the successive drafts of this letter we have tried to state a central moral imperative: that the arms race should be stopped and disarmament begun. The implementation of this imperative is open to a wide variety of approaches. Hence we have chosen our own language in this paragraph, not wanting either to be identified with one specific political initiative or to have our words used against specific political measures.

86. Cf. President Reagan's "Speech to the National Press Club" (November 18, 1981) and "Address at Eureka College" (May 9, 1982), Department of State, *Current Policy* #346 and #387.

urged us to condemn all aspects of nuclear deterrence. This urging has been based on a variety of reasons, but has emphasized particularly the high and terrible risks that either deliberate use or accidental detonation of nuclear weapons could quickly escalate to something utterly disproportionate to any acceptable moral purpose. That determination requires highly technical judgments about hypothetical events. Although reasons exist which move some to condemn reliance on nuclear weapons for deterrence, we have not reached this conclusion for the reasons outlined in this letter.

*193.*    Nevertheless, there must be no misunderstanding of our profound skepticism about the moral acceptability of any use of nuclear weapons. It is obvious that the use of any weapons which violate the principle of discrimination merits unequivocal condemnation. We are told that some weapons are designed for purely "counterforce" use against military forces and targets. The moral issue, however, is not resolved by the design of weapons or the planned intention for use; there are also consequences which must be assessed. It would be a perverted political policy or moral casuistry which tried to justify using a weapon which "indirectly" or "unintentionally" killed a million innocent people because they happened to live near a "militarily significant target."

*194.*    Even the "indirect effects" of initiating nuclear war are sufficient to make it an unjustifiable moral risk in any form. It is not sufficient, for example, to contend that "our" side has plans for "limited" or "discriminate" use. Modern warfare is not readily contained by good intentions or technological designs. The psychological climate of the world is such that mention of the term "nuclear" generates uneasiness. Many contend that the use of one tactical nuclear weapon could produce panic, with completely unpredictable consequences. It is precisely this mix of political, psychological, and technological uncertainty which has moved us in this letter to reinforce with moral prohibitions and prescriptions the prevailing political barrier against resort to nuclear weapons. Our support for enhanced command and control facilities, for major reductions in strategic and tactical nuclear forces, and for a "no first use" policy (as set forth in this letter) is meant to be seen as a complement to our desire to draw a moral line against nuclear war.

*195.*    Any claim by any government that it is pursuing a morally acceptable policy of deterrence must be scrutinized with the greatest care. We are prepared and eager to participate in our country in the ongoing public debate on moral grounds.

*196.*    The need to rethink the deterrence policy of our nation, to make the revisions necessary to reduce the possibility of nuclear war, and to move toward a more stable system of national and international security will demand a substantial intellectual, political, and moral effort. It also will require, we believe, the willingness to open ourselves to the providential care, power and word of God, which call us to recognize our common humanity and the bonds of mutual responsibility which exist in the international community in spite of political differences and nuclear arsenals.

*197.*    Indeed, we do acknowledge that there are many strong voices within our own episcopal ranks and within the wider Catholic community in the United States which challenge the strategy of deterrence as an adequate response to the arms race today. They highlight the historical evidence that deterrence has not, in fact, set in motion substantial processes of disarmament.

*198.*    Moreover, these voices rightly raise the concern that even the conditional acceptance of nuclear deterrence as laid out in a letter such as this might be inappropriately used by some to reinforce the policy of arms buildup. In its stead, they call us to raise a prophetic challenge to the community of faith—a challenge which goes beyond nuclear deterrence, toward more resolute steps to actual bilateral disarmament and peacemaking. We recognize the intellectual ground on which the argument is built and the religious sensibility which gives it its strong force.

*199.*    The dangers of the nuclear age and the enormous difficulties we face in moving toward a more adequate system of global security, stability and justice require steps beyond our present conceptions of security and defense policy. In the following section we propose a series of steps aimed at a more adequate policy for preserving peace in a nuclear world.

# III

# The Promotion of
# Peace: Proposals and
# Policies

*200.* In a world which is not yet the fulfillment of God's kingdom, a world where both personal actions and social forces manifest the continuing influence of sin and disorder among us, consistent attention must be paid to preventing and limiting the violence of war. But this task, addressed extensively in the previous section of this letter, does not exhaust Catholic teaching on war and peace. A complementary theme, reflected in the Scriptures and the theology of the Church and significantly developed by papal teaching in this century, is the building of peace as the way to prevent war. This traditional theme was vividly reasserted by Pope John Paul in his homily at Coventry Cathedral:

> Peace is not just the absence of war. It involves mutual respect and confidence between peoples and nations. It involves collaboration and binding agreements. Like a cathedral, peace must be constructed patiently and with unshakable faith.[87]

*201.* This positive conception of peacemaking profoundly influences many people in our time. At the beginning of this letter we affirmed the need for a more fully developed theology of peace. The basis of such a theology is found in the papal teaching of this century. In this section of our pastoral we wish to illustrate how the positive vision of peace contained in Catholic teaching provides direction for policy and personal choices.

## A. Specific Steps to Reduce the Danger of War

202. The dangers of modern war are specific and visible; our

---

87. John Paul II, "Homily at Bagington Airport," Coventry, #2, *Origins* 12 (1982):55.

teaching must be equally specific about the needs of peace. Effective arms control leading to mutual disarmament, ratification of pending treaties,[88] development of nonviolent alternatives, are but some of the recommendations we would place before the Catholic community and all men and women of good will. These should be part of a foreign policy which recognizes and respects the claims of citizens of every nation to the same inalienable rights we treasure, and seeks to ensure an international security based on the awareness that the creator has provided this world and all its resources for the sustenance and benefit of the entire human family. The truth that the globe is inhabited by a single family in which all have the same basic needs and all have a right to the goods of the earth is a fundamental principle of Catholic teaching which we believe to be of increasing importance today. In an interdependent world all need to affirm their common nature and destiny; such a perspective should inform our policy vision and negotiating posture in pursuit of peace today.

## 1. ACCELERATED WORKS FOR ARMS CONTROL, REDUCTION AND DISARMAMENT

*203.*    Despite serious efforts, starting with the Baruch plans and continuing through SALT I and SALT II, the results have been far too limited and partial to be commensurate with the risks of nuclear war. Yet efforts for negotiated control and reduction of arms must continue. In his 1982 address to the United Nations, Pope John Paul II left no doubt about the importance of these efforts:

> Today once again before you all I reaffirm my confidence in the power of true negotiations to arrive at just and equitable solutions.[89]

*204.*    In this same spirit, we urge negotiations to halt the testing, production, and deployment of new nuclear weapons systems. Not only should steps be taken to end development and deployment, but the numbers of existing weapons must be reduced in a manner which lessens the danger of war.

*205.*    Arms control and disarmament must be a process of verifiable agreements especially between two superpowers. While we do not advocate a policy of unilateral disarmament, we believe the urgent

---

88. The two treaties are the Threshold Test Ban Treaty signed July 3, 1974, and the Treaty on Nuclear Explosions for Peaceful Purposes (P.N.E.) signed May 28, 1976.

89. John Paul II, "Message to U.N. Special Session 1982," #8.

need for control of the arms race requires a willingness for each side to take some first steps. The United States has already taken a number of important independent initiatives to reduce some of the gravest dangers and to encourage a constructive Soviet response; additional initiatives are encouraged. By independent initiatives we mean carefully chosen limited steps which the United States could take for a defined period of time, seeking to elicit a comparable step from the Soviet Union. If an appropriate response is not forthcoming, the United States would no longer be bound by steps taken. Our country has previously taken calculated risks in favor of freedom and of human values; these have included independent steps taken to reduce some of the gravest dangers of nuclear war.[90] Certain risks are required today to help free the world from bondage to nuclear deterrence and the risk of nuclear war. Both sides, for example, have an interest in avoiding deployment of destabilizing weapons systems.

*206.*     There is some history of successful independent initiatives which have beneficially influenced the arms race without a formal public agreement. In 1963 President Kennedy announced that the United States would unilaterally forgo further nuclear testing; the next month Soviet Premier Nikita Khrushchev proposed a limited test ban which eventually became the basis of the U.S.-Soviet partial test ban treaty. Subsequently, both superpowers removed about 10,000 troops from Central Europe and each announced a cut in production of nuclear material for weapons.

*207.*     a) Negotiation on arms control agreements in isolation, without persistent and parallel efforts to reduce the political tensions which motivate the buildup of armaments, will not suffice. The United States should therefore have a continuing policy of maximum political engagement with governments of potential adversaries, providing for repeated, systematic discussion and negotiation of areas of friction. This policy should be carried out by a system of periodic, carefully prepared meetings at several levels of government, including summit meetings at regular intervals. Such channels of discussion are too important to be regarded by either of the major powers as a concession or an event made dependent on daily shifts in international developments.

*208.*     b) The Nuclear Non-Proliferation Treaty of 1968 (NPT) acknowledged that the spread of nuclear weapons to hitherto non-nuclear states (horizontal proliferation) could hardly be prevented in the long run in the absence of serious efforts by the nuclear states to control

---

90. Mr. Weinberger's letter to Bishop O'Connor specifies actions taken on command and control facilities designed to reduce the chance of unauthorized firing of nuclear weapons.

and reduce their own nuclear arsenals (vertical proliferation). Article VI of the NPT pledged the superpowers to serious efforts to control and to reduce their own nuclear arsenals; unfortunately, this promise has not been kept. Moreoever, the multinational controls envisaged in the treaty seem to have been gradually relaxed by the states exporting fissionable materials for the production of energy. If these tendencies are not constrained, the treaty may eventually lose its symbolic and practical effectiveness. For this reason the United States should, in concert with other nuclear exporting states, seriously reexamine its policies and programs and make clear its determination to uphold the spirit as well as the letter of the treaty.

## 2. CONTINUED INSISTENCE ON EFFORTS TO MINIMIZE THE RISK OF ANY WAR

*209.*    While it is right and proper that priority be given to reducing and ultimately eliminating the likelihood of nuclear war, this does not of itself remove the threat of other forms of warfare. Indeed, negotiated reduction in nuclear weapons available to the superpowers could conceivably increase the danger of non-nuclear wars.

*210.*    a) Because of this we strongly support negotiations aimed at reducing and limiting conventional forces and at building confidence between possible adversaries, especially in regions of potential military confrontations. We urge that prohibitions outlawing the production and use of chemical and biological weapons be reaffirmed and observed. Arms control negotiations must take account of the possibility that conventional conflict could trigger the nuclear confrontation the world must avoid.

*211.*    b) Unfortunately, as is the case with nuclear proliferation, we are witnessing a relaxation of restraints in the international commerce in conventional arms. Sales of increasingly sophisticated military aircraft, missiles, tanks, anti-tank weapons, anti-personnel bombs, and other systems by the major supplying countries (especially the Soviet Union, the United States, France, and Great Britain) have reached unprecedented levels.

*212.*    Pope John Paul II took specific note of the problem in his U.N. address:

> The production and sale of conventional weapons throughout the world is a truly alarming and evidently growing phenomenon . . . . Moreover the

traffic in these weapons seems to be developing at an increasing rate and seems to be directed most of all toward developing countries.[91]

*213.*    It is a tragic fact that U.S. arms sales policies in the last decade have contributed significantly to the trend the Holy Father deplores. We call for a reversal of this course. The United States should renew earlier efforts to develop multilateral controls on arms exports, and should in this case also be willing to take carefully chosen independent initiatives to restrain the arms trade. Such steps would be particularly appropriate where the receiving government faces charges of gross and systematic human rights violations.[92]

*214.*    c) Nations must accept a limited view of those interests justifying military force. True self-defense may include the protection of weaker states, but does not include seizing the possessions of others, or the domination of other states or peoples. We should remember the caution of Pope John Paul II: "In alleging the threat of a potential enemy, is it really not rather the intention to keep for itself a means of threat, in order to get the upper hand with the aid of one's own arsenal of destruction?"[93] Central to a moral theory of force is the principle that it must be a last resort taken only when *all* other means of redress have been exhausted. Equally important in the age of modern warfare is the recognition that the justifiable reasons for using force have been restricted to instances of self-defense or defense of others under attack.

## 3. THE RELATIONSHIP OF NUCLEAR AND CONVENTIONAL DEFENSES

*215.*    The strong position we have taken against the use of nuclear weapons, and particularly the stand against the initiation of nuclear war in any form, calls for further clarification of our view of the requirements for conventional defense.

*216.*    Nuclear threats have often come to take the place of efforts to deter or defend against non-nuclear attack with weapons that are themselves non-nuclear, particularly in the NATO-Warsaw Pact confrontation. Many analysts conclude that, in the absence of nuclear

---

91. Ibid. Cf. United States Catholic Conference, *At Issue #2: Arms Export Policies—Ethical Choices* (Washington, D.C.: 1978) for suggestions about controlling the conventional arms trade.

92. The International Security Act of 1976 provides for such human rights review.

93. John Paul II, "Address to the United Nations General Assembly," *Origins* 9 (1979):268.

deterrent threats, more troops and conventional (non-nuclear) weapons would be required to protect our allies. Rejection of some forms of nuclear deterrence could therefore conceivably require a willingness to pay higher costs to develop conventional forces. Leaders and peoples of other nations might also have to accept higher costs for their own defense, particularly in Western Europe, if the threat to use nuclear weapons first were withdrawn. We cannot judge the strength of these arguments in particular cases. It may well be that some strengthening of conventional defense would be a proportionate price to pay, if this will reduce the possibility of a nuclear war. We acknowledge this reluctantly, aware as we are of the vast amount of scarce resources expended annually on instruments of defense in a world filled with other urgent, unmet human needs.

*217.*     It is not for us to settle the technical debate about policy and budgets. From the perspective of a developing theology of peace, however, we feel obliged to contribute a moral dimension to the discussion. We hope that a significant reduction in numbers of conventional arms and weaponry would go hand in hand with diminishing reliance on nuclear deterrence. The history of recent wars (even so-called "minor" or "limited" wars) has shown that conventional war can also become indiscriminate in conduct and disproportionate to any valid purpose. We do not want in any way to give encouragement to a notion of "making the world safe for conventional war," which introduces its own horrors.

*218.*     Hence, we believe that any program directed at reducing reliance on nuclear weapons is not likely to succeed unless it includes measures to reduce tensions, and to work for the balanced reduction of conventional forces. We believe that important possibilities exist which, if energetically pursued, would ensure against building up conventional forces as a concomitant of reductions in nuclear weapons. Examples are to be found in the ongoing negotiations for mutual balanced force reductions, the prospects for which are certainly not dim and would be enhanced by agreements on strategic weapons, and in the confidence-building measures still envisaged under the Helsinki agreement and review conference.

*219.*     We must re-emphasize with all our being, nonetheless, that it is not only nuclear war that must be prevented, but war itself. Therefore, with Pope John Paul II we declare:

> Today, the scale and the horror of modern warfare—whether nuclear or not—makes it totally unacceptable as a means of settling differences be-

tween nations. War should belong to the tragic past, to history; it should find no place on humanity's agenda for the future.[94]

Reason and experience tell us that a continuing upward spiral, even in conventional arms, coupled with an unbridled increase in armed forces, instead of securing true peace will almost certainly be provocative of war.

## 4. CIVIL DEFENSE

*220.*    Attention must be given to existing programs for civil defense against nuclear attack, including blast and fall-out shelters and relocation plans. It is unclear in the public mind whether these are intended to offer significant protection against at least some forms of nuclear attack or are being put into place to enhance the credibility of the strategic deterrent forces by demonstrating an ability to survive attack. This confusion has led to public skepticism and even ridicule of the program and casts doubt on the credibility of the government. An independent commission of scientists, engineers, and weapons experts is needed to examine if these or any other plans offer a realistic prospect of survival for the nation's population or its cherished values, which a nuclear war would presumably be fought to preserve.

## 5. EFFORTS TO DEVELOP NON-VIOLENT MEANS OF CONFLICT RESOLUTION

*221.*    We affirm a nation's right to defend itself, its citizens, and its values. Security is the right of all, but that right, like everything else, must be subject to divine law and the limits defined by that law. We must find means of defending peoples that do not depend upon the threat of annihilation. Immoral means can never be justified by the end sought; no objective, however worthy of good in itself, can justify sinful acts or policies. Though our primary concern through this statement is war and the nuclear threat, these principles apply as well to all forms of violence, including insurgency, counter-insurgency, "destabilization," and the like.

*222.*    a) The Second Vatican Council praised "those who renounce the use of violence in the vindication of their rights and who resort to methods of defense which are otherwise available to weaker parties, provided that this can be done without injury to the rights and duties

---

94. John Paul II, "Homily at Bagington Airport," Coventry, 2; cited, p. 55.

of others or of the community itself."[95] To make such renunciation effective and still defend what must be defended, the arts of diplomacy, negotiation, and compromise must be developed and fully exercised. Non-violent means of resistance to evil deserve much more study and consideration than they have thus far received. There have been significant instances in which people have successfully resisted oppression without recourse to arms.[96] Non-violence is not the way of the weak, the cowardly, or the impatient. Such movements have seldom gained headlines, even though they have left their mark on history. The heroic Danes who would not turn Jews over to the Nazis and the Norwegians who would not teach Nazi propaganda in schools serve as inspiring examples in the history of non-violence.

223.    Non-violent resistance, like war, can take many forms depending upon the demands of a given situation. There is, for instance, organized popular defense instituted by government as part of its contingency planning. Citizens would be trained in the techniques of peaceable non-compliance and non-cooperation as a means of hindering an invading force or non-democratic government from imposing its will. Effective non-violent resistance requires the united will of a people and may demand as much patience and sacrifice from those who practice it as is now demanded by war and preparation for war. It may not always succeed. Nevertheless, before the possibility is dismissed as impractical or unrealistic, we urge that it be measured against the almost certain effects of a major war.

224.    b) Non-violent resistance offers a common ground of agreement for those individuals who choose the option of Christian pacifism even to the point of accepting the need to die rather than to kill, and those who choose the option of lethal force allowed by the theology of just war. Non-violent resistance makes clear that both are able to be committed to the same objective: defense of their country.

225.    c) Popular defense would go beyond conflict resolution and compromise to a basic synthesis of beliefs and values. In its practice, the objective is not only to avoid causing harm or injury to another creature, but, more positively, to seek the good of the other. Blunting the aggression of an adversary or oppressor would not be enough. The goal is winning the other over, making the adversary a friend.

---

95. *Pastoral Constitution,* #78.

96. G. Sharp, *The Politics of Nonviolent Action* (Boston: 1973); R. Fisher and W. Ury, *Getting to Yes: Negotiating Agreement Without Giving In* (Boston: 1981).

*226.* ⌐ It is useful to point out that these principles are thoroughly compatible with—and to some extent derived from—Christian teachings and must be part of any Christian theology of peace. Spiritual writers have helped trace the theory of non-violence to its roots in scripture and tradition and have illustrated its practice and success in their studies of the church fathers and the age of martyrs. Christ's own teachings and example provide a model way of life incorporating the truth, and a refusal to return evil for evil.

*227.* Non-violent popular defense does not insure that lives would not be lost. Nevertheless, once we recognize that the almost certain consequences of existing policies and strategies of war carry with them a very real threat to the future existence of humankind itself, practical reason as well as spiritual faith demand that it be given serious consideration as an alternative course of action.

*228.* d) Once again we declare that the only true defense for the world's population is the rejection of nuclear war and the conventional wars which could escalate into nuclear war. With Pope John Paul II, we call upon educational and research institutes to take a lead in conducting peace studies: "Scientific studies on war, its nature, causes, means, objectives and risks have much to teach us on the conditions for peace . . ."[97] To achieve this end, we urge that funds equivalent to a designated percentage (even one-tenth of one percent) of current budgetary allotments for military purposes be set aside to support such peace research.

*229.* In 1981, the Commission on Proposals for the National Academy of Peace and Conflict Resolution recommended the establishment of the U.S. Academy of Peace, a recommendation nearly as old as this country's constitution. The commission found that "peace is a legitimate field of learning that encompasses rigorous, interdisciplinary research, education, and training directed toward peacemaking expertise."[98] We endorse the commission's recommendation and urge all citizens to support training in conflict resolution, non-violent resistance, and programs devoted to service to peace and education for peace. Such an academy would not only provide a center for peace studies and activities, but also be a tangible evidence of our nation's sincerity in its often professed commitment to international peace and the abolition of war. We urge universities, particularly Catholic

---

97. John Paul II, "World Day of Peace Message 1982," #7, cited, p. 476.

98. *To Establish the United States Academy of Peace: Report of the Commission on Proposals for the National Academy of Peace and Conflict Resolution* (Washington, D.C.: 1981), pp. 119-20.

universities, in our country to develop programs for rigorous, inter-disciplinary research, education and training directed toward pea-cemaking expertise.

*230.*    We, too, must be prepared to do our part to achieve these ends. We encourage churches and educational institutions, from pri-mary schools to colleges and institutes of higher learning, to undertake similar programs at their own initiative. Every effort must be made to understand and evaluate the arms race, to encourage truly trans-national perspectives on disarmament, and to explore new forms of international cooperation and exchange. No greater challenge or higher priority can be imagined than the development and perfection of a theology of peace suited to a civilization poised on the brink of self-destruction. It is our prayerful hope that this document will prove to be a starting point and inspiration for that endeavor.

## 6. THE ROLE OF CONSCIENCE

*231.*    A dominant characteristic of the Second Vatican Council's evaluation of modern warfare was the stress it placed on the require-ment for proper formation of conscience. Moral principles are effective restraints on power only when policies reflect them and individuals practice them. The relationship of the authority of the state and the conscience of the individual on matters of war and peace takes a new urgency in the face of the destructive nature of modern war.

*232.*    a) In this connection we reiterate the position we took in 1980. Catholic teaching does not question the right in principle of a government to require military service of its citizens provided the government shows it is necessary. A citizen may not casually disregard his country's con-scientious decision to call its citizens to acts of "legitimate defense." Moreover, the role of Christian citizens in the armed forces is a service to the common good and an exercise of the virtue of patriotism, so long as they fulfill this role within defined moral norms.[99]

*233.*    b) At the same time, no state may demand blind obedience. Our 1980 statement urged the government to present convincing reasons for draft registration, and opposed reinstitution of conscrip-tion itself except in the case of a national defense emergency. More-over, it reiterated our support for conscientious objection in general and for selective conscientious objection to participation in a partic-

---

99. United States Catholic Conference, *Statement on Registration and Conscription for Military Service* (Washington, D.C.: 1980). Cf. also *Human Life in Our Day*, cited, pp. 42-45.

ular war, either because of the ends being pursued or the means being used. We called selective conscientious objection a moral conclusion which can be validly derived from the classical teaching of just-war principles. We continue to insist upon respect for and legislative protection of the rights of both classes of conscientious objectors. We also approve requiring alternative service to the community—not related to military needs—by such persons.

## B. Shaping a Peaceful World

*234.*   Preventing nuclear war is a moral imperative; but the avoidance of war, nuclear or conventional, is not a sufficient conception of international relations today. Nor does it exhaust the content of Catholic teaching. Both the political needs and the moral challenge of our time require a positive conception of peace, based on a vision of a just world order. Pope Paul VI summarized classical Catholic teaching in his encyclical, *The Development of Peoples*: "Peace cannot be limited to a mere absence of war, the result of an ever precarious balance of forces. No, peace is something built up day after day, in the pursuit of an order intended by God, which implies a more perfect form of justice among men and women."[100]

## 1. WORLD ORDER IN CATHOLIC TEACHING

*235.*   This positive conception of peace sees it as the fruit of order; order, in turn, is shaped by the values of justice, truth, freedom and love. The basis of this teaching is found in sacred scripture, St. Augustine and St. Thomas. It has found contemporary expression and development in papal teaching of this century. The popes of the nuclear age, from Pius XII through John Paul II have affirmed pursuit of international order as the way to banish the scourge of war from human affairs.[101]

*236.*   The fundamental premise of world order in Catholic teaching is a theological truth: the unity of the human family—rooted in

---

100. Paul VI, *The Development of Peoples* (1967), #76.

101. Cf. V. Yzermans, ed., *Major Addresses of Pius XII*, 2 vols. (St. Paul: 1961) and J. Gremillion, *The Gospel of Peace and Justice*, cited.

common creation, destined for the kingdom, and united by moral bonds of rights and duties. This basic truth about the unity of the human family pervades the entire teaching on war and peace: for the pacifist position it is one of the reasons why life cannot be taken, while for the just-war position, even in a justified conflict bonds of responsibility remain in spite of the conflict.

*237.*    Catholic teaching recognizes that in modern history, at least since the Peace of Westphalia (1648) the international community has been governed by nation-states. Catholic moral theology, as expressed for example in chapters 2 and 3 of *Peace on Earth*, accords a real but relative moral value to sovereign states. The value is real because of the functions states fulfill as sources of order and authority in the political community; it is relative because boundaries of the sovereign state do not dissolve the deeper relationships of responsibility existing in the human community. Just as within nations the moral fabric of society is described in Catholic teaching in terms of reciprocal rights and duties—between individuals, and then between the individual and the state—so in the international community *Peace on Earth* defines the rights and duties which exist among states.[102]

*238.*    In the past twenty years Catholic teaching has become increasingly specific about the content of these international rights and duties. In 1963, *Peace on Earth* sketched the political and legal order among states. In 1966, *The Development of Peoples* elaborated on order of economic rights and duties. In 1979, Pope John Paul II articulated the human rights basis of international relations in his "Address to the United Nations General Assembly."

*239.*    These documents and others which build upon them, outlined a moral order of international relations, i.e., how the international community *should* be organized. At the same time this teaching has been sensitive to the actual pattern of relations prevailing among states. While not ignoring present geopolitical realities, one of the primary functions of Catholic teaching on world order has been to point the way toward a more integrated international system.

*240.*    In analyzing this path toward world order, the category increasingly used in Catholic moral teaching (and, more recently, in the social sciences also) is the interdependence of the world today. The theological principle of unity has always affirmed a human interdependence; but today this bond is complemented by the growing

---

102. Cf. John XXIII, *Peace on Earth* (1963), esp. #80-145.

political and economic interdependence of the world, manifested in a whole range of international issues.[103]

*241.*    An important element missing from world order today is a properly constituted political authority with the capacity to shape our material interdependence in the direction of moral interdependence. Pope John XXIII stated the case in the following way:

> Today the universal common good poses problems of world-wide dimensions, which cannot be adequately tackled or solved except by the efforts of public authority endowed with a wideness of powers, structure and means of the same proportions: that is, of public authority which is in a position to operate in an effective manner on a world-wide basis. The moral order itself, therefore, demands that such a form of public authority be established.[104]

*242.*    Just as the nation-state was a step in the evolution of government at a time when expanding trade and new weapons technologies made the feudal system inadequate to manage conflicts and provide security, so we are now entering an era of new, global interdependencies requiring global systems of governance to manage the resulting conflicts and ensure our common security. Major global problems such as worldwide inflation, trade and payments deficits, competition over scarce resources, hunger, widespread unemployment, global environmental dangers, the growing power of transnational corporations, and the threat of international financial collapse, as well as the danger of world war resulting from these growing tensions—cannot be remedied by a single nation-state approach. They shall require the concerted effort of the whole world community. As we shall indicate below, the United Nations should be particularly considered in this effort.

*243.*    In the nuclear age, it is in the regulation of interstate conflicts and ultimately the replacement of military by negotiated solutions that the supreme importance and necessity of a moral as well as a political concept of the international common good can be grasped. The absence of adequate structures for addressing these issues places even greater responsiblity on the policies of individual states. By a mix of political vision and moral wisdom, states are called to interpret the national interest in light of the larger global interest.

---

103. A sampling of the policy problems and possibilities posed by interdependence can be found in: R. O. Keohane and J. S. Nye, Jr., *Power and Interdependence* (Boston: 1977); S. Hoffmann, *Primacy or World Order* (New York: 1978); The Overseas Development Council, *The U.S. and World Development* 1979; 1980; 1982 (Washington, D.C.).

104. John XXIII, *Peace on Earth* (1963), #137.

*244.*  We are living in a global age with problems and conflicts on a global scale. Either we shall learn to resolve these problems together, or we shall destroy one another. Mutual security and survival require a new vision of the world as one interdependent planet. We have rights and duties not only within our diverse national communities but within the larger world community.

## 2. THE SUPERPOWERS IN A DISORDERED WORLD

*245.*    No relationship more dramatically demonstrates the fragile nature of order in international affairs today than that of the United States and the Soviet Union. These two sovereign states have avoided open war, nuclear or conventional, but they are divided by philosophy, ideology and competing ambitions. Their competition is global in scope and involves everything from comparing nuclear arsenals to printed propaganda. Both have been criticized in international meetings because of their policies in the nuclear arms race. [105]

*246.*    In our 1980 pastoral letter on Marxism, we sought to portray the significant differences between Christian teaching and Marxism; at the same time we addressed the need for states with different political systems to live together in an interdependent world:

> The Church recognizes the depth and dimensions of the ideological differences that divide the human race, but the urgent practical need for cooperative efforts in the human interest overrules these differences. Hence Catholic teaching seeks to avoid exacerbating the ideological opposition and to focus upon the problems requiring common efforts across the ideological divide: keeping the peace and empowering the poor. [106]

*247.*    We believe this passage reflects the teaching of *Peace on Earth*, the continuing call for dialogue of Pope Paul VI and the 1979 address of Pope John Paul II at the United Nations. We continue to stress this theme even while we recognize the difficulty of realizing its objectives.

*248.*    The difficulties are particularly severe on the issue of the arms race. For most Americans, the danger of war is commonly defined primarily in terms of the threat of Soviet military expansionism and the consequent need to deter or defend against a Soviet military threat. Many assume that the existence of this threat is

---

105. This has particularly been the case in the two U.N. Special Sessions on Disarmament, 1979, 1982.

106. United States Catholic Conference, *Marxist Communism* (Washington, D.C.: 1980), p. 19.

permanent and that nothing can be done about it except to build and maintain overwhelming or at least countervailing military power.[107]

*249.*    The fact of a Soviet threat, as well as the existence of a Soviet imperial drive for hegemony, at least in regions of major strategic interest, cannot be denied. The history of the Cold War has produced varying interpretations of which side caused which conflict, but whatever the details of history illustrate, the plain fact is that the memories of Soviet policies in Eastern Europe and recent events in Afghanistan and Poland have left their mark in the American political debate. Many peoples are forcibly kept under communist domination despite their manifest wishes to be free. Soviet power is very great. Whether the Soviet Union's pursuit of military might is motivated primarily by defensive or aggressive aims might be debated, but the effect is nevertheless to leave profoundly insecure those who must live in the shadow of that might.

*250.*    Americans need have no illusions about the Soviet system of repression and the lack of respect in that system for human rights, or about Soviet covert operations and pro-revolutionary activities. To be sure, our own system is not without flaws. Our government has sometimes supported repressive governments in the name of pre-serving freedom, has carried out repugnant covert operations of its own, and remains imperfect in its domestic record of ensuring equal rights for all. At the same time, there is a difference. NATO is an

---

107. The debate on U.S.-Soviet relations is extensive; recent examples of it are found in: A. Ulam, "U.S.-Soviet Relations: Unhappy Coexistence," *America and the World, 1978; Foreign Affairs* 57 (1979):556-71; W. G. Hyland, "U.S.-Soviet Relations: The Long Road Back," *America and the World, 1981; Foreign Affairs* 60 (1982):525-50; R. Legvold, "Containment Without Confrontation," *Foreign Policy* 40 (1980):74-98; S. Hoffmann, "Muscle and Brains," *Foreign Policy* 37 (1979-80):3-27; P. Hassner, "Moscow and The Western Alliance," *Problems of Communism* 30 (1981):37-54; S. Bialer, "The Harsh Decade: Soviet Policies in the 1980s," *Foreign Affairs* 59 (1981):999-1020; G. Kennan, *The Nuclear Delusion: Soviet-American Relations in the Atomic Age* (New York: 1982); N. Podhoretz, *The Present Danger* (New York: 1980); P. Nitze, "Strategy in the 1980s," *Foreign Affairs* 59 (1980):82-101; R. Strode and C. Gray, "The Imperial Dimension of Soviet Military Power," *Problems of Communism* 30 (1981):1-15; International Institute for Strategic Studies, *Prospects of Soviet Power in the 1980s,* Parts I and II, Adelphi Papers #151 and 152 (London: 1979); S. S. Kaplan, ed., *Diplomacy of Power: Soviet Armed Forces as a Political Instrument* (Washington, D.C.: 1981); R. Barnet, *The Giants: Russia and America* (New York: 1977); M. McGwire, *Soviet Military Requirements,* The Brookings Institution (Washington, D.C.: 1982); R. Tucker, "The Purposes of American Power," *Foreign Affairs* 59 (1980/81):241-74; A. Geyer, *The Idea of Disarmament: Rethinking the Unthinkable* (Washington, D.C.: 1982). For a review of Soviet adherence to treaties cf.: "The SALT Syndrome Charges and Facts: Analysis of an 'Anti-SALT Documentary,'" report prepared by U.S. government agencies (State, Defense, CIA, ACDA and NSC), reprinted in *The Defense Monitor* 10, #8A, Center for Defense Information.

alliance of democratic countries which have freely chosen their association; the Warsaw Pact is not.

*251.*    To pretend that as a nation we have lived up to all our own ideals would be patently dishonest. To pretend that all evils in the world have been or are now being perpetrated by dictatorial regimes would be both dishonest and absurd. But having said this, and admitting our own faults, it is imperative that we confront reality. The facts simply do not support the invidious comparisons made at times, even in our own society, between our way of life, in which most basic human rights are at least recognized even if they are not always adequately supported, and those totalitarian and tyrannical regimes in which such rights are either denied or systematically suppressed. Insofar as this is true, however, it makes the promotion of human rights in our foreign policy, as well as our domestic policy, all the more important. It is the acid test of our commitment to our democratic values. In this light, any attempts to justify, for reasons of state, support for regimes that continue to violate human rights is all the more morally reprehensible in its hypocrisy.

*252.*    A glory of the United States is the range of political freedoms its system permits us. We, as bishops, as Catholics, as citizens, exercise those freedoms in writing this letter, with its share of criticisms of our government. We have true freedom of religion, freedom of speech, and access to a free press. We could not exercise the same freedoms in contemporary Eastern Europe or in the Soviet Union. Free people must always pay a proportionate price and run some risks—responsibly—to preserve their freedom.

*253.*    It is one thing to recognize that the people of the world do not want war. It is quite another thing to attribute the same good motives to regimes or political systems that have consistently demonstrated precisely the opposite in their behavior. There are political philosophies with understandings of morality so radically different from ours, that even negotiations proceed from different premises, although identical terminology may be used by both sides. This is no reason for not negotiating. It is a very good reason for not negotiating blindly or naively.

*254.*    In this regard, Pope John Paul II offers some sober reminders concerning dialogue and peace:

> [O]ne must mention the tactical and deliberate lie, which misuses language, which has recourse to the most sophisticated techniques of propaganda, which deceives and distorts dialogue and incites to aggression . . . while certain parties are fostered by ideologies which, in spite of their declarations, are opposed to the dignity of the human person, ideologies which

see in struggle the motive force of history, that see in force the source of rights, that see in the discernment of the enemy the ABC of politics, dialogue is fixed and sterile. Or, if it still exists, it is a superficial and falsified reality. It becomes very difficult, not to say impossible, therefore. There follows almost a complete lack of communication between countries and blocs. Even the international institutions are paralyzed. And the setback to dialogue then runs the risk of serving the arms race. However, even in what can be considered as an impasse to the extent that individuals support such ideologies, the attempt to have a lucid dialogue seems still necessary in order to unblock the situation and to work for the possible establishment of peace on particular points. This is to be done by counting upon common sense, on the possibilities of danger for everyone and on the just aspirations to which the peoples themselves largely adhere.[108]

255.    The cold realism of this text, combined with the conviction that political dialogue and negotiations must be pursued, in spite of obstacles, provides solid guidance for U.S.-Soviet relations. Acknowledging all the differences between the two philosophies and political systems, the irreducible truth is that objective mutual interests do exist between the superpowers. Proof of this concrete if limited convergence of interest can be found in some vitally important agreements on nuclear weapons which have already been negotiated in the areas of nuclear testing and nuclear explosions in space as well as the SALT I agreements.

256.    The fact that the Soviet union now possesses a huge arsenal of strategic weapons as threatening to us as ours may appear to them does not exclude the possibility of success in such negotiations. The conviction of many European observers that a *modus vivendi* (often summarized as "detente") is a practical possibility in political, economic, and scientific areas should not be lightly dismissed in our country.

257.    Sensible and successful diplomacy, however, will demand that we avoid the trap of a form of anti-Sovietism which fails to grasp the central danger of a superpower rivalry in which both the U.S. and the U.S.S.R. are the players, and fails to recognize the common interest both states have in never using nuclear weapons. Some of those dangers and common interests would exist in any world where two great powers, even relatively benign ones, competed for power, influence, and security. The diplomatic requirement for addressing the U.S.-Soviet relationship is not romantic idealism about Soviet intentions and capabilities but solid realism which recognizes that everyone will lose in a nuclear exchange.

258.    As bishops we are concerned with issues which go beyond diplomatic requirements. It is of some value to keep raising in the realm

---

108. John Paul II, "World Day of Peace Message 1983," #7.

of the political debate truths which ground our involvement in the affairs of nations and peoples. Diplomatic dialogue usually sees the other as a potential or real adversary. Soviet behavior in some cases merits the adjective reprehensible, but the Soviet people and their leaders are human beings created in the image and likeness of God. To believe we are condemned in the future only to what has been the past of U.S.-Soviet relations is to underestimate both our human potential for creative diplomacy and God's action in our midst which can open the way to changes we could barely imagine. We do not intend to foster illusory ideas that the road ahead in superpower relations will be devoid of tension or that peace will be easily achieved. But we do warn against that "hardness of heart" which can close us or others to the changes needed to make the future different from the past.

## 3. INTERDEPENDENCE: FROM FACT TO POLICY

*259.*    While the nuclear arms race focuses attention on the U.S.-Soviet relationship, it is neither politically wise nor morally justifiable to ignore the broader international context in which that relationship exists. Public attention, riveted on the big powers, often misses the plight of scores of countries and millions of people simply trying to survive. The interdependence of the world means a set of interrelated human questions. Important as keeping the peace in the nuclear age is, it does not solve or dissolve the other major problems of the day. Among these problems the pre-eminent issue is the continuing chasm in living standards between the industrialized world (East and West) and the developing world. To quote Pope John Paul II:

> So widespread is the phenomenon that it brings into question the financial, monetary, production and commercial mechanisms that, resting on various political pressures, support the world economy. These are proving incapable either of remedying the unjust social situations inherited from the past or of dealing with the urgent challenges and ethical demands of the present.[109]

*260.*    The East-West competition, central as it is to world order and important as it is in the foreign policy debate, does not address this moral question which rivals the nuclear issue in its human significance. While the problem of the developing nations would itself require a pastoral letter, Catholic teaching has maintained an analysis of the problem which should be identified here. The analysis acknowledges internal causes of poverty, but also concentrates on the way the larger

---

109. John Paul II, "The Redeemer of Man," #16, *Origins* 8 (1980):635.

international economic structures affect the poor nations. These particularly involve trade, monetary, investment and aid policies.

*261.*    Neither of the superpowers is conspicuous in these areas for initiatives designed to address "the absolute poverty" in which millions live today.[110]

*262.*    From our perspective and experience as bishops, we believe there is a much greater potential for response to these questions in the minds and hearts of Americans than has been reflected in U.S. policy. As pastors who often appeal to our congregations for funds destined for international programs, we find good will and great generosity the prevailing characteristics. The spirit of generosity which shaped the Marshall Plan is still alive in the American public.

*263.*    We must discover how to translate this personal sense of generosity and compassion into support for policies which would respond to papal teaching in international economic issues. It is precisely the need to expand our conception of international charity and relief to an understanding of the need for social justice in terms of trade, aid and monetary issues which was reflected in Pope John Paul II's call to American Catholics in Yankee Stadium:

> Within the framework of your national institutions and in cooperation with all your compatriots, you will also want to seek out the structural reasons which foster or cause the different forms of poverty in the world and in your own country, so that you can apply the proper remedies. You will not allow yourselves to be intimidated or discouraged by over-simplified explanations which are more ideological than scientific—explanations which try to account for a complex evil by some single cause. But neither will you recoil before the reforms—even profound ones—of attitudes and structures that may prove necessary in order to recreate over and over again the conditions needed by the disadvantaged if they are to have a fresh chance in the hard struggle of life. The poor of the United States and of the world are your brothers and sisters in Christ.[111]

*264.*    The Pope's words highlight an intellectual, moral, and political challenge for the United States. Intellectually, there is a need to rethink the meaning of national interest in an interdependent world. Morally, there is a need to build upon the spirit of generosity present in the U.S. public, directing it toward a more systematic response to the major issues affecting the poor of the world. Politically, there is

---

110. The phrase and its description are found in R. S. McNamara, *Report to the Board of Governors of the World Bank* 1978; cf. also 1979; 1980 (Washington, D.C.).

111. John Paul II, "Homily at Yankee Stadium," #4, *Origins* 9 (1979):311.

a need for U.S. policies which promote the profound structural reforms called for by recent papal teaching.

*265.*    Precisely in the name of international order papal teaching has, by word and deed, sought to promote multilateral forms of cooperation toward the developing world. The U.S. capacity for leadership in multilateral institutions is very great. We urge much more vigorous and creative response to the needs of the developing countries by the United States in these institutions.

*266.*    The significant role the United States could play is evident in the daily agenda facing these institutions. Proposals addressing the relationship of the industrialized and developing countries on a broad spectrum of issues, all in need of "profound reforms," are regularly discussed in the United Nations and other international organizations. Without U.S. participation, significant reform and substantial change in the direction of addressing the needs of the poor will not occur. Meeting these needs is an essential element for a peaceful world.

*267.*    Papal teaching of the last four decades has not only supported international institutions in principle, it has supported the United Nations specifically. Pope Paul VI said to the U.N. General Assembly:

> The edifice which you have constructed must never fail; it must be perfected and made equal to the needs which world history will present. You mark a stage in the development of mankind for which retreat must never be admitted, but from which it is necessary that advance be made.[112]

*268.*    It is entirely necessary to examine the United Nations carefully, to recognize its limitations and propose changes where needed. Nevertheless, in light of the continuing endorsement found in papal teaching, we urge that the United States adopt a stronger supportive leadership role with respect to the United Nations. The growing interdependence of the nations and peoples of the world, coupled with the extra-governmental presence of multinational corporations, requires new structures of cooperation. As one of the founders of and major financial contributors to the United Nations, the United States can, and should, assume a more positive and creative role in its life today.

*269.*    It is in the context of the United Nations that the impact of the arms race on the prospects for economic development is highlighted. The numerous U.N. studies on the relationship of development and disarmament support the judgment of Vatican II cited earlier in this letter: "The arms race is one of the greatest curses on the human

---

112. Paul VI, "Address to the General Assembly of the United Nations" (1965), #2.

race and the harm it inflicts upon the poor is more than can be endured."[113]

270.   We are aware that the precise relationship between disarmament and development is neither easily demonstrated nor easily reoriented. But the fact of a massive distortion of resources in the face of crying human need creates a moral question. In an interdependent world, the security of one nation is related to the security of all. When we consider how and what we pay for defense today, we need a broader view than the equation of arms with security.[114] The threats to the security and stability of an interdependent world are not all contained in missiles and bombers.

271.   If the arms race in all its dimensions is not reversed, resources will not be available for the human needs so evident in many parts of the globe and in our own country as well. But we also know that making resources available is a first step; policies of wise use would also have to follow. Part of the process of thinking about the economics of disarmament includes the possibilities of conversion of defense industries to other purposes. Many say the possibilities are great if the political will is present. We say the political will to reorient resources to human needs and redirect industrial, scientific, and technological capacity to meet those needs is part of the challenge of the nuclear age. Those whose livelihood is dependent upon industries which can be reoriented should rightfully expect assistance in making the transition to new forms of employment. The economic dimension of the arms race is broader than we can assess here, but these issues we have raised are among the primary questions before the nation.[115]

272.   An interdependent world requires an understanding that key policy questions today involve mutuality of interest. If the monetary and trading systems are not governed by sensitivity to mutual needs, they can be destroyed. If the protection of human rights and the promotion of human needs are left as orphans in the diplomatic arena, the stability we seek in increased armaments will eventually

---

113. *Pastoral Constitution*, #81.

114. Cf. Hoffman, cited; Independent Commission on Disarmament and Security Issues, *Common Security* (New York: 1982).

115. For an analysis of the policy problems of reallocating resources, cf: Bruce M. Russett, *The Prisoners of Insecurity* (San Francisco: 1983). Cf.: *Common Security*, cited; Russett, cited; *U.N. Report on Disarmament and Development* (New York: 1982); United Nations, *The Relationship Between Disarmament and Development: A Summary*, Fact Sheet #21 (New York: 1982).

be threatened by rights denied and needs unmet in vast sectors of the globe. If future planning about conservation of and access to resources is relegated to a pure struggle of power, we shall simply guarantee conflict in the future.

273.    The moral challenge of interdependence concerns shaping the relationships and rules of practice which will support our common need for security, welfare, and safety. The challenge tests our idea of human community, our policy analysis, and our political will. The need to prevent nuclear war is absolutely crucial, but even if this is achieved, there is much more to be done.

# IV

# The Pastoral
# Challenge and Response

## A. The Church: A Community of Conscience, Prayer and Penance

274.    Pope John Paul II, in his first encyclical, recalled with gratitude the teaching of Pius XII on the Church. He then went on to say:

> Membership in that body has for its source a particular call, united with the saving action of grace. Therefore, if we wish to keep in mind this community of the People of God, which is so vast and so extremely differentiated, we must see first and foremost Christ saying in a way to each member of the community: "Follow Me." It is the community of the disciples, each of whom in a different way—at times very consciously and consistently, at other times not very consciously and very consistently—is following Christ. This shows also the deeply "personal" aspect and dimension of this society.[116]

275.    In the following pages we should like to spell out some of the implications of being a community of Jesus' disciples in a time when our nation is so heavily armed with nuclear weapons and is engaged in a continuing development of new weapons together with strategies for their use.

276.    It is clear today, perhaps more than in previous generations, that convinced Christians are a minority in nearly every country of the world—including nominally Christian and Catholic nations. In our own country we are coming to a fuller awareness that a response

---

116. John Paul II, "The Redeemer of Man," #21, cited, p. 641. Much of the following reflects the content of A. Dulles, *A Church to Believe in: Discipleship and the Dynamics of Freedom* (New York: 1982), ch. 1.

to the call of Jesus is both personal and demanding. As believers we can identify rather easily with the early Church as a company of witnesses engaged in a difficult mission. To be disciples of Jesus requires that we continually go beyond where we now are. To obey the call of Jesus means separating ourselves from all attachments and affiliation that could prevent us from hearing and following our authentic vocation. To set out on the road to discipleship is to dispose oneself for a share in the cross (cf. Jn. 16:20). To be a Christian, according to the New Testament, is not simply to believe with one's mind, but also to become a doer of the word, a wayfarer with and a witness to Jesus. This means, of course, that we never expect complete success within history and that we must regard as normal even the path of persecution and the possibility of martyrdom.

277.    We readily recognize that we live in a world that is becoming increasingly estranged from Christian values. In order to remain a Christian, one must take a resolute stand against many commonly accepted axioms of the world. To become true disciples, we must undergo a demanding course of induction into the adult Christian community. We must continually equip ourselves to profess the full faith of the Church in an increasingly secularized society. We must develop a sense of solidarity, cemented by relationships with mature and exemplary Christians who represent Christ and his way of life.

278.    All of these comments about the meaning of being a disciple or a follower of Jesus today are especially relevant to the quest for genuine peace in our time.

## B. Elements of a Pastoral Response

279.    We recommend and endorse for the faithful some practical programs to meet the challenge to their faith in this area of grave concern.

## 1. EDUCATIONAL PROGRAMS AND FORMATION OF CONSCIENCE

280.    Since war, especially the threat of nuclear war, is one of the central problems of our day, how we seek to solve it could determine the mode, and even the possibility, of life on earth. God made human beings stewards of the earth; we cannot escape this responsibility. Therefore we urge every diocese and parish to implement balanced

and objective educational programs to help people at all age levels to understand better the issues of war and peace. Development and implementation of such programs must receive a high priority during the next several years. They must teach the full impact of our Christian faith. To accomplish this, this pastoral letter in its entirety, including its complexity, should be used as a guide and a framework for such programs, as they lead people to make moral decisions about the problems of war and peace, keeping in mind that the applications of principles in this pastoral letter do not carry the same moral authority as our statements of universal moral principles and formal Church teaching.

*281.*   In developing educational programs, we must keep in mind that questions of war and peace have a profoundly moral dimension which responsible Christians cannot ignore. They are questions of life and death. True, they also have a political dimension because they are embedded in public policy. But the fact that they are also political is no excuse for denying the Church's obligation to provide its members with the help they need in forming their consciences. We must learn together how to make correct and responsible moral judgments. We reject, therefore, criticism of the Church's concern with these issues on the ground that it "should not become involved in politics." We are called to move from discussion to witness and action.

*282.*   At the same time, we recognize that the Church's teaching authority does not carry the same force when it deals with technical solutions involving particular means as it does when it speaks of principles or ends. People may agree in abhorring an injustice, for instance, yet sincerely disagree as to what practical approach will achieve justice. Religious groups are as entitled as others to their opinion in such cases, but they should not claim that their opinions are the only ones that people of good will may hold.

*283.*   The Church's educational programs must explain clearly those principles or teachings about which there is little question. Those teachings, which seek to make explicit the gospel call to peace and the tradition of the Church, should then be applied to concrete situations. They must indicate what the possible legitimate options are and what the consequences of those options may be. While this approach should be self-evident, it needs to be emphasized. Some people who have entered the public debate on nuclear warfare, at all points on the spectrum of opinion, appear not to understand or accept some of the clear teachings of the Church as contained in papal or conciliar documents. For example, some would place almost no limits

on the use of nuclear weapons if they are needed for "self-defense.'
Some on the other side of the debate insist on conclusions which
may be legitimate options but cannot be made obligatory on the basis
of actual Church teaching.

## 2. TRUE PEACE CALLS FOR "REVERENCE FOR LIFE"

*284*.    All of the values we are promoting in this letter rest ultimately
in the disarmament of the human heart and the conversion of the
human spirit to God who alone can give authentic peace. Indeed, to
have peace in our world, we must first have peace within ourselves.
As Pope John Paul II reminded us in his 1982 World Day of Peace
message, world peace will always elude us until peace becomes a
reality for each of us personally. "It springs from the dynamism of
free wills guided by reason towards the common good that is to be
attained in truth, justice and love."[117] Interior peace becomes possible
only when we have a conversion of spirit. We cannot have peace with
hate in our hearts.

*285*.    No society can live in peace with itself, or with the world,
without a full awareness of the worth and dignity of every human
person, and of the sacredness of all human life (Jas. 4:1-2). When
we accept violence in any form as commonplace, our sensitivities
become dulled. When we accept violence, war itself can be taken
for granted. Violence has many faces: oppression of the poor, dep-
rivation of basic human rights, economic exploitation, sexual exploitation and pornography, neglect or abuse of the aged and the
helpless, and innumerable other acts of inhumanity. Abortion in particular blunts a sense of the sacredness of human life. In a society
where the innocent unborn are killed wantonly, how can we expect
people to feel righteous revulsion at the act or threat of killing non-
combatants in war?

*286*.    We are well aware of the differences involved in the taking
of human life in warfare and the taking of human life through abortion.
As we have discussed throughout this document, even justifiable
defense against aggression may result in the indirect or unintended
loss of innocent human lives. This is tragic, but may conceivably be
proportionate to the values defended. Nothing, however, can justify
direct attack on innocent human life, in or out of warfare. Abortion
is precisely such an attack.

---

117. John Paul II, "World Day of Peace Message 1982," #4, cited, p. 475.

*287.*   We know that millions of men and women of good will, of all religious persuasions, join us in our commitment to try to reduce the horrors of war, and particularly to assure that nuclear weapons will never again be used, by any nation, anywhere, for any reason. Millions join us in our "no" to nuclear war, in the certainty that nuclear war would inevitably result in the killing of millions of innocent human beings, directly or indirectly. Yet many part ways with us in our efforts to reduce the horror of abortion and our "no" to war on innocent human life in the womb, killed not indirectly, but directly.

*288.*   We must ask how long a nation willing to extend a constitutional guarantee to the "right" to kill defenseless human beings by abortion is likely to refrain from adopting strategic warfare policies deliberately designed to kill millions of defenseless human beings, if adopting them should come to seem "expedient." Since 1973, approximately 15 million abortions have been performed in the United States, symptoms of a kind of disease of the human spirit. And we now find ourselves seriously discussing the pros and cons of such questions as infanticide, euthanasia, and the involvement of physicians in carrying out the death penalty. Those who would celebrate such a national disaster can only have blinded themselves to its reality.

*289.*   Pope Paul VI was resolutely clear: *If you wish peace, defend life.*[118] We plead with all who would work to end the scourge of war to begin by defending life at its most defenseless, the life of the unborn.

## 3. PRAYER

*290.*   A conversion of our hearts and minds will make it possible for us to enter into a closer communion with our Lord. We nourish that communion by personal and communal prayer, for it is in prayer that we encounter Jesus, who is our peace, and learn from him the way to peace.

*291.*   In prayer we are renewed in faith and confirmed in our hope in God's promise.

*292.*   The Lord's promise is that he is in our midst when we gather in prayer. Strengthened by this conviction, we beseech the risen Christ to fill the world with his peace. We call upon Mary, the first disciple and the Queen of Peace, to intercede for us and for the people of our

---

118. Paul VI, "World Day of Peace Message 1977."

time that we may walk in the way of peace. In this context, we encouage devotion to Our Lady of Peace.

293. ⌐ As believers, we understand peace as a gift of God. This belief prompts us to pray constantly, personally and communally, particularly through the reading of scripture and devotion to the rosary, especially in the family. Through these means and others, we seek the wisdom to begin the search for peace and the courage to sustain us as instruments of Christ's peace in the world. ⌐

294.    The practice of contemplative prayer is especially valuable for advancing harmony and peace in the world. For this prayer rises, by divine grace, where there is total disarmament of the heart and unfolds in an experience of love which is the moving force of peace. Contemplation fosters a vision of the human family as united and interdependent in the mystery of God's love for all people. This silent, interior prayer bridges temporarily the "already" and "not yet," this world and God's kingdom of peace.

295.    The Mass in particular is a unique means of seeking God's help to create the conditions essential for true peace in ourselves and in the world. In the eucharist we encounter the risen Lord, who gave us his peace. He shares with us the grace of the redemption, which helps us to preserve and nourish this precious gift. Nowhere is the Church's urgent plea for peace more evident in the liturgy than in the Communion Rite. After beginning this rite of the Mass with the Lord's Prayer, praying for reconciliation now and in the kingdom to come, the community asks God to "grant us peace in our day," not just at some time in the distance future. Even before we are exhorted "to offer each other the sign of peace," the priest continues the Church's prayer for peace, recalling the Lord Jesus Christ's own legacy of peace:

> Lord Jesus Christ, you said to your apostles: I leave you peace, my peace
> I give you. Look not on our sins, but on the faith of your Church, and
> grant us the peace and unity of your kingdom.

Therefore we encourage every Catholic to make the sign of peace at Mass an authentic sign of our reconciliation with God and with one another. This sign of peace is also a visible expression of our commitment to work for peace as a Christian community. We approach the table of the Lord only after having dedicated ourselves as a Christian community to peace and reconciliation. As an added sign of commitment, we suggest that there always be a petition for peace in the general intercessions at every eucharistic celebration.

296.    We implore other Christians and everyone of good will to join us in this continuing prayer for peace, as we beseech God for

peace within ourselves, in our families and community, in our nation, and in the world.

## 4. PENANCE

*297.*   Prayer by itself is incomplete without penance. Penance directs us toward our goal of putting on the attitudes of Jesus himself. Because we are all capable of violence, we are never totally conformed to Christ and are always in need of conversion. The twentieth century alone provides adequate evidence of our violence as individuals and as a nation. Thus, there is continual need for acts of penance and conversion. The worship of the Church, particularly through the sacrament of reconciliation and communal penance services, offers us multiple ways to make reparation for the violence in our own lives and in our world.

*298.*   As a tangible sign of our need and desire to do penance we, for the cause of peace, commit ourselves to fast and abstinence on each Friday of the year. We call upon our people voluntarily to do penance on Friday by eating less food and by abstaining from meat. This return to a traditional practice of penance, once well observed in the U.S. Church, should be accompanied by works of charity and service toward our neighbors. Every Friday should be a day significantly devoted to prayer, penance, and almsgiving for peace.

*299.*   It is to such forms of penance and conversion that the Scriptures summon us. In the words of the prophet Isaiah:

> Is not the sort of fast that pleases me, to break unjust fetters and undo the thongs of the yoke, to let the oppressed go free and break every yoke, to share your bread with the hungry, and shelter the homeless poor, to clothe the person you see to be naked and not turn from your own kin? Then will your light shine like the dawn and your wound be quickly healed over. If you do away with the yoke, the clenched fist, the wicked word, if you give your bread to the hungry and relief to the oppressed, your light will rise in the darkness, and your shadows become like noon (Is. 58:6-8; 10).

*300.*   The present nuclear arms race has distracted us from the words of the prophets, has turned us from peace-making, and has focused our attention on a nuclear buildup leading to annihilation. We are called to turn back from this evil of total destruction and turn instead in prayer and penance toward God, toward our neighbor, and toward the building of a peaceful world:

> I set before you life or death, a blessing or a curse. Choose life then, so that you and your descendants may live in the love of Yahweh your God, obeying His voice, clinging to Him; for in this your life consists, and on

this depends your long stay in the land which Yahweh swore to your fathers
Abraham, Isacc and Jacob, He would give them (Dt. 30:19–20).

## C. Challenge and Hope

*301.*    The arms race presents questions of conscience we may not
evade. As American Catholics, we are called to express our loyalty
to the deepest values we cherish: peace, justice and security for the
entire human family. National goals and policies must be measured
against that standard.

*302.*    We speak here in a specific way to the Catholic community.
After the passage of nearly four decades and a concomitant growth
in our understanding of the ever growing horror of nuclear war, we
must shape the climate of opinion which will make it possible for
our country to express profound sorrow over the atomic bombing in
1945. Without that sorrow, there is no possibility of finding a way
to repudiate future use of nuclear weapons or of conventional weapons
in such military actions as would not fulfill just-war criteria.

*303.*    **To Priests, Deacons, Religious and Pastoral Ministers:**
We recognize the unique role in the Church which belongs to priests
and deacons by reason of the sacrament of holy orders and their
unique responsibility in the community of believers. We also recognize the valued and indispensable role of men and women religious.
To all of them and to all other pastoral ministers we stress that the
cultivation of the gospel vision of peace as a way of life for believers
and as a leaven in society should be a major objective. As bishops,
we are aware each day of our dependence upon your efforts. We are
aware, too, that this letter and the new obligations it could present
to the faithful may create difficulties for you in dealing with those
you serve. We have confidence in your capacity and ability to convert
these difficulties into an opportunity to give a fuller witness to our
Lord and his message. This letter will be known by the faithful only
as well as you know it, preach and teach it, and use it creatively.

*304.*    **To Educators:** We have outlined in this letter Catholic teaching on war and peace, but this framework will become a living
message only through your work in the Catholic community. To teach
the ways of peace is not "to weaken the nation's will" but to be
concerned for the nation's soul. We address theologians in a particular
way, because we know that we have only begun the journey toward
a theology of peace; without your specific contributions this des-

perately needed dimension of our faith will not be realized. Through your help we may provide new vision and wisdom for church and state.

*305.*    We are confident that all the models of Catholic education which have served the Church and our country so well in so many ways will creatively rise to the challenge of peace.

*306.*    **To Parents:** Your role, in our eyes, is unsurpassed by any other; the foundation of society is the family. We are conscious of the continuing sacrifices you make in the efforts to nurture the full human and spiritual growth of your children. Children hear the gospel message first from your lips. Parents who consciously discuss issues of justice in the home and who strive to help children solve conflicts through non-violent methods enable their children to grow up as peacemakers. We pledge our continuing pastoral support in the common objective we share of building a peaceful world for the future of children everywhere.

*307.*    **To Youth:** Pope John Paul II singles you out in every country where he visits as the hope of the future; we agree with him. We call you to choose your future work and professions carefully. How you spend the rest of your lives will determine, in large part, whether there will any longer be a world as we know it. We ask you to study carefully the teachings of the Church and the demands of the gospel about war and peace. We encourage you to seek careful guidance as you reach conscientious decisions about your civic responsibilities in this age of nuclear military forces.

*308.*    We speak to you, however, as people of faith. We share with you our deepest conviction that in the midst of the dangers and complexities of our time God is with us, working through us and sustaining us all in our efforts of building a world of peace with justice for each person.

*309.*    **To Men and Women in Military Service:** Millions of you are Catholics serving in the armed forces. We recognize that you carry special responsibilities for the issues we have considered in this letter. Our perspective on your profession is that of Vatican II: "All those who enter the military service in loyalty to their country should look upon themselves as the custodians of the security and freedom of their fellow-countrymen; and where they carry out their duty properly, they are contributing to the maintenance of peace."[119]

---

119. *Pastoral Constitution,* #79.

*310.*   It is surely not our intention in writing this letter to create problems for Catholics in the armed forces. Every profession, however, has its specific moral questions and it is clear that the teaching on war and peace developed in this letter poses a special challenge and opportunity to those in the military profession. Our pastoral contact with Catholics in military service, either through our direct experience or through our priests, impresses us with the demanding moral standards we already see observed and the commitment to Catholic faith we find. We are convinced that the challenges of this letter will be faced conscientiously. The purpose of defense policy is to defend the peace; military professionals should understand their vocation this way. We believe they do, and we support this view.

*311.*   We remind all in authority and in the chain of command that their training and field manuals have long prohibited, and still do prohibit, certain actions in the conduct of war, especially those actions which inflict harm on innocent civilians. The question is not whether certain measures are unlawful or forbidden in warfare, but which measures: to refuse to take such actions is not an act of cowardice or treason but one of courage and patriotism.

*312.*   We address particularly those involved in the exercise of authority over others. We are aware of your responsibilities and impressed by the standard of personal and professional duty you uphold. We feel, therefore, that we can urge you to do everything you can to assure that every peaceful alternative is exhausted before war is even remotely considered. In developing battle plans and weapons systems, we urge you to try to ensure that these are designed to reduce violence, destruction, suffering, and death to a minimum, keeping in mind especially non-combatants and other innocent persons.

*313.*   Those who train individuals for military duties must remember that the citizen does not lose his or her basic human rights by entrance into military service. No one, for whatever reason, can justly treat a military person with less dignity and respect than that demanded for and deserved by every human person. One of the most difficult problems of war involves defending a free society without destroying the values that give it meaning and validity. Dehumanization of a nation's military personnel by dulling their sensibilities and generating hatred toward adversaries in an effort to increase their fighting effectiveness robs them of basic human rights and freedoms, degrading them as persons.

*314.*   Attention must be given to the effects on military personnel themselves of the use of even legitimate means of conducting war. While attacking legitimate targets and wounding or killing opposed combat forces may be morally justified, what happens to military persons required to carry out these actions? Are they treated merely as instruments of war, insensitive as the weapons they use? With what moral or emotional experiences do they return from war and attempt to resume normal civilian lives? How does their experience affect society? How are they treated by society?

*315.*    It is not only basic human rights of adversaries that must be respected, but those of our own forces as well. We re-emphasize, therefore, the obligation of responsible authorities to ensure appropriate training and education of combat forces and to provide appropriate support for those who have experienced combat. It is unconscionable to deprive those veterans of combat whose lives have been severely disrupted or traumatized by their combat experiences of proper psychological and other appropriate treatment and support.

*316.*    Finally, we are grateful for the sacrifice so many in military service must make today and for the service offered in the past by veterans. We urge that those sacrifices be mitigated so far as possible by the provision of appropriate living and working conditions and adequate financial recompense. Military persons and their families must be provided continuing opportunity for full spiritual growth, the exercise of their religious faith, and a dignified mode of life.

*317.*    We especially commend and encourage our priests in military service. In addition to the message already addressed to all priests and religious, we stress the special obligations and opportunities you face in direct pastoral service to the men and women of the armed forces. To complement a teaching document of this scope, we shall need the sensitive and wise pastoral guidance only you can provide. We promise our support in facing this challenge.

*318.*    **To Men and Women in Defense Industries:** You also face specific questions, because the defense industry is directly involved in the development and production of the weapons of mass destruction which have concerned us in this letter. We do not presume or pretend that clear answers exist to many of the personal, professional and financial choices facing you in your varying responsibilities. In this letter we have ruled out certain uses of nuclear weapons, while also expressing conditional moral acceptance for deterrence. All Catholics, at every level of defense industries, can and should use the moral principles of this letter to form their consciences. We realize that different judgments of conscience will face different people, and we recognize the possibility of diverse concrete judgments being made in this complex area. We seek as moral teachers and pastors to be available to all who confront these questions of personal and vocational choice. Those who in conscience decide that they should no longer be associated with defense activities should find support in the Catholic community. Those who remain in these industries or earn a profit from the weapons industry should find in the Church guidance and support for the ongoing evaluation of their work.

*319.*    **To Men and Women of Science:** At Hiroshima Pope John Paul said: "Criticism of science and technology is sometimes so severe that it comes close to condemning science itself. On the contrary, science and technology are a wonderful product of a God-given human creativity, since they have provided us with wonderful possibilities and we all gratefully benefit from them. But we know that this potential is not a neutral one: it can be used either for man's progress or for his degradation."[120] We appreciate the efforts of scientists, some of whom first unlocked the secret of atomic power and others of whom have developed it in diverse ways, to turn the enormous power of science to the cause of peace.

*320.*    Modern history is not lacking scientists who have looked back with deep remorse on the development of weapons to which they contributed, sometimes with the highest motivation, even believing that they were creating weapons that would render all other weapons obsolete and convince the world of the unthinkableness of war. Such efforts have ever proved illusory. Surely, equivalent dedication of scientific minds to reverse current trends, and to pursue concepts as bold and adventuresome in favor of peace as those which in the past have magnified the risks of war, could result in dramatic benefits for all of humanity. We particularly note in this regard the extensive efforts of public education undertaken by physicians and scientists on the medical consequences of nuclear war.

*321.*    We do not, however, wish to limit our remarks to the physical sciences alone. Nor do we limit our remarks to physical scientists. In his address at the United Nations University in Hiroshima, Pope John Paul II warned about misuse of "the social sciences and the human behavioral sciences when they are utilized to manipulate people, to crush their mind, souls, dignity and freedom . . ."[121] The positive role of social science in overcoming the dangers of the nuclear age is evident in this letter. We have been dependent upon the research and analysis of social scientists in our effort to apply the moral principles of the Catholic tradition to the concrete problems of our

---

120. John Paul II, "Address to Scientists and Scholars," #3, cited, p. 621.
121. Ibid.

day. We encourage social scientists to continue this work of relating moral wisdom and political reality. We are in continuing need of your insights.

*322.*    **To Men and Women of the Media:** We have directly felt our dependence upon you in writing this letter; all the problems we have confronted have been analyzed daily in the media. As we have grappled with these issues, we have experienced some of the responsibility you bear for interpreting them. On the quality of your efforts depends in great measure the opportunity the general public will have for understanding this letter.

*323.*    **To Public Officials:** Vatican II spoke forcefully of "the difficult yet noble art of politics."[122] No public issue is more difficult than avoiding war; no public task more noble than building a secure peace. Public officials in a democracy must both lead and listen; they are ultimately dependent upon a popular consensus to sustain policy. We urge you to lead with courage and to listen to the public debate with sensitivity.

*324.*    Leadership in a nuclear world means examining with great care and objectivity every potential initiative toward world peace, regardless of how unpromising it might at first appear. One specific initiative which might be taken now would be the establishment of a task force including the public sector, industry, labor, economists and scientists with the mandate to consider the problems and challanges posed by nuclear disarmament to our economic well-being and industrial output. Listening includes being particularly attentive to the consciences of those who sincerely believe that they may not morally support warfare in general, a given war, or the exercise of a particular role within the armed forces. Public officials might well serve all of our fellow citizens by proposing and supporting legislation designed to give maximum protection to this precious freedom, true freedom of conscience.

*325.*    In response to public officials who both lead and listen, we urge citizens to respect the vocation of public service. It is a role easily maligned but not easily fulfilled. Neither justice nor peace can be achieved with stability in the absence of courageous and creative public servants.

*326.*    **To Catholics as Citizens:** All papal teaching on peace has stressed the crucial role of public opinion. Pope John Paul II specified the tasks before us: "There is no justification for not raising the

---

122. *Pastoral Constitution,* #75.

question of the responsibility of each nation and each individual in the face of possible wars and of the nuclear threat."[123] In a democracy, the responsibility of the nation and that of its citizens coincide. Nuclear weapons pose especially acute questions of conscience for American Catholics. As citizens we wish to affirm our loyalty to our country and its ideals, yet we are also citizens of the world who must be faithful to the universal principles proclaimed by the Church. While some other countries also possess nuclear weapons, we may not forget that the United States was the first to build and to use them. Like the Soviet Union, this country now possesses so many weapons as to imperil the continuation of civilization. Americans share responsibility for the current situation, and cannot evade responsibility for trying to resolve it.

*327.*    The virtue of patriotism means that as citizens we respect and honor our country, but our very love and loyalty make us examine carefully and regularly its role in world affairs, asking that it live up to its full potential as an agent of peace with justice for all people.

> Citizens must cultivate a generous and loyal spirit of patriotism, but without being narrow-minded. This means that they will always direct their attention to the good of the whole human family, united by the different ties which bind together races, people, and nations.[124]

*328.*    In a pluralistic democracy like the United States, the Church has a unique opportunity, precisely because of the strong constitutional protection of both religious freedom and freedom of speech and the press, to help call attention to the moral dimensions of public issues. In a previous pastoral letter, *Human Life In Our Day*, we said: "In our democratic system, the fundamental right of political dissent cannot be denied, nor is rational debate on public policy decisions of government in the light of moral and political principles to be discouraged. It is the duty of the governed to analyze responsibly the concrete issues of public policy."[125] In fulfilling this role, the Church helps to create a community of conscience in the wider civil community. It does this in the first instance by teaching clearly within the Church the moral principles which bind and shape the Catholic conscience. The Church also fulfills a teaching role, however, in striving to share the moral wisdom of the Catholic tradition with the larger society.

---

123. John Paul II, "Address at Hiroshima," #2, *Origins* 10 (1981):620.

124. *Pastoral Constitution*, #75.

125. *Human Life in Our Day*, cited, p. 41.

*329.*    In the wider public discussion, we look forward in a special way to cooperating with all other Christians with whom we share common traditions. We also treasure cooperative efforts with Jewish and Islamic communities, which possess a long and abiding concern for peace as a religious and human value. Finally, we reaffirm our desire to participate in a common public effort with all men and women of good will who seek to reverse the arms race and secure the peace of the world.

# Conclusion

*330.* As we close this lengthy letter, we try to answer two key questions as directly as we can.

*331.* Why do we address these matters fraught with such complexity, controversy and passion? We speak as pastors, not politicians. We are teachers, not technicians. We cannot avoid our responsibility to lift up the moral dimensions of the choices before our world and nation. The nuclear age is an era of moral as well as physical danger. We are the first generation since Genesis with the power to virtually destroy God's creation. We cannot remain silent in the face of such danger. Why do we address these issues? We are simply trying to live up to the call of Jesus to be peacemakers in our own time and situation.

*332.* What are we saying? Fundamentally, we are saying that the decisions about nuclear weapons are among the most pressing moral questions of our age. While these decisions have obvious military and political aspects, they involve fundamental moral choices. In simple terms, we are saying that good ends (defending one's country, protecting freedom, etc.) cannot justify immoral means (the use of weapons which kill indiscriminately and threaten whole societies). We fear that our world and nation are headed in the wrong direction. More weapons with greater destructive potential are produced every day. More and more nations are seeking to become nuclear powers. In our quest for more and more security, we fear we are actually becoming less and less secure.

*333.* In the words of our Holy Father, we need a "moral about-face." The whole world must summon the moral courage and technical means to say "no" to nuclear conflict; "no" to weapons of mass destruction; "no" to an arms race which robs the poor and the vulnerable; and "no" to the moral danger of a nuclear age which places

293

before humankind indefensible choices of constant terror or surrender. Peacemaking is not an optional commitment. It is a requirement of our faith. We are called to be peacemakers, not by some movement of the moment, but by our Lord Jesus. The content and context of our peacemaking is set, not by some political agenda or ideological program, but by the teaching of his Church.]

*334.*     Thus far in this pastoral letter we have made suggestions we hope will be helpful in the present world crisis. Looking ahead to the long and productive future of humanity for which we all hope, we feel that a more all-inclusive and final solution is needed. We speak here of the truly effective international authority for which Pope John XXIII ardently longed in *Peace on Earth*,[126] and of which Pope Paul VI spoke to the United Nations on his visit there in 1965.[127] The hope for such a structure is not unrealistic, because the point has been reached where public opinion sees clearly that, with the massive weaponry of the present, war is no longer viable. There *is* a substitute for war. There is negotiation under the supervision of a global body realistically fashioned to do its job. It must be given the equipment to keep constant surveillance on the entire earth. Present technology makes this possible. It must have the authority, freely conferred upon it by all the nations, to investigate what seems to be preparations for war by any one of them. It must be empowered by all the nations to enforce its commands on every nation. It must be so constituted as to pose no threat to any nation's sovereignty. Obviously the creation of such a sophisticated instrumentality is a gigantic task, but is it hoping for too much to believe that the genius of humanity, aided by the grace and guidance of God, is able to accomplish it? To create it may take decades of unrelenting daily toll by the world's best minds and most devoted hearts, but it shall never come into existence unless we make a beginning now.

*335.*     As we come to the end of our pastoral letter we boldly propose the beginning of this work. The evil of the proliferation of nuclear arms becomes more evident every day to all people. No one is exempt from their danger. If ridding the world of the weapons of war could be done easily, the whole human race would do it gladly tomorrow. Shall we shrink from the task because it is hard?

*336.*     We turn to our own government and we beg it to propose to the United Nations that it begin this work immediately; that it

---

126. John XXIII, *Peace on Earth* (1963), #137.

127. Paul VI, "Address to the General Assembly of the United Nations," (1965), #2.